The Life and Letters of Sydney Dobell, Ed., by E.J

Sydney Dobell

ÆTAT 41.

faults of our favourite, to gain credit to our praise of his excellences;'—but we justify ourselves against the over-sceptical critic by an appeal to the same authority, who tells us that, 'to leave things out of a book merely because people say they will not be believed, is meanness.'

We can only plead that we have endeavoured to 'nothing extenuate,' and to let the man as he was, speak, in great measure, directly for himself. His deficiencies will appear in the self-revelations of his letters, which also bear frequent, though rarely adequate, witness to the indefinable, and, to all who came in contact with it, the magnetic nobility of a nature too highly strung to be universally appreciated.

Sydney Dobell's last book was published in 1856, when he was in his thirty-third year. After that time physical conditions made it impossible for him to complete any important literary work. But even the fragmentary results of his intermittent labour should have a peculiar interest, in an age so strongly marked as our own by the eager revival of those religious and philosophical speculations to which so much of his energy was directed.

BOOK III.

1851 TO 1854. AGED 27 TO 30.

BOOK IV.

1854 TO 1857. AGED 30 TO 33.

ILLUSTRATIONS.

century as a leader of political Reform in the City
of London, and as the founder of a 'Church'
which aimed to be on the Primitive Christian
model.[1]

This teacher seems by the natural force of his
character to have inspired his whole family,
especially his daughters, with an enthusiastic
reverence—a feeling which Mrs. Dobell in great
measure communicated to her children, educating
them as champions of their grandfather's religious,
political and social principles. There were certain
characteristics of her eldest son in which she
rejoiced to recognise the stamp of her father—his
stern devotion to duty, perseverance in opposing
difficulties, patience under trials, and power of
holding to convictions with an almost dogged
tenacity, his aptitude alike for command and for
persuasion; above all, the combination of a keen
logical and, in some directions, inconoclastic intellect with a child-like reverence for what he was
led to regard as the essentials of the Faith.

In reading the records of Sydney Dobell's boy-

---

[1] See Appendix A. to Book I. for an account of Mr. Samuel
Thompson, which has been furnished by a younger grandson, Mr.
Clarence Dobell.

Appendix B. reprints a pamphlet, which gives a brief statement of
the principles and objects of 'the Church' founded by Mr. Thompson.

was narrowing in the atmosphere of sectarian theology and social exclusiveness. These changes —the effects of which we shall find more tangible in his various political attitudes—were probably due in part to the influences of travel and the companionship of other minds, but they resulted mainly from the natural development of his own, in studying which the leading interest of these volumes must lie.

Among memoranda written concerning his son's early boyhood, we find the following characteristic reference by John Dobell:

I used frequently to talk to him of how delightful and blessed it would be if any child would resolve to live as pure, virtuous and holy a life, as dedicated to the will and service of God, as Jesus. I used to say to him that if one could ever be found again who was spotless and holy, it was with me a pleasing speculation and hope that such a character might, even in this life, be called out as a special instrument of Our Heavenly Father for some great purpose with His Church, or with the Jews.

The feeling of Mrs. Dobell, (a woman of exceptional strength of character, and a passionately loving mother,) in regard to her eldest child, is shown in the following extract:

In my eyes he was indeed precious, precious in that

wine-merchant.—(About this time Sydney was described as of 'very astonishing understanding,' as 'preferring mental diversion to eating and drinking,' as 'very inventive with tales,' and as possessing 'literary powers extensive and generalising, but too heedless to attend to particulars!)'— The new home was in the City, the child pined from want of pure air and had occasionally to be sent away into the country. The distress of these partings from his parents, and of being thrown among comparative strangers, remained vividly impressed upon his mind in later life.

When about four years old he was sent to an uncle's house at Loughborough, and the self-command for which his father's notes had already credited him seems to have given way during the coach-journey; for he ever after remembered the passion of crying into which he broke at intervals when he pictured to himself his parents sitting together, and saying 'our poor little boy.' On his return he was pronounced to be 'more reserved and increased in morbid sensibility.'

These early years were years of struggle and difficulty for the parents. John Dobell's health was extremely delicate. In the autumn of 1828, after an illness, from which he had never expected

—the boy being then eight years old—his father writes :

I have never known Sydney to tell an untruth . . . His distinctions sometimes are so nice and correct that to an inattentive person he might give an impression of untruth . . . He has a scientific inclination, and is quick in observing mechanism . . . He learns astronomy . . . He attends the Sunday meeting (of the members of Mr. Thompson's Church), and I find understands much that he hears.

A few months later he is spoken of as 'thin and delicate,' as 'giving the effect of the mind being too much for the body,' and as showing 'great fondness for, and determination to gain religious knowledge.' 'He has now twice,' his father says, 'asked what the Sunday subject[1] would be, and then has sat down with his Bible, to read and think about it. The other day, after reading the 1st of Acts he took a piece of paper and wrote as follows ':

I think why Jesus was taken up in the presence of Peter and John &c., was to confirm in their minds what Jesus had told them concerning his death and the other things he had preached to them, and the short time he was with them might not have been sufficient to quite confirm them, and, as he was taken from them, this was given as a finishing confirmance.

[1] Each Sunday the subject chosen for discussion at the next Church meeting was announced.

he is limited in extent, eternal at the same time that he
is limited in duration, that he is supreme and independent at the same time that he is inferior and dependent.

Next follows a long description of 'how to tell
the quantity of calcareous earth in marle.' Then
'April 28, one silkworm came out, afterwards two
or three every day.'

'Report of the Controversy of Porter and
Bagot: Mr. Porter maintains that Jesus Christ
lived in heaven with God before the beginning of
the world.'

'Hydro-oxygen microscope—ask the man about
the human eye. Take him some wings and stings
and tongues of insects.'

Even earlier books, made of folded paper, note
the dates on which the first leaves come out on
different trees, the first flowers blossom, record
some observations of habits or appearance of bird
or animal, and contain, here and there, a verse 'To
the Snowdrop,' 'To Mamma on her Birthday,'
&c. &c.

At the beginning of 1834 Mr. Dobell writes
that 'Sydney reads all Miss Martineau's books on
Political Economy, and devours any other book I
give him. He seems to understand all he reads
and does, and catches some things sooner than I do.'

CHAPTER II.

BOYHOOD, 1835–1839.

In the autumn of 1835 Mr. Dobell removed with his family to Cheltenham. The house taken there —which was, for a few years, both home and place of business, was large, tolerably open to the country, and had a paddock and good garden attached to it, so that there was ample play-room for the children.

This was an anxious and much occupied time in the life of the parents. One of the few entries concerning his eldest son—then in his twelfth year —made by the father, contains a copy of some verses addressed to Emily Fordham, who, about nine years later, became Sydney Dobell's wife. She had some time before spent one day with the family at Peckham Rye. Her husband often in later life spoke, both comically and pathetically, of the despair which on that occasion had filled his heart, as he looked down on the sleeve of his holland blouse with a sense of the impossibility

a school where they could have been satisfied that those best interests would be safe.

Besides this, being himself, after the early elementary routine, self-educated, and—as he possessed a good deal of originality of mind and natural refinement—having reason to be moderately satisfied with the result in his own case, John Dobell was, not unnaturally, disposed to bring up his children, or to let them bring themselves up, in the same fashion, without what would now be considered adequate assistance from good masters, or even from a sufficient variety of good books.

In mature life Sydney Dobell often expressed profound regret at the time and labour lost in unassisted study; but he was neither blind nor thankless in regard to immunities from temptation to evil, and influences towards all that was pure and noble, afforded by this home education, under the eyes of most anxiously conscientious parents.

A disadvantage more serious than the negative one, of absence of systematic help in his studies, was the being prematurely subjected to the weight and stress of business life.

In this way we must account for what is curiously notable in going through the records of his youth—the very few evidences of boyish love

tions quick. His general knowledge is very great, as he understands and remembers everything he devours, and his mental appetite is very keen. I have great reason to bless an All-gracious Father for such a domestic treasure.

At the beginning of 1837 is written :

He still devours every book he can get near, and the driest study seems a pleasure to him. Among other amusements, he is forming a new system of Classification of Birds.

A few months later the same record notes that 'Sydney is learning Latin twice a week from Mr. ———. The first instruction he has had in anything, except from his parents.'

In March 1838, when he is close upon fourteen, his father writes that he has grown a great fellow, that he now takes other part in the business than the work of the counting-house, that he is learning Greek and continuing Latin and French, that he has become curiously critical in his taste as regards poetry and composition, is fond of attempting dramatic writing, and has written a little drama entitled ' Napoleon '—some passages of which are in the father's judgment ' very fine.'

From this date poems of the boy's writing— some of considerable length—were, from time to time, printed in the Cheltenham papers.

familiar footing, but his feeling for Sir Arthur always remained a thing by itself.

The Diaries kept between the ages of twelve and fifteen record observations and speculations in Natural History and Natural Science, and minutely describe different aspects of sky and cloud scenery; while business memoranda occur among scraps of poetry, comments on important Biblical texts, and lists of 'Books I must read.'

From a few specimens, taken almost at random, the reader may judge of the calibre of their contents.

We observed to-day that a stream nearly one cubit broad, minus four inches, running at the rate of about one cubit in two seconds, and not more than half an inch deep, would by its force carry stones (of different shapes), some roundish, others square &c., of the size of a large pea and rather larger, a considerable distance. Might not then the erratic blocks of granite found at great distances from their mountains have been carried by a larger stream; for instance, if half an inch carry a grain, what will ten feet do?

.   .   .   .   .   .

As I was settling to my lessons in French this morning, I saw a largish hawk quivering at a little distance and striking at a small bird that kept flying this way and that in confusion. At this moment about five or six

thrust her head, when the cuckoo was seized with vertigo.'
Was not this opening of the mouth the effect of the egg,
just ready to put in the robin's nest, and the thrusting of
the robin's head down it her anxiety to break the egg?

. . . . . .

. . . June 18. Last night about nine o'clock, while
it was light, I was witness to a splendid phenomenon.
About N.W. from our parlour there was a large black
cloud, unbroken and deep black, reaching to about 25°
above the horizon. Above the cloud was the clear blue
sky, specked here and there with little white clouds.
Venus was shining brightly, not a breath stirred, the
clouds seemed motionless, it was one of the most beautiful
of evenings. I was gazing on the scene when suddenly
the black cloud was lit up by a stream of red light that
ran along the middle of it. Again it was dark as before,
but in about five minutes was lit up by a red light
springing up as from several different furnaces at different
parts of the cloud. There was no flame, but the bright
glare, as of hidden fires, lighted up the cloud, and made
what before seemed a black even mass resemble a mountain of chasms and cliffs. The fire uniformly seemed to
glare from the bottom of the cloud, sending its flames
upwards. The fire never left the cloud, but confined itself
to it; it kept on discharging for a quarter of an hour: as
I before said it looked, not like flames, but the vivid light
sent from a red and furious fire raging in its bowels.

Scores of similar passages occur; but we take
up a Diary of 1838, when the writer was fourteen

two alterations, one expungement, and the addition of a
verse, pronounced it good, copied and signed it ' Corrector,'
folded it, and directed it to the Free-press Office . . .
After tea read some more of ' Merchant of Venice' aloud :
it is a beautiful play, without any peculiarly broadly and
strikingly defined character, except Shylock (who is his
Richard III. in miniature, only wanting the vast designs,
and his mischief being necessarily, from the difference of
their stations and circumstances, on a smaller scale), yet
sustains the interest throughout, and exhilarates the
spirits, which have so many times given all up for lost,
with a happy end.   But 'tis a pity that the Launcelot scenes
should come between almost every fine and stirring scene
in the first act; this draws off and divides the attention
and breaks the chain of occurrences, thereby lessening the
interest in all by dividing it. Went to bed at half-past nine.

October 31.   Up at half-past seven ; business of the
morning as usual till half-past eight, breakfast.   Went
out till eleven to see Collins about bottles.   Came home,
wrote bills ; dinner at one.   After dinner began posting
the accounts of the month.   After tea finished ' Merchant
of Venice ' aloud.   The objection to the Launcelot scenes
does not apply to the last two or three acts, though it
were to be wished that, at the end, part of Portia and
Nerissa's gross bantering were left out.

This year closed with an illness—called by his
father typhus and by his mother nervous fever—of
which a night adventure,[1] involving a good deal of

---

[1] The house was broken into.

stered
brought
to get
gentle,
been so
It was
were po
people,

She
away t
sights
house;
revive,
that sh
father—
—and
' wrapp
suppose
how wo
able to
been tak

I thin
taken him
greater cha
covered, a
might have
or fight ag
did not ; a

have been Mr. Dobell's only reasonable ground of objection to the engagement. Miss Fordham's father, a man of intellect and culture, had belonged to 'the Church' founded by Mr. Thompson, and still held its principles, though he had withdrawn from direct membership. He was, also, an energetic social and political reformer—what in those days was considered an Ultra-Liberal, well acquainted with Godwin, Cobbett, and other celebrities of that time. Belonging to an influential Cambridgeshire family, he was lord of the three manors of Sandon, Luffnell, and Cromer, and, till an unsuccessful lawsuit impoverished him, possessed of considerable property.

His daughter Emily, perhaps a favourite among his numerous children, from the time she was four years old, when she used to be tied on a little pony, of which her father held the rein, was the frequent companion of his rides round and about the home-fields. Leading a secluded and yet a free and cheerful life, associating almost exclusively with family connections, yet having, within those limits, a fairly wide circle, the girl grew up in a singular simplicity of innocence and ignorance of evil. But for constitutional delicacy, her youth might have been a peculiarly happy and prosperous one.

And the sun hath a face for that happy place
   Which never he knows elsewhere,
As a villager gay, in his harvest array,
   He strides through the morning air :

Pane by pane, through hamlet and lane,
   He peepeth in every one ;
And right fair speech hath his love for each,
   That brave old neighbourly sun.

A village home for me,
   And the village peace that plays
In the calm delights of its holy nights .
   And the thoughts of its quiet days.

And a village home for me,
   When my village life is o'er ;
And the village hum at eve may come
   On my list'ning ear no more.

That sleep so calm and sound,
   How the weary heart would love,
With the village graves around
   And the village bells above :

And the village blessing borne
   On balm of Sabbath air,
And tears in simple eyes that mourn
   At village hour of prayer,
As they point to the stone with moss overgrown
   And think of the sleeper there.

A village home, a village home,
   With a village stream and tree,
Where the hearths are clean, and the graves are green,
   Oh, a village home for me !

creasing pressure of occupation made the practice
impossible, kept a Diary which was, from time
to time, read by Miss Fordham, for whom indeed
it was written.   This Diary contrasts strongly with
the earlier note-books and journals.   It briefly
records the studies and other occupations of each
day; mentions the books he is reading, and sometimes comments on their contents; but the chief
burden is of religious argument, exhortation and
aspiration, and every sentence testifies to the absolute sincerity with which he regarded the bond
between himself and Miss Fordham as 'not for time
but for Eternity.'

Soon after speaking of his son's engagement,
Mr. Dobell writes:

'Sydney, while in London,[1] voluntarily joined
the Church '—meaning that he became a professed
member of it—and adds: 'There could be no
external allurement, for Emily is not a member,
and the Church is not prosperous nor fascinating.'

'The Church' had of late been harassed and
weakened by internal dissensions.   Almost all its
influential members were Mr. Thompson's sons-in-
law, and family quarrels had embittered 'Church'
differences.

---

[1] On his way to or from Cambridgeshire.

how ' his greatest delight always was to interest me
in all good and beautiful things, and to rouse me
to high views of the highest duties of life.' They
studied out-doors together, botany, ornithology,
geology ; and she speaks of his keen pleasure in
any discovery in regard to the habits of beast, bird,
or insect. His presents to her, beyond the constant gifts of flowers, were almost always of books,
such books as, out of those his limited resources
enabled him to buy, he thought would be most
helpful to her.

About this time he mentions that his mother
had been seriously conversing with him, as to what
he would be, 'a Barrister or what?' His natural
answer, under the circumstances, was that he
wished to be what would soonest put him in a
position to claim his promised wife, and the idea
of any further study for the Bar was, of course,
abandoned.

Lessons and accounts continued chiefly to fill
his days. All records in his Diary of out-door
exercise—'fencing in the garden,' 'making a re-
doubt with the boys,' 'cutting a canal through an
island in the little stream which runs at the bottom
of Detmore field,' and enjoying the high spirits of
his horse, shown in ' plunging, rearing and kick-

that bane of educated women (or rather of women only half educated, their heads and not their hearts) Pedantry . . . You feel you could like her as much as a woman as you do as an authoress.'

' Woman,' he wrote in another part of his Diary, ' is to me, when read aright, perfection, or at least, the perfection of loveableness. . . . I love above all things in a woman's character, the spirit of devotedness and self-forgetfulness.'

It must have been at this time that he began to commit to memory the New Testament, for his Diaries constantly mention what portion of Scripture has been occupying him. He also, says, after telling Miss Fordham how he is often detained for long chats, at houses where he calls on business, by people anxious to ' convert ' him :

' We shall all get to be quite learned Theologians presently : as Papa reads the Bible, I always now follow the Greek text, so whenever a difficult passage occurs in the English, we refer to the Greek.'

His great desire for leisure for more extensive study, and the longing for plenty of time to read with which he sees and hears of books, is often alluded to.

pronounces ' the prose in some parts very good
indeed, the only pity is he should be such a fool as
to spoil it all by his confounded doggrel rhyme.'

A little later he mentions having got hold of
Defoe's ' Religious Courtship,' which he character-
ises as ' a *devilish* old volume.'

Two letters exchanged in June of this year,
1840, between Mr. Fordham and his future son-in-
law indicate a good deal of the inner history of
the time.

Mr. Fordham, having read two or three of the
letters recently received by his daughter, wrote to
remonstrate on the ' painful and excessive feelings '
which, he considered, they betrayed and encouraged. ' All the difference,' he asserts,

between an unhappy and a happy man, and therefore
between a wise and a foolish man,— lies in the proper
government of our passions. . . . Religion, too, which has
for its *sole* object the happiness of man, *above all other
things* teaches us the absolute necessity of self-government, and the cultivation of calm and tranquil feelings,
as being the sources of all true felicity; knowing that
God is the author of all things, in whom, when we do
what is right in His sight, we ought to place implicit
confidence. I felt very sorry when I read your letters,
because I perceive (what you must be conscious of your-

would

cribe.

that

which

V... of God,

that God

send to

religion

important

her which

and caused me

sufficient from our

that such a vast

not quote E.'s

permission to do

and I quote them

as I do that the

unity of principle,

I would not do less

a person to have an idea of an extensive landscape by constantly looking through a telescope at one of its objects.

One evening he mentioned having, at the wish of 'the boys' lectured to them (extempore) on the History of the Reformation: and this practice of extempore speaking was continued.

As his children grew up, Mr. Dobell adopted the habit of holding Sunday meetings, on the principle of 'the Church'-meetings. On one of these occasions his eldest son rising to speak on a subject which always occupied a good deal of his attention—that of Prophecy—spoke on till (just, as he used laughingly to relate, when he found himself well-warmed to his subject and beginning to master his fast-crowding ideas), his eldest sister was deputed to enquire whether he would be much longer, as he had already been speaking upwards of two hours!

Some of his criticisms on Priestley's 'Institutes' are worth quoting. Though written by him as a boy of sixteen, they are characteristic of the views held to the end of his life. Where so much changed it is interesting to note those essentials which remained unchanged.

I think, he says, that Priestley's great mistake lies in supposing that God in creating and legislating for the

strength, and amid circumstances which at the same time
that they brighten the steel test its durability and temper.
But, lest the rough iron should revolt at the grindstone,
which must sharpen it for God's sake, He has given one
bright example of what it might become, one shining proof,
that the trials of this world are not, though heavy, too
weighty to be overcome, one glorious witness that the steel
need not break in the tempering.

The study of Mosheim's ' Ecclesiastical History,'
of ' the Wine-book with maps,' of French, Latin,
and Greek, with the inevitable accounts, form the
occupation of many days.   Then comes a passage
—written apparently in answer to some expressions of pity in one of Miss Fordham's letters—
concerning Feargus O'Connor.   If she considered
all the circumstances of the case she would, she is
told, ' feel more contempt than pity.'

Can there be anything more pusillanimous than his
conduct ?   He has for years been employed in exciting
discord which he, the coward, has not courage enough to
face, and urging others on to danger at the first appearance of which he flies. . . .

The very first week of being in jail ' in the people's
cause,' he whines like a spoiled child put in the corner,
and prays for death to relieve him from his sufferings !
Shame on him !   Instead of the bold dashing ' Man of the
People ' we saw in prosperity, here he is, under the prospect

The friend of Papa's who called on Colburn for the manuscript, says he is the intimate friend of Campbell, the great poet, and that, should Papa approve, he will show 'Napoleon' to him. This is capital! I would sooner have *his* approval, who is a real poet, than half-a-dozen Mr. Colburns.

Soon after he gives a detailed and spirited account of an attack made upon him by a clergyman, for not attending public worship in any of the Cheltenham Churches or Chapels. His manner of receiving and repulsing this attack, of an evidently more zealous than wise adversary, is characteristic, but too lengthy for quotation.

Another entry in his Diary mentions a long gossip with a gentleman who 'was an admirer of Napoleon, had travelled all over Europe, and could curse Sir Hudson Lowe from the bottom of his heart.'

The opinion given by Campbell of the manuscript that had been submitted to him—'he prophesies that I shall make my way as a writer, and that with care there is no doubt of my becoming a poet'—was at that time a source of pleasant satisfaction. Later in life the notion of a 'poet' made 'with care' appealed strongly to his sense of the ridiculous.

feeble and commonplace in conversation, whom
you would never suspect of writing such beautiful
poetry,' by 'the gentleman who showed my pieces
to Campbell, a most agreeable man to converse
with.'

As the summer waned he began to look forward with almost painful intensity to the September visit to Cambridgeshire—and frankly expressed
his hope that Miss Fordham's eldest brother may
not be at home, because he feared he was an early
riser, and would spoil the dear mornings 'while
the dews are deep,' the memory of which breathes
through a poem, written twenty years later,
addressed to a little girl then growing up amid the
scenes of his wife's girlhood.[1]

September 7 (Miss Fordham's birthday) he says
how long the day has seemed to him because he
had 'crowded into it the thoughts and memories,
the hopes and fears, of years past and years to
come.'

Noting the date on which his son starts for
Cambridgeshire, the father writes: 'Sydney is still
very thin, though he looks broad. I think this
love-affair is too much for his nerves—the constant

---

[1] 'Love,' p. 316, vol. ii., collected edition of Poems.

Mr. —— he wrote, seems to him to forget the end for which all punishment is given.

What we call punishment we ought rather to call help and assistance. . . . The undoubted end of religion being the formation of a certain sort of character. . . . When we are even forbidden ' to judge ' our brother, shall we dare to judge God ?

> ' Say here He gives too little, there too much,
> Snatch from His hands the balance and the rod,
> Rejudge His justice, be the God of God ? '

The same evening he commented on St. Paul's saying, that he had ' faith towards God that there should be a resurrection of the dead, both of the just and the unjust,' adding ' yet some men will be wiser than Paul, and say that the righteous only shall be raised.'

As the winter came on there was rather a larger proportion of study; chiefly Latin and Greek, the Bible, and various theological and controversial works. By and by he had ' the luxury ' of being laid up for a few days: ' able to be still, and to think at leisure and uninterruptedly.' But at the close of this year, 1840, he was again energetically engaged in business, and seizing with avidity all opportunities of study: while the increasing persistency and consistency of his petitions

CHAPTER V.

FROM SEVENTEEN TO TWENTY.   1841–1844.

It is difficult to give any true notion of the stress
and tension of this period of Sydney Dobell's life
without touching things almost too sacred for handling; and yet, without some reference to these
inner phases of his mind, no indication can be
given of one of the causes of the early and disastrous break down of his physical system.

Ten years later, in connection with his wife's
ill-health, he wrote : ' About three or four years
before our marriage I adopted an excessive practice
of prayer. . . . My poor E. easily fell into my
enthusiastic arguments . . .'

' Pray without ceasing,' ' Ask, and you shall
receive,' seem to have been adopted in all simplicity as command and promise.   The child and boy
had been brought up in a firm belief in the definite
and immediate efficacy of prayer.   But the excessive practice of it was not a thing inculcated by his

to him.   And, on this one point, it was conviction, not resolution, that was wanting.   The practice once acquired, it needed a voice from Heaven, speaking with power and authority, to convince him of the duty of abandoning it.

He wrote in one of his poems ('The Harps of Heaven') :—

> On a solemn day
> I clomb the shining bulwark of the skies :
> Not by the beaten way,
> But climbing by a prayer,
> That like a golden thread hung by the giddy stair
> Fleck'd on the immemorial blue,
> By the strong step-stroke of the brave and few,
> Who, stirr'd by echoes of far harmonies,
> Must either lay them down and die of love,
> Or dare
> Those empyrean walls that mock their starward eyes.

And it was as the golden way by which we mount from earth to heaven, as the golden chain which binds earth to heaven, that he regarded prayer : and of this chain he could not persuade himself, for any earthly consideration, to loosen his hold.

' He looked ill when we first met,' his wife says, ' and I never knew him long free from some kind of suffering during the years of our engagement.' Since his death many of those who knew him in his youth have expressed their wonder that he

that the more diligently he occupies himself with such things the sooner that happy time may come.

In March of this year, 1841, Miss Fordham was seriously ill; and the receipt of a letter from her father instead of from herself caused a sudden shock that was followed by an aftertime of supreme anxiety.

Commenting on this in his Diary, he says how far easier this is to bear than would have been the slightest illness of the heart. Nevertheless, by the time Miss Fordham was well again, even casual acquaintances commented on his worn look. While feeling it almost sacrilege to cease from prayerful thought of her, he had, of course, gone through the business routine of the days. On her recovery he was to have been allowed to visit her, but family arrangements made this inconvenient, and the meeting was postponed till she came to Cheltenham.

In regard to dissensions following on a disputed will, he wrote to her: ' Do not fall into the error (which has caused so much unhappiness around you), of thinking that those who treat us ill must necessarily be devoid of every good feeling, must be " evil spirits," because towards us they have committed evil.'

Then, after a good deal more on the same subject, said—'I daresay you may think I have written a great deal about a little, but it is not a little thing to me . . . I long that you should be free from the least tinge of that spirit—so different from His who said, " Love your enemies," " do good to them that hate you," " bless them that curse you," " overcome evil with good." '

When, by and by, Miss Fordham was staying with his family, they seem to have occupied a good deal of the time they had together in Scripture reading, and especially in the study of those prophecies supposed to indicate the time of Christ's Reign upon Earth as at hand.

The summer of 1841 was spent in Cheltenham, with only occasional days in the country. In his Diary, after Miss Fordham had left, he says how he has changed in the last two years : how, two years ago, ' to be in the open air, under the blue sky, to tread the turf, to feel the smile of God's sunshine and the breath of His wind seemed enough for happiness : ' but now, dear as these things still are to him, they are no longer ' enough.' Asking Miss Fordham to study the Epistle of St. James, he remarks in what a special way it seemed to him to abound in a spirit of universal benevolence, kindli-

ness, courteousness, and anxiety for others. He
gave her, in the same letter, a little physiological
disquisition, urging her to take more nourishing
food, saying that what was sufficient nourishment
while the mind was inert, is not sufficient now that
she attempts mental exertion : ' some being taken
by the brain, enough is not left for the body.' He
begs her to strengthen her mind by moderate exertion ; leaving off always before she is tired, and so
gradually accustoming herself to more arduous
study.

An election occurring this summer, caused
great political excitement in Cheltenham. The
young Dobells had been brought up to believe that
those aspiring in a special manner to be ' children
of God' should keep aloof from such agitations ;
and Sydney, when experiencing disappointment in
regard to a matter near his heart, questioned himself, with quaint simplicity, as to whether he ought
not to receive this as a deserved chastisement for
having too warmly interested himself in the contest.

One July afternoon he speaks of having spent
in the garden, adding, ' My brain has been over-
exerted the last few days, I think, and wants a
" bait." ' Soon after he wrote that, in looking

hrough his Diary, it had occurred to him, that
were it to be read by those who look no higher
,han earth, they might well ask scornfully how it
was that they, in many things, succeeded as well
as did the offerer of such constant and fervid petitions. The answer he makes is :

God governs the world He has formed by certain great
and perfect organic laws. By obedience to these an end
may be obtained so long as it is within their scope. But
for those who have consecrated their hearts to the attain-
ment of unworldly excellence, a new set of laws, or rather
a neglected chapter of the one great Code, arises, and in a
manner supersedes the merely organic enactments. By
these we are led to depend upon the moving cause of
immaterial things, by these new sequences are introduced
into the chain of our events, we are led to look higher than
before, and are linked with that Heaven towards which all
our noble aspirations tend.

The visit to Cambridgeshire was this year postponed till the end of September.

When speaking of his return, his father approv-
ingly records that Sydney had managed during his
holiday, to spend two Sundays in London with ' the
Church,' and mentions admiringly that he has
written ' in two pieces of days, Emily all the time
at the same table, and himself only seventeen, a

poem of five hundred lines—an imaginary legend, to account for the names of some of the places in the neighbourhood.'

To this date belong the following lines, in acknowledgment of a note from Sir Arthur Faulkner, announcing his brother's death:

To Sir A. B. F.

If to the tortures of a heart uncalm
A sympathising friendship would be balm;
If when the storm is high and skies are dark,
It would be sweet to meet a kindred bark;
If we may hold community in care,
And sorrow is a burden hearts may share—
Think, while empaled in its funereal gloom,
Thy heart sits watching a fraternal tomb,
Mine, while it echoes every sorrowing tone
And in thy dying friend deplores its own,
Whispers thee how earth's tears are only given
To melt the film that blinds our eyes to Heaven,
And like the flowret bathed in summer dew,
Teach the seared heart to bud and bloom anew.

The 'tyrant' business grew more tyrannical as the months went on. Any but the baldest and briefest entries in his Diary are often, he says, impossible.

Miss Fordham spent great part of the summer of 1842 with the Dobell family in the country.

Late in the autumn of 1842, his father wrote:

Sydney has become a beautiful orator. He can
peak on the spur of the moment really eloquently.
Iis studied speeches are full of matter, eloquently
xpressed, and delivered with grace and dignity.'

It is also mentioned that a classical tutor who
;ave him lessons once a week, expressed surprise
it the amount he had learnt from Æschylus, and
.hat the Bible with Lexicon in hand was studied
:very evening.

The year 1843, of which there is little record,
must have had much such a history as its predecessor. He spoke at the ' Church '-meetings on
any occasion of being able to spend a Sunday in
London, and contributed to a manuscript magazine
circulated among members of ' the Church.' He
wrote, also, a great deal of poetry: some of which
was published in ' Chambers's Journal ' and other
periodicals. Amid a good deal of what would,
probably, strike a critic as not above the mark
likely to be reached by a talented youth, occur
verses and lines suggestive of greater things. The
unpublished poems, mostly addressed to Miss
Fordham, and written with an idea of being sung,
are musical, and often contain some happy phrase
—but, as wholes, are not strikingly original or
remarkable.   .

In his own opinion, both his father, and his grandfather on the father's side, having possessed something of 'fatal facility' in verse—these early attempts showed little beyond an inherited faculty, and were of little value or promise.

It has, no doubt, been impossible after reading the mass of intimate records of the inner life of Sydney Dobell's youth, from which the foregoing chapters have been compiled, and failing any counterbalancing knowledge of its lighter aspects, not to produce a one-sided and painful picture of a time that remains in his mother's memory as one of, on the whole, bright, buoyant, various, and vigorous activity.

His nature was always free both from that pale and colourless indifference, and from that gloomy asceticism, which have no pulse, no palate, no eye or ear, for the sensuous glories and stirring delights of this life.

Physical exercise and intellectual encounter were alike welcome to him. He had that pleasure in the use of all his faculties natural to a well constituted organisation. From an hour's skating on a brilliant winter morning, or a gallop over turf on a spirited horse, he could have derived no keener exhilaration if such pursuits had been the chief interests of his existence.

Someone has said that all ' life ' of which we have any experience is only a process of gradual destruction. If so, the ' life ' in this case was of greatly more than average strength, and the process of destruction unduly rapid in proportion to that strength.

It was not deficiency of matter, but excess of spirit—or whatever is the consuming element within us—that too early wore him out.

Four lines from ' In Memoriam,' seem to suggest a more representative idea of Sydney Dobell's youth than can be given by any amount of detail:

> High nature, amorous of the good,
>   But touched with no ascetic gloom :
>   And passion pure in snowy bloom
> Through all the years of April blood.

APPENDIX TO BOOK I.

A.

AMONG the bold and original thinkers who lived in the latter part of the eighteenth and beginning of the present century, Samuel Thompson was one of the freest and most fearless: but although he was well acquainted with the ideas which influenced the conclusions of Voltaire, Rousseau, Hume, and Paine, the path of free enquiry and free thought brought him to a result exactly opposite to that arrived at by the more celebrated freethinkers of his day. His conviction only became more deeply rooted that, in the life and teaching of Christ must be found the secret of human improvement, happiness and hope. At the same time he was impressed by the fact that for at least sixteen centuries the practice of Christianity had not been fairly and honestly tried by any but exceptional men; that no society had seriously endeavoured to put into practice the principles taught by Jesus, and that no Church had restricted its creed or ceremonial to such as were enjoined by the actual teaching of Christ and his contemporaries. For, although the Evangelical portion of the reformed Church and the bulk of English dissenters had thrown aside the observances of Rome, they had all, even including the Quakers, retained the creeds, the dogmas, and more or less of the formulæ handed down by Roman tradition, and owing their concrete form to the decisions of Roman Councils.

Mr. Thompson was a man of action, and he straightway began practically to apply the twofold conviction. First, by trying to make his personal life and conduct conform to the teaching of Christ; secondly, by collecting a band of friends who, while separately endeavouring to practise the same Christian life, conducted their public religious observances according to rules based upon Bible teaching alone.[1]

He started on his religious pilgrimage with the creed of an orthodox Churchman; but the natural result of his plan was that the society was occupied for many years by frank and fearless discussions concerning all the great problems of religion : the New Testament, rationally understood, being accepted as the ultimate authority and guide.

The themes since discussed in periodicals like the 'Nineteenth Century,' 'Contemporary' and 'Fortnightly' Reviews were matters of frequent conversation among these men; and although the speakers were many of them self-educated, and the style of argument more crude than it would be to-day—yet strong native intelligence and entire simplicity enabled them to anticipate almost every thought and idea that has found expression some seventy years later, while the consistent result of their enquiry was an ever deepening reverence and love for, and faith in, the Founder of Christianity.

The manner in which Mr. Thompson reached this result— not by the beaten track of dogmatic assumption, but by the path of free enquiry and through the thorny ways of scepticism— peculiarly fitted him to influence unbelievers. Among his writings is an essay on the 'Evidences of Christianity,' in which the subject is treated from the point of view of a man of the world : a fresh and vigorous treatment which enables him to use the very arguments that are still found most potent to turn the position of his adversaries, but which no man who had not thrown off the ordinary forms and observances of religion could use with similar force. . . .

A vast amount of what is usually styled orthodox belief was thus set aside, as not actually authorised by the Gospels or necessary to Christianity, and the chief dogma retained was the

[1] They held that public prayer was not only not enjoined, but was forbidden, by Christ—so interpreting Matthew vi. 6.

acknowledgment of Christ as the divine authority for all our conclusions touching the practice, end, and aim of human life.

A Church was formed consisting of members who were pledged to treat one another as equals. The persons composing this body belonged to various social grades. One or two country gentlemen of property, a few merchants, many tradesmen, with a few artisans and servants. So long as the members were in earnest the system worked more easily than might have been expected—and is remembered by those who endeavoured to work it out as something perhaps too good to last, but not wholly impracticable for this world.

It is stated by many observers that the effect of this scheme of life upon the persons practising it was very striking: it imparted a gentle dignity of manner, and an accuracy of thought and expression, to those who by birth, breeding and outward circumstance would have been otherwise common, and even vulgar, in their habits and conversation. But in all questions of the relation between a man and the principles he holds, it is difficult to distinguish which is the author, whether the man begets the principles or the principles make the man, or whether, as is most probable, one reacts on the other.

Mr. Thompson is described by all who saw or heard him as singularly gifted by nature, both in mind and person. A commanding presence, an expressive and beautiful countenance, united to singular eloquence and facility in debate, were qualifications which would probably have secured him a more brilliant history had he chosen any career but that of a religious reformer.

It should be borne in mind that he worked with no advantages of wealth or position. His origin was humble. He carried into the bread-winning activity of his life the same energy and perseverance, the same shrewdness and high principles combined, and the same reforming tendencies that characterised him in other pursuits.

He was idolised by his friends, feared by his opponents, but respected by all who came in contact with him, whether friends or foes, and this marked personal influence the man himself attributed entirely to the principles which guided his every action.

Spectators who remember his once familiar face on the platforms where were assembled the early leaders of reform, affirm that though the men who surrounded him were chiefly men of superior rank, his face and bearing shone out among them, as of one belonging to a higher and nobler race. This effect was, probably, due to the fact, that his peculiar principles had led him to discard all personal ambition and worldly aim in political life—he resolutely refused the share that was offered him in any of the material advantages of party triumphs. His one end in participating in the reform movement was to aid men to be free to follow the truth—and he, therefore, appeared on the scene in a serene attitude of mind which would naturally be reflected in the countenance and mark him out as distinct from the ordinary politician.

But Mr. Thompson had faults as well as virtues, and his followers were but fallible mortals, unequal to grapple with the gigantic difficulties which beset their endeavour to maintain a system so ideal as that which they had called into being. 'The Church,' founded on the model of the Christian Church of the first century, was already old before its time, and repeated in a few short years the history of its great predecessor.

Success and rapidly increasing numbers, together with the principle of absolute social union and equality, naturally brought to the surface the great question of Church fellowship and Church power—where they should begin? how far they should extend? And some of the younger members, with a certain show of logic, revived the old Judaic idea of exclusiveness,[1] according to which 'the Church' was to be regarded as a community set apart by God, consecrated to a superior existence, separated from and distinct from 'the world.' . . .

[1] This idea was carried to greater extremes by Sydney Dobell's father than by any other member of 'the Church.'

This theory, which was no part of Samuel Thompson's original system, led to differences among the members, and, ultimately, after his death, caused ' the Church' to collapse and, practically, cease to exist.

Sydney Dobell was born at a time when this religious scheme appeared to be successful: his father and mother were both participators in the movement; they left London before its failure, carrying with them a vivid memory of its better days.

A statement of this twofold series of facts, first, Mr. Thompson, his strong, clear and masculine view of Christianity, and his application of that view to the daily life of a Christian gentleman; secondly, ' the Church,' and its assumption of exclusive superiority, is a necessary adjunct to a Biography of Sydney Dobell—as containing the seeds which again blossomed into his noble Christian personality, and as accounting for the peculiar circumstances of his early intellectual life.

B.

A BRIEF ACCOUNT OF THE CHURCH OF GOD, KNOWN AS FREE-THINKING CHRISTIANS : ALSO, AN ABSTRACT OF THE PRINCIPLES WHICH THEY BELIEVE, AND THE LAWS OF CHURCH FELLOWSHIP THEY HAVE ADOPTED.

Cast thy bread upon the waters: for thou shalt find it after many days.—In the morning sow thy seed, and in the evening withhold not thine hand: for thou knowest not whether shall prosper, either this or that. *Eccl.* xi. 1, 6.

Yea, and why even of yourselves judge ye not what is right? *Luke* xii. 57.

Prove all things; hold fast that which is good. 1 *Thess.* v. 21.

PREFACE.

A CAREFUL perusal of the following pages, will, it is presumed, convince every reader, that the parties from whom it emanates, yield to none in devotedness to the truth as it is in Jesus, or in veneration for the Sacred Scriptures.

Their progress has been from Trinitarianism and the many doctrinal errors usually associated with it; from Priestcraft, whether in the form of an open pretension to spiritual supremacy, or in the insidious guise of exclusive religious teacher or lecturer; and from the rites and forms that accompany Priestcraft—albeit, at one time, they venerated many of those things—towards the purity of the faith, as it was once delivered to the saints.

In the present day, a powerful hierarchy is striving to move heaven and earth, in order to roll back the tide of religious enlightenment, and to banish from the world those sacred principles of religious freedom which were established by the labours, and sealed by the blood, of many righteous servants of God.

This is a sign of the times not to be mistaken. It is, moreover, the signal for all who prize religious freedom, and all who are convinced that the revelation through Jesus Christ is a perfect work, and that the religion dispensed by hirelings is not that Gospel, to unite as one man, even as their divine master has commanded them, and hold to the truth and support every man his brother, and so build their eternal happiness upon that Rock, against which the gates of hell shall never prevail.

London, March, 1841.

A BRIEF ACCOUNT ETC.

THE first members of this Church were part of the Congregation of Mr. Winchester, the celebrated advocate of the doctrine of the ' Universal Restoration ;' but it was during the ministry of his successor, Mr. Vidler, that they were led to deny the doctrine of the Trinity, and the correctness of having paid or exclusive teachers in the Church. This produced a separation, and those who seceded held their first meetings in the year 1798.

The object which these seceders proposed to themselves, as stated in a declaration published at the time, was ' to make the conduct and example of the first Christians, so far as they

followed the commands of Jesus Christ and his Apostles, their
only rule.' In furtherance of this object, they held many
meetings, which they devoted to the reading and examination
of the New Testament, 'for the purpose,' as they leave on
record, 'of collecting and arranging the laws, form of government, discipline, and essential principles of the Church of God,
as set forth by the Apostles of Christ.'

The result of these meetings was, that on the 24th day of
March, 1799, a special meeting was held, at which, 'after solemn
preparation and prayer,' those present resolved themselves into
a Church, elected an elder and deacons, and agreed upon the
place and times of meeting, and the religious exercises in which
they should in future engage. In the following year they published a book entitled, ' *The true design of the Church of God,
and the government thereof, exhibited by a succession of laws
founded upon the authority of Jesus Christ and his Apostles,
faithfully extracted from the New Testament. Published for
the Church meeting in Old Change, London*, 1800.'

The name first chosen by this Church, to distinguish themselves from the rest of the religious world was, HUMBLE EN-
QUIRERS AFTER TRUTH, they afterwards adopted that of FREE-
THINKING CHRISTIANS. This latter name was chosen to imply
at once, their conviction that the free exercise of reason is
essential to a correct understanding and appreciation of divine
truth, and their belief in Jesus Christ, as the messenger of God.
But, as a Church founded solely upon the laws and authority of
the Scriptures, they consider their proper and scriptural desig-
nation to be CHURCH OF GOD.

The foregoing statement will shew the esteem in which the
members of this Church have ever held those great principles,
emphatically called Protestant,—the right of private judgment,
and the sufficiency of the Scriptures. In accordance with these
principles they maintain the utmost freedom of enquiry, and
freedom of speech in their religious association; and, they feel
bound to reject, as contrary to the will of God, any doctrine

concerning religion, whether of faith or practice, which does not agree with the Scriptures correctly interpreted. To the question, who is to judge concerning religious doctrine and Scripture interpretation? they reply—every man, individually and for himself, not as a right merely, but as a most imperative duty. It is impossible one man can be another's substitute in matters of religion, or that the responsibility attached to the duty of individual judgment can be evaded.

In submitting the following statement, the formation of a creed, or of articles of faith, is not intended. Any such attempt would be in evident contradiction to the principles just stated. Neither do this Church profess to advance new truths—for those things cannot be new which the Scriptures taught so many ages since; nor yet, strange and unheard of opinions concerning revealed religion, for they hold no opinion which may not be found amongst one or other of the Churches of the religious world, either as cherished truths or as distinguishing principles : but, what follows is presented as an abstract of the views of revealed truth, both in religious doctrine and church organisation, to which the members of this Church have been led. They have long possessed these views, they prize them highly, and desiring their furtherance submit them to the consideration of others.

There is one God, and only one, the sole Creator and sovereign disposer of all things, material and spiritual,—the Jehovah of the Old Testament, the God and Father of our Lord Jesus Christ.

God revealed His being and His will to the first families of the earth, providing thus for the moral and religious necessities of His rational creatures, as He had already provided for the physical wants and necessities of all creation.

Abraham and his posterity were, subsequently, chosen to be the depositaries of revealed truth, and the Jewish people were instituted the people and the Church of God, Moses and the Prophets promulgating and enforcing the law of God. But perfect as this dispensation was, in respect of the objects proposed, and the circumstances of its recipients, it always pointed to a more perfect dispensation when the Messiah should come, and the Gospel should be proclaimed, first to the Jews, and afterwards to all the nations of the earth.

Jesus of Nazareth was that Messiah—that Son of God— that beloved Son, concerning whom, the heavens declared ' hear ye him '—a man, not a supernal being. To do good and to teach the truths of religion in simplicity and perfection, were his meat and his drink. The love of God, and love, or benevolence, towards mankind, were declared, by him, to be the sum of all religion; he denounced that profession of religion which consists in mere faith, or apparent sanctity, without fruits; he taught that the true worshippers should worship God in spirit and in truth; he taught the forgiveness of sins upon repentance; the resurrection of the dead; and the future righteous judgment of all mankind.

This same Jesus suffered death at the hands of the Jewish people, and was raised from the dead by the mighty power of God—the reward of his own perfect obedience, and the certain confirmation of the truth of everything which he had taught.

After his resurrection from the dead, he was with his Apostles many days, and fully instructed them in all things pertaining to his kingdom. He commanded them to preach the glad tidings of this kingdom to all nations of the earth, beginning at Jerusalem;—for this great work they were endued with power from on high, and in obeying this command their lives were spent.

The labours of the Apostles were realised in a twofold result —the conversion of unbelievers; and the establishment of the Church of God under Jesus Christ, as the head and chief of a new dispensation. Neither of these objects was attained without the accomplishment of the other; and therefore, in whatever city or place their testimony was received, all who believed were united together, and organised as assemblies, or parts of the Church of God, and, these churches now became the depositaries of the truths of divine revelation, and occupied that place in the dispensations of Providence which had been previously occupied by the descendants of Abraham, and the Church under Moses.

The Church of God is, thus, a continuous institution, and one and the same Church in all ages. Unity is its distinguishing feature. All who complied with the conditions which the messengers of God required were united with those of like faith; and whatever assembly obeyed the laws of God, without any admixture of human authority, however separated by time or place, were parts of His Church.

Under this new dispensation, of which Jesus and the Apostles were the agents, the distinction of Jew and Gentile, slave and freeman, man and woman, secures no peculiar or spiritual privileges in the sight of God, or in His Church; descent from Abraham, and national consanguinity, are overruled by the relationship and brotherhood of a common faith, and common obedience to one Lord and master. Equality, therefore, is the condition of members of the Church of God.

In order to become a member of the Church of God, the Apostles required those who believed in Jesus to repent of their past sins, and resolve in future to obey the revealed will of God. As the messengers of God, they proposed no other conditions; and those who complied with these conditions, are declared to have received justification, that is, forgiveness from God of all past sin; to be accepted by Him, that is, received into His Church; and, to be His elect, that is, chosen by Him for a life of religion and holiness. These are the only scriptural doctrines of salvation, justification, and election.

To this Church, the Apostles prescribed the form of Church government under which it should exist; the mode of religious improvement and instruction which it should adopt; and the

nature and kind of religious worship which, as a Church, it
should render to God.

THE FORM OF GOVERNMENT, or CHURCH ESTABLISHMENT,
instituted by the Apostles, was as simple as it was perfect. It
consisted of elders, that is overseers; of deacons, that is, servants; and of messengers. An elder was ordained in each
assembly of the Church of God, not as a lord over God's
heritage—not for the purpose of personal gain, or as a means of
livelihood, or for worldly influence—neither as constrained to
an irksome duty—but, as a brother among brethren, to preserve
the order of the meetings, and, by example and precept, induce
and secure a willing obedience to the laws of God. Deacons
were appointed, either as aids to the elder, or when any affairs
were to be transacted to which the whole body could not
attend: and messengers were chosen when it was necessary
to communicate, personally, with distant churches. Such is
the Church Establishment of the New Testament. All that
system of spiritual domination, which has exercised, and still
exercises so much influence in the Christian world, is wholly,
and *avowedly*, without the authority of the Apostles of Jesus;
and, though essential for the support and influence of a class,
is utterly subversive of the rights of believers, and the constitution of the Church of God.

THE METHOD OF RELIGIOUS INSTRUCTION, and means of increase in the knowledge of religious truth, established by the
Apostles in the Church of God, consisted mainly, in private
converse, and mutual admonition and exhortation; but, when
assembled in one place, as a Church, the speakers were to
speak, two or three, and the rest to judge. Paid or exclusive
teachers, under any name or guise, were unheard of;—the
distinction of clergy and laity, priest and people was unknown;
no such orders or distinctions existed in the apostolic Churches,
nor can they now exist in the Church without the entire destruction of those principles upon which it was founded.

THE RELIGIOUS WORSHIP commanded by Jesus, and instituted by his Apostles, in the Church of God, under the Gospel dispensation, was equally consistent with the attributes of the Divine Being, and the rational nature of His offspring. It consists in obedience to God, uninfluenced by temporary considerations; in faithfulness to the commands of Jesus, however tempted to swerve from them; in care and disinterested labour for the preservation of the principles and the purity of the Church, purchased by the sufferings and sacrifices of the holy servants of God; in benevolence, forbearance, meekness, integrity; in an open profession of the truth, and conduct emanating from faith in the promises of God;—such is the worship, and such are the spiritual sacrifices which the Church of God are continually to offer up. But, public social prayers, Sabbaths, holy days, and all other forms and ceremonies, are devoid of sanction from the New Testament. All authorised rites and ceremonies ceased with the Jewish temple worship.

To the Church thus established, all the promises of God, and all the exhortations of the Apostles to believers, are addressed; either to that Church as a whole, or to the assemblies or individuals who are part of that whole. To be united with this Church must have been the highest privilege, and the first duty of everyone who believed in Jesus Christ as the Son of God; for the existence of an independent, or isolated believer, or of a class of persons accepting revealed religion, and yet not united with others of like faith, is, in no one case, contemplated. The religion of Jesus, as expounded by himself and his Apostles, is not, as a whole, either applicable or practicable under any other circumstance than that of Church fellowship.

Such is the religion of Jesus Christ, according to the New Testament, and such are the characteristic and essential principles of the Church of God, as established by divinely appointed messengers. To become a Church of God, one only and obvious means exists, or ever did, or could exist, acceptance of the conditions propounded by God through His messengers. These conditions can be learned nowhere but in the New Testament.

He who prescribed these conditions alone can change or modify them,—no such power exists on earth; apostolical descent is a fiction, the spiritual authority claimed by hierarchies, priests, or their agents, mere assumption. If in the days of the Apostles any Church which set aside the commands of God, as inconvenient or inexpedient, or which adopted any invention of man as a religious duty, ceased to be of the Church of God, so must it be in the present time. The blessing of the Gospel can be received, only by complying with the conditions of the Gospel, and the advantages of revelation realised, only in the proportion in which its truths and principles are correctly understood and faithfully applied.

CHAPTER I.

In 1844, just after his twentieth birthday, letters were exchanged between Sydney Dobell and his future father-in-law, in regard to the date of his marriage.

Worldly prospects were not brilliant on either side. The lawsuit before referred to had recently caused Mr. Fordham great losses, and resulted in his having to leave the old home at Sandon-bury. The move was only to another part of the Fordham estate, Odsey; but a change, which transferred to comparative strangers the scenes of so many meetings and partings, of so many associations—' the dear green gate, the Terrace, the woods, the lanes, above all that window and the rose-tree growing by it—' was felt as no light loss.

From the new home — Odsey House—Mr. Fordham wrote, in April 1844, that he regarded the enquiry made of him as a very proper one, but

feared his answer would not be altogether satisfactory. 'However,' he continued :—

when my legal affairs are settled, which I think will be
the case in about another month or two, and when, probably, poor G.'s [1] fate in this world will also be determined—by the Disposer of all events—one way or another,
I hope to be able to answer your enquiries more explicitly.
As to the postponement of your marriage—I can enter
too readily into your just feelings and honourable mo-
tives to desire it of you, after five years of most patient
and affectionate courtship, in which you have always conducted yourself towards E. and myself and Mrs. Fordham,
in a manner highly creditable to your profession of our
holy religion.   But I cannot do more than I can : or
more than I think my duty requires of me in justice to
all my large family.   It would not be becoming in me to
recommend any precise period for your marriage, because,
as I do not know anything of *your* pecuniary means, nor
of the plans and intentions of your Father, I am entirely
unqualified to give you advice.

Matters admitted of such arrangement as
enabled the young people to begin their married
life, though on a very modest scale, for, on the
15th of July of this year Mr. Dobell writes :
' Sydney's courtship, which began five years ago,
is now nearly ended.   He and his eldest brother

---

[1] His eldest son, who was dying of consumption.

and sister started for London, outside the coach, on Saturday last, and it is intended that he should be married at Royston, on Thursday the 18th.' Mr. Dobell goes on to explain circumstances which prevent either his or his wife's presence at the ceremony; then says: 'Emily joined the Church some months ago. Dear Sydney is still exemplary for piety and virtue; but has certainly not advanced much lately in exhibiting or exercising any increased talent or intellectual powers.' This his father accounts for by saying, that 'his love affair has been carried on with such unvarying attention to E——, as exclusively to occupy his mind,' and adds: ' This it is that makes us more readily assent to his marriage, though so young. He looks horridly thin and pale. His mind fidgets away his physical powers.'

After expressing his good wishes for his son, and his hope, 'that Reason not Poetry may guide him to the performance of Duty,' Mr. Dobell remarks, that 'business is certainly not Sydney's element; in a profession, or as a literary man, he might have distinguished himself, but we could not order or arrange it otherwise.'

The same entry mentions that Campbell the poet, 'who was buried last week in Poets' Corner,

Westminster Abbey, a hundred nobles attending,'
' called on Sydney two or three times last autumn.'
The connection of ideas is not far to seek. Then
follows comment on what has been already named,
' a habit of night-meditation and prayer, to the loss
of rest, in addition to much time spent that way
in the day, when he can get alone.' . . . ' 'Tis
certainly a majestic mind,' his father concludes,
' but I fear he is weakening it by extremes.'

The father hoped that ' Reason not Poetry
might guide his son to the performance of Duty.'
His son learnt and lived another lesson. Poetry,
as he conceived it, never being in opposition to
Reason or Duty. It became his creed, that in all
things ' so made and done' as to be lifted above
the ordinary and imperfect, towards the ideal and
perfect, there is Poetry.

The last little poem he wrote was an attempt to
express this:

> To fulfil the Law
> In Gospel, force the seeds of use to flower
> In beauty, to enman invisible truth
> And then transfigure—this is Poetry.

On the day following that of his last quoted
entry, Mr. Dobell refers to a letter just received
from his son H——, saying that Sydney had sur-

prised them all by making a beautiful 'speech,' at 'Church,' on the just past Sunday.

'He did not get to town till nine o'clock on the Saturday night,' his father comments,

drenched with rain, and no one knew of his intention to speak. Another extraordinary exhibition of his talent and character, when you consider how most folks' minds and feelings would have been absorbed. . . . Up to this time the purity and holiness of Sydney's character is all I could wish. May he go on to perfection !

'Heresy, popularly and scripturally considered,' had been the subject of the speech ; which in the opinion of the 'Church-elders ' was admirable and beautiful.

Sydney did not know what the subject was when he entered the Church ; but was applied to to speak, owing to the absence of the member who was to have done so.

The marriage took place on July 18 ; and the young people went home the same day to ' a pleasant little house, looking direct on the Cotswold Hills,' where his father and mother were waiting to receive them. The holiday which would have been so desirable, was, probably, not possible.

During the many years, beginning when he was twelve, that Sydney Dobell had been in his father's Cheltenham office, it has already been indicated that he was in constant association there with many of the men and women of exceptional culture and character who frequented that town.

A certain charm of manner, the outcome of a singularly genial nature, together with a growing, though as yet chiefly local, literary notoriety, and the remarkable talent of his conversation, broke down in his case those class distinctions which, thirty years ago, were especially strong in such places as Cheltenham. The peculiarities, too, of the family principles and practice piqued curiosity and excited interest. He was treated with most consideration and distinction by those from whom these things meant most and were best worth having, and, in nearly all instances, won as much affection as admiration.

On his marriage, the wives of two or three of those gentlemen with whom his intimacy had been closest—ladies who belonged to the higher society of the place—called upon his wife, and an attempt was made to draw her and her husband into their circle.

The reasons for which all such attempts were resisted, and the manner of that resistance, are so significantly characteristic of the influence on Sydney Dobell's character of his up-bringing, that they call for some detailed explanation.

At this time he still held firmly to the opinions in which he had been educated ; and, among them, to that one already alluded to—the belief that Scripture forbids friendly domestic association with those whose views of life and religion we consider erroneous : who belong not to ' the Church,' but to ' the world.' Of the dangers of ' worldly association,' and the duty of observing strictly the doctrines of ' separation,' his father persistently warned and admonished him.

The elder Dobell's own practice had been sincerely and stringently consonant with his beliefs ; often to the detriment of his worldly position. ' Business is not brisk,' he had written to his son two or three years before, ' I cannot account for it, except, as usual, in our secluded life and habits. However, if so, principle cannot give way to profit.' He had abstained from all social intercourse of any intimate kind, and from all active and direct interference in politics. Peculiarities of a highly nervous temperament made his course in this respect accordant with his predispositions, and, therefore, comparatively easy. But his son's temperament was altogether different, being pre-eminently open and social.

Even at a very early age he showed in con-

versation unusual self-possession and composure of
manner, as well as great facility of expression.   He
always enjoyed intercourse with his kind, and,
therefore, must have felt keenly what he wrote to
one of those ladies who were most kindly persistent
in their attentions to his wife :

In cases like this where to generous friendship and
the greatest kindness we are obliged to return what
seems—but believe me only *seems*—coldness and dis-
courtesy, to act as we believe we ought to act, is a work
of no slight pain, no slight or trifling self-denial.   To
come to the point at once—one among the many odd
notions for which people laugh at us, but which, despite
the laughter, and despite the daily pain it may be to
fulfil its demands, we still hold as an imperative and
cherished duty, is this—and I put it in its broadest and
most offensive form because, in *any* form, I know that
unless you could go with me along all the long line by
which we arrive at it, you cannot help condemning and
contemning it—not to mix with any society however high
and excellent, however intellectually and morally superior
to ourselves, which does not hold our own peculiar tenets
of religion.   Nobody here holds them ; therefore we can
mix with nobody . . . There are few points in duty and
religion on which we think like the rest of the world.
This, I have no doubt, you will say is a great misfortune
and a sad piece of foolery ; but still, while we cannot help
thinking as we do, I know Mrs. G——'s tone of mind too

well to doubt that she would agree with me in the necessity
of our acting up to our own convictions, however painful
to ourselves that course of action may be.

He goes on to explain more fully the peculiarities of the family faith and practice; but the
matter is more clearly stated in the following
extract from a letter, written, on going to live in a
new neighbourhood, three or four years later:

Peculiar beliefs and opinions oblige me sometimes to
deviate from ordinary usages, and I wish you to be in a
position to put down any appearance of eccentricity to the
account of its true cause. I belong—the connection is
hereditary—to a very small religious sect—' small' for
we do not consider it our mission to proselytise—very
much resembling the Quakers. Among the tenets which
we hold in common with them is that one—bigoted and
self-sufficient I know it appears, when stated in this unexplained unvarnished manner—which limits our associations and domestic intercourse to members of our own
sect. But, believe me, we adopt this principle of separation
not in any hypersanctified spirit of pharasaical imperti-
nence, nor with any assumption of superior goodness.
We use it simply as a means to an end; not as the end
itself. But do not mistake me. Although this peculiar
principle of ours compels us to decline the invitations
of many in whose virtues, character and talents we should
delight, it by no means precludes us from receiving at our
own houses the members of every party, and the disciples

of every sect. Taking, or *endeavouring* to take, the
Scriptures of the New Testament as the sole source of
every doctrine and every precept, we look upon the direction ‘ to be given to hospitality ’ (in the true sense of
φιλόξενος) as a very prominent feature in the outline of
Christian duty. Those therefore who, having a courage
or a kindliness superior to ceremony, pay us the compliment of overlooking our want of reciprocity, we consider
it a pleasure and a privilege to receive. At the same
time if this compliment is withheld, we do not feel ourselves neglected.

I have chosen thus briefly to place the true state of
the case before you (even at the risk of appearing vastly
egotistical), because I feel it will set any future intercourse
between us on a right footing, and because I should be
sorry to seem apathetic or to return courtesy by coldness.

The lady to whom the earlier explanation
was made must have received it in a manner
highly creditable to her good feeling ; acknowledging her reply, he says : ‘ I feel it to be really admirable that you should be able to meet in the kindly
spirit of friendship what must seem to you most
genuine folly.’ But he has again to impose upon
himself the ungracious task of declining a proposition for such friendly visiting as she had hoped
might not be inconsistent with the peculiar views
of her young friends. “ You can easily guess,’ he

says, 'that in a town like this invitations are not
unfrequent ; and you will, I know, agree with me
that to talk of " principle " on such matters to a
mere " fashionable " is a " casting of pearls before
swine." My simple reply, therefore, to such
personages is—" I never go out." But, to say this
with truth, I must strictly abide by my saying.'

He had always—after boyhood ended—a keen
sense of the incomprehensible and even 'ridiculous'
aspect of the family views and conduct, on this
head, in the eyes of the general public. It has
been said that his temperament peculiarly disposed
him towards the social and genial side of things ;
and it is easier to see and to deplore the disadvantages under which his exclusive nurture and training laid him, the manner in which it weighted him
for the race of life, the disagreeable and difficult
positions in which it placed him, than to estimate
the value of the purity of atmosphere thus secured,
and of the bracing moral discipline implied in the
necessity so constantly ' to testify' to what he held
right and true.

His power of seeing things as they appeared to
others, of laughing with those who laughed and
weeping with those who wept, kept alive in him a
spirit of large and kindly tolerance, made narrow-

minded bigotry impossible, and therefore reduced to a minimum any injury to character from these early influences.

As he matured and his experience enlarged he, of course, saw what warping of his own nature, and crippling of his powers of usefulness, must have ensued from strict adherence to such practice as was inculcated by the doctrine of ' separation '—as held and practised by his father. In later years he might have said, with Sir Thomas Browne, ' My conversation is, like the sun's, with all men, and with a friendly aspect to good and bad ; . . . There is no man's mind of so discordant and jarring a temper to which a tuneable disposition may not strike a harmony.' Nevertheless, he all his life thankfully appreciated and did ample justice to much that had been admirable in his early training.

In the course of the autumn of 1844 his father's note-book mentions that ' Sydney has written and published anonymously a little song he made one morning at breakfast, that we might give an opinion unbiassed as to its *plainness,* as I have latterly told him that his pieces are too obscure, and from being highly imaginative not obvious in meaning.'

There is, also, frequent allusion to the young wife's want of strength, and attacks of suffering.— ' Sydney and his wife have been on a visit to Odsey to see her family, but E—— has been ill all the time. . .'

From childhood and through girlhood, Miss Fordham's health had been very fragile, and now, the external conditions of her life being, of course, far less favourable than when

Her equal way was all among her own,

it caused her husband increasing anxiety.

Absorbed though she was in happy love, she, nevertheless, suffered from the change from the free life of a large family in a country home, passed more out-doors than in, riding, driving, gardening —a happy girl's life, unconscious and irresponsible, singularly unfettered by restraint and untouched by criticism—to the life that must have seemed, when compared with the old life, that of a caged bird; in a tiny house, one of a row of similar houses, on the outskirts of Cheltenham.

CHAPTER II.

EARLY MARRIED LIFE. 1845–1849.

On the first anniversary of his son's wedding-day,
Mr. Dobell mentions that he has sent Sydney some
verses, to which others of affectionate and compli-
mentary acknowledgment were *immediately* returned.
The immediateness is emphasised : rapidity and
facility were highly esteemed by the parents, and
their son was easily able to gratify them by displays
of quick-wittedness.   But his own theory soon
became that, not to do many things and those
quickly, but to do the duty of each hour or day as
perfectly as possible, was the really educational
manner of life—the way to throw some glamour of
poetry over the prose of common existence.   The
argument ' that will do well enough,' was one he
never let pass unchallenged : holding that a thing
was never done ' well enough ' if not done as well
as the doer had power to do it.

Late in the year 1846, Mr. Dobell wrote, that his

son, in passing through London that summer, on
his way to Cambridgeshire, had made another able
address to 'the Church': but had looked so ill
that friends had persuaded him to consult a London
physician; whose unfavourable opinion, led first to
a prolonged holiday, and then to the lightening of
his business engagements, and an arrangement,
that, to secure country-air, he and his wife should
lodge in a small farm-house, near Detmore.

These country quarters were, doubtless, delightful to the young people in comparison with the
little suburban residence; but the place was hardly
fit, except in fine summer weather—for anyone not
in robust health; and disastrously unfit to be the
scene of such an illness as that by which, in the
first month of 1847, Sydney Dobell was prostrated;
and from the effects of which—though all the
important work of his life was done afterwards—he
never completely recovered.

His father's note-books minutely detail the
course of this illness (rheumatic fever), which nearly
proved fatal; but, after many days, there was some
improvement: and, a fortnight later, his father
wrote :—

The poor dear skeleton as he lies in bed can talk a
little, rationally and intellectually, on moral and reflective

subjects, but his memory of locality and individuality is most shocking.   He cannot understand where he is, does not remember a quarter of an hour afterwards that he has seen you, but if you utter a wrong sentiment he can correct you, or approve a right one.

Soon after this, came a serious relapse, another physician was called in, and little hope of recovery was entertained, the state both of heart and lungs causing the gravest apprehension.

There occurs at this crisis, a curious passage in his father's note-book.   He writes that his son had said, when alone with him that morning :—

' You said the other day : " Oh, you will be better in a few days," and I know your manner and that if you wish (he meant pray) for a thing you gererally realize it, but please don't do so now.'   Then in a broken way he tried to repeat and explain, because I pretended not exactly to comprehend the dear boy's meaning.   Alas ! I *did* comprehend, but I *will* pray an ever-gracious God, that He may even now preserve our dear pure-hearted son.

That his son wished him to refrain from praying for the prolongation of his life because he did not wish to live seems to be intimated.   If this were so, it is strangely at variance with what is known of him in later life, when, under no pressure of sorrow, anxiety, disappointment, or suffering, did

he seem to desire death, or to hold life otherwise
than dear. But he was young then, in acute suffering, his long apprenticeship to which was but
just beginning, and his illness was of a kind that
made him incredulous of ever again being anything but a burden and a pain to those who loved
him.

For four months, alternations of hope and fear,
of amendment and relapse, are chronicled; and
during this time, in spite of his mother's unflagging
and self-forgetting devotion, his wife's fragile health
was irremediably over-taxed. To physical exertion
beyond anything to which she was equal, and to
want of sleep, was, of course, added, what told
upon her peculiarities of constitution more than
these, the terrible mental strain of such a long-
continued anxiety. An already over-wrought
nervous system was irrecoverably damaged: her
husband, on coming to himself, was shocked at
the change he saw in her: and her life for the
future was, physically, little but pain and weariness.

It was not till May—the illness having begun
early in January—that the patient could be moved
for change of air. He was then taken to Birdlip,
a little hill-top village, about seven miles from

Cheltenham, which, looking down over rich masses
of hanging beech-woods, commands a splendid
view of the vale of Gloucester. He was fascinated
by the beauty of this district, and often afterwards
returned to it. What he felt then, emerging, after
those months, from his fever-phantom haunted
room, into the May-world, how its every sight and
sound appealed to him, he never afterwards forgot;
but on many a future ride up that same road recalled how it had all looked to him then, with what
expressive faces the wealth of hedge-row flowers
had seemed to regard him, with what over-keen
exquisiteness the beauty of all things had pene-
trated him.

In the pure hill-air he rapidly regained tone;
and after a short stay at Birdlip, went for further
recovery into Cambridgeshire; returning in July to
the neighbourhood of Cheltenham.

The rheumatic fever was supposed to have left
some weakness of action, or other affection, of the
heart, which accounted for strange attacks of
sudden illness to which he was from this time
subject; but he was soon in full and varied work.
Though a large proportion of every week was
consumed by attendance to the business of his
father's counting-house, he during this summer

began to plan 'The Roman,' wrote occasional
articles for 'The Critic'—a literary venture just
then started,—and was a contributor to one or two
Magazines and Reviews.   An eloquent and elaborate paper on Palestine and the Jews—a subject
which always had for him a peculiar interest, and
which just then was occupying a good deal of
attention—was written at this period.

Meanwhile the under-current of his life was
often one of deep sorrow and anxiety, owing to
the failure of any medical treatment to ward off
his wife's attacks of suffering.

Many reasons combined to make him now—in
his four-and-twentieth year—desirous of a more
independent life than he had yet led.   It is easily
conceivable that one of these reasons was the
strong craving for more leisure to devote to
literary work.   He was loved by both his parents
with unusual intensity: their admiration of him
and expectations from him were very high, and at
the same time, very clearly defined; and any sub-
stitution of an ideal of his own for that which
from his childhood had been held up to him,
naturally brought upon him remonstrance, passionate, because the love out of which it sprang
was passionate.

A sentence pencilled in one of his early note-books may be quoted here: 'Habit of obedience necessary to be early formed. Therefore before reason can comprehend the Will of God another will is necessary; but when reason is gained God becomes the Parent, and the parent sinks to brotherhood.'

In 1848 his father consented to give up to him a branch-business he had lately opened at Glou-cester, but was not able to dispense with his services in Cheltenham on three days in the week. This concession was greatly valued, as implying comparative independence, and was the beginning of his connection with Gloucester, to which inter-esting old city he became substantially attached. His father expressed affectionate regret that he could not afford to give him a totally easy life; but he had four other sons and five daughters.

The young people now went to live at a house called Lark-Hay, in the village of Hucclecote, on the old Roman Road, three or four miles from Gloucester. And here during the summer of 1848, in a little study, looking over fields and orchards to the slopes of Chosen Hill, a great part of 'The Roman' was written. Business was diligently attended to. His means would not just now admit of a horse or pony being kept, and the walk to and from Gloucester, as the beginning and end of an exhausting day in that city, or in Cheltenham, proved an over-great fatigue. Days spent in business, in study, or in composition, with insufficient attention to the needs of the body, were too often followed by nights of watching and nursing, as his wife's illness steadily increased, and its course was marked by more frequent and more severe paroxysms of suffering. Late in the autumn came the natural result of this state of things—a sudden and violent seizure of an alarming kind, 'spasmodic action of the heart,' his father conjectured. His wife, distracted with fear, sent for his parents, and for the medical man under whose care she herself was at the time—Dr. Ker, of Cheltenham, between whom and Sydney Dobell a cordial friendship, then already beginning, lasted till the poet's death. This illness seems to have been as short as it was sharp and mysterious; but it led to another change of residence. Lark-Hay was thought to lie too low for a rheumatic constitution, and his wife felt too much shaken by the sudden blow to remain at so great a distance from help in case of the recurrence of any similar attack.

The autumn of this year seems to have been of

remarkable beauty. In the middle of September
he writes in his note-book of a most exquisite
day: 'The freshness of spring, the balm of summer, the riches of autumn, and over all these a
radiance inexpressibly its own.' Of a December
day he speaks as having the amenity of spring,
and its twilight the gentle calm of a summer
evening.

The following 'Memorandum of a Storm' also
occurs at this time :

> The clouds green with anger drew up in a semicircle
> above the city. Suddenly the great tower of the old
> Cathedral turned livid and stared like a dead face. The
> clouds poisonous and green became black with the black-
> ness of a bruise. It was as dark as evening; just then a
> white dove flew across the city.

About Christmas of this year, 1848, John
Dobell mentions that his son has moved to
Coxhorne House, Charlton Kings, near Cheltenham,
not half a mile from Detmore. 'A large house,' he
comments, 'and *I* think more than their circumstances warrant; otherwise I am glad to have him
near us.'

CHAPTER III.

LITERARY ACTIVITY, 1849.

' COXHORNE,' in which this year began, was held by
Sydney Dobell for five years. It was a comfortable and roomy house, ample enough to tempt
him to his favourite indulgence—the exercise of
hospitality. It had a beautiful environment of
shrubberies, orchards, and fields, with, what was
always a delight to him, a rookery among its old
trees. The slopes of the Cotswold Hills, commanding great variety both of near and of distant
beauty, rose within easy reach behind it, and to
these, when his wife's health allowed her to accompany him, he loved to make long summer-day
excursions. This place became very dear to him :
his wife remembers his kissing its gate, his cheek
moist with tears, when, for the last time, as the
gate of his own home, he leant on and looked over
it. He was keenly pleased when—twenty years
and more afterwards—his youngest brother took
it, and made it his home.

'The Roman' was finished, 'Balder' chiefly written, and a good deal of other literary work done, during this residence at Coxhorne; but business was not neglected for literature : which, it was always an article of his creed, should never be adopted as a bread-winning profession.

It may be well to mention here, at the beginning of a new phase of his life, that the income on which at this time, and for a few following years, he found himself able to be both hospitable and charitable, was what would by many be felt as 'impossibly' small, it never exceeded and did not always amount to 400*l.* a year.   It will be understood, therefore, that his own and his wife's habits continued to be simple and frugal, and their personal expenses limited to the minimum of what was suitably possible.

An extract from 'The Roman,' published in 'Tait's Magazine,' had excited a good deal of attention, and was, probably, the first motive of a correspondence between its author and the Rev. George Gilfillan—the first allusion to which, in Mr. Dobell senior's note-book, mentions 'the high praise for originality of talent, &c.,' lavished upon his son by this correspondent.

The correspondence now begun was carried on

for some years, but Sydney Dobell's letters have come into the hands of the Editors only in a very fragmentary state.   Always enthusiastic in his sentiments, and unreserved in their expression, the tone of these letters shows that he had conceived a warm admiration for Mr. Gilfillan both as a writer and as a critic.   It is not, therefore, difficult (at least not difficult for those who have had any kindred experience) to enter to some extent into the feelings of the ambitious young writer receiving for the first time, from one to whose judgment he attached value and importance, the kind of eulogy freely bestowed by Mr. Gilfillan: who pronounced his work to have the royal stamp—of genius—upon the whole of it; and prophesied that its author was to be 'another Shelley, of a manlier, Christian type.'   If Sydney Dobell's maturer estimate of his friend's critical acumen and literary taste was less enthusiastic than that shown in his early letters, he always retained a grateful and affectionate feeling towards one who had been the first to hold out to him a hand of generous welcome and encouragement.

The following letter seems to be one of the earliest written to Mr. Gilfillan:

To the Rev. George Gilfillan.

Coxhorne House : May 3, 1849.

All on earth at once.   All of the same key and colour.
May flowers, spring sunshine, summer birds, and—your
letter.   Don't laugh.   Don't mistake me either and,
because I name them together, suppose that I confound
for one moment these Divine and human utterances.

Sitting here at my little study window, the hills above,
the orchards beneath, the rich sweet valley spread out in—
shall I say intolerable ?—loveliness, Nature is before me
like an ineffable Temple and you, a Hierophant at the
gates, say ' *enter.*'   But though we may not confound what
we worship with what we love, must I confess that this
May morning is not less bright to me for knowing you
believe ' I am also of Arcady ' ?

I am not ashamed to tell you that your words have
given me great happiness—whoso has been in *great doubt*
can fancy how lively—and it is due to that free philan-
thropy which has thrown such largess to an importunate
stranger, to say that *happiness* is, I believe and trust, the
poorest part of the alms.   If in after years I should ever
be called ' Poet' you will know that my success is, in some
sort, your work.   And in that knowledge I feel that such
a nature as yours will be best thanked.

And yet I cannot help paying, even here, a little
interest on that debt of gratitude which you have laid on
me, by your chapter—given and promised—on ' Faults.'
I cannot say how much I am already relieved.   I have had

always—you must not think me self-sufficient—an un-
conquerable ever-welling confidence that *some* of my
thoughts were sterling.   But over and around me hung
such a cloud of indefinite imperfections that I fancied my
scattered diamond dust could never shine.   Wherever I
looked in the wide uncertainty *possibilities* of fatal error
loomed out,—'discordia semina' of things which—as I
dreaded—the very heat of mental exercise might ripen
into ineradicable deformities.

Less blind than 'inscia Dido,' I felt indeed that something sat on me, but shuddered to ask of what complexion
it might be.   Your words will be an anodyne to this morbid
state of doubt, and, by giving feature and colour to what I
have to avoid, give also a strength and free purpose to my
steps in the right track ; and knowing this—and all the
cognates and consequences of this—I hope my friend will
not regret, now or hereafter, the time he has so generously
spent on me.   I will not unprofitably add to that 'time'
by one word more than respect to his wishes makes necessary.   And only that respect should compel me to write
a line which would decrease by one shade the immateriality
of our friendship, and 'clothe upon' the insubstantial with
the flesh and bones of time, place and circumstance.

You say I have never mentioned 'who and what I am.'
It never struck me that *I* was of any importance in our
correspondence.   Whenever I write, the feeling of being a
receiver, an instrument, a *mouthpiece*, has always been so
strong on me that I should as soon have accompanied a
draught from our hill-streams with a chip of the rock it

ran through as have associated—when offering you a
poem—the thought with a portrait of the thinker. . . .

I will trouble you with only one or two points in my
home-spent life, and only with them because they may be
explanatory of other matters. I say 'my home-spent life.'
My Father had (and has) a passion for home education.
I am one of ten, not one of whom has ever seen school
or college. Thus, you see, *etymologically* at least, I am
decidedly no scholar. We have had, of course, 'the best
masters,' but the liberality of the Home Curriculum,
though it may give cultivation is, I daresay, unfavourable
to erudition.

Again he writes, as a sort of postscript to the
foregoing, after apologizing for 'such a locust
plague of letters':

You will find that I have not amended all the lines to
which you put interrogations, but have confined myself to
those which you have directly condemned. And even one
of these I have suffered to pass. You have forgotten it,
doubtless. You marked it as a plagiarism from Shakespeare :—

> Sublime, as if a god of old had stepped
> Warm from his marble pedestal.

With my morbid fear of any approach to the *confines*
of plagiarism, I would have struck out this line without a
pang, but for one recollection. I remember that I owed
that line to a critique of Mrs. Jamieson's, in her 'Visits
and Sketches.' She says 'The Paris of Canova looks as it

he *would* step from his pedestal if he *could*, the Apollo Belvidere as if he *could* if he *would*.' The sentence—I read it years ago—struck me very much at the time, and has been a canon of artistic criticism to me ever since: and I feel sure my idea had its origin there.

In another letter he says:

In reading the scene I send, you will, of course, do me the favour to lay any political opinions aside. Whether a Republic for Italy be politically right or wrong we will, if you please, at present set aside; or reserve for some distant conflict of wits, if ever I should have the adventurous happiness to be a party to such a tourney. It is as a *critic* that I come to you with the reverence of discipleship. You will see, at a glance, the kind of problem which the scene has to solve. Given the Monk—the Apostle of rebellion—and two happy half-contented *strangers*—to convert the said strangers into practical workable *rebels* with as little *à priori* commission of self as possible. . . . My own impression is, that the great fault of my scene is a disproportion of means to ends. A plethora of cause. A bombarding of sparrows. But the scene which Tait published (in which the Monk had tried his eloquence on an assembly and miserably failed) perhaps renders it more natural that he should over-do on the next attempt in the determination to succeed. Besides, some of his revelations will be useful in other parts of the poem —in elucidating other parts, I mean. And enthusiasts are poor syllogists.

To this same year 1849, appear to belong the passages which follow from the same correspondence :

Every time I write in *rhyme* I vow it shall be the last. I feel I could have made something of this vision[1] in my usual blank metre.

I am looking forward to two great feasts ! My wife is to give me, in honour of my twenty-fifth birthday (rather late you will say, seeing it occurred last April), Doctor Carlyle's literal translation of Dante. I can't wait till my Italian is good enough to read him. Then I am going to read Bailey's ' Festus,' of which I, as yet, know nothing but by report. Envy me.

I am fresh, however, from another banquet of which I should have shouted to you even from the triclinium, but— well, I can't tell why. I always blush to hear a young man *praising*. Genius sets years at defiance, for it is an instinct ; but praise presupposes judicial inquest, and judicature experience.

In another letter, after acknowledging the receipt from his friend of ' that magnificent Paper of yours,' he says :

In much of it you have expressed—and right nobly— ideas that have long filled my mind. That thought that science is but the expansion of our perplexities, that ' the mystery of the atom has been but transferred to the universe,' has often overwhelmed me.

[1] Of Quirinus, in ' The Roman.'

The unknown becomes more awful from the fact that there are things which we are allowed to know. The hopelessness of the secret becomes more utter when we find it in the enigma of all worlds. There is a Divine mockery in this sealing of the seven Thunders—the permission to ask only those who are forbidden to reply. 'The Lord shall laugh.' I count such truths invaluable in these days. Truths that reduce us to the alternatives—Revelation or Despair. The idea of the invisible becoming visible to the spirits of the Resurrection, and the visible ceasing to be 'the things which do appear,' is very wonderful and very grand, and not—I think—inconsistent with either Scripture or Philosophy. Every step in thought, experiment, or (still better) experience, of these simulacra on which we look indisposes one more and more to accept, invent, or reject a theory about them. But I am increasingly disposed to think that immortality will rather add to our perceptions by enlarging than transmuting them; that a new faculty, a new sense, will receive the incomprehensible and hear the inaudible; meanwhile the known will take its allotted place in the harmony of the unknown, and the competent soul, complete in godlike capabilities, will feel at last *how* every note in 'the things seen which are temporal' chords with every other in the Divine symphony of 'the things not seen which are eternal.'

When 'The Roman' was finished, its writer went with his wife[1] on a short visit to London—to

[1] It may be mentioned that these last words may always be supplied by the reader, for during the one-and-thirty years of their

arrange for its publication; and thence to the wife's old home—Sandon—now rented by her eldest sister's husband. He had taken with him to town a few letters of introduction from Mr. Gilfillan. His interview with Mr. Carlyle was very memorable to him, and was often spoken of at greater length than it is recorded in the following letter. He was at first, he used to say, somewhat stunned and bewildered by the tremendous eloquence poured forth—the point of which appeared to be to urge him to adopt any handicraft, rather than literature, as his occupation in life; but, by and by, gathering himself together, he confuted the candour of this tirade by an appeal to Mr. Carlyle's own practice, which was received with the kindliest good-humour. Of the word warfare of later interviews something has already since his death been written by an ear-witness.

To the Rev. George Gilfillan.

Sandon Bury, near Royston, Herts: December 12, 1849.

I feel sure that if you have thought of me at all, you have not misinterpreted my long silence. You took it for granted that, in my anxiety to save you unnecessary

married life Mr. and Mrs. Sydney Dobell were never for four-and-twenty consecutive hours apart.

trouble, I forebore to give you the result of any of your
kind introductions till I could send you a history of all.
Happy was I to have so good an excuse for neglecting
you. The roar of that Babylon of Babylons distracted
me. *I could not hear myself think.* A burning ring
of living sound seemed to revolve about my brain. Beyond its hot horizon I neither saw, thought, felt, or hoped.
One could almost believe the old fable of the wanderings of
the spirit, and that my country soul cowered into its re-
cesses before that hideous mêlée of wheels . . .

I set down writing to you as one of the pleasures of
Sandon. And here at last I am at peace. Here in the
scene of my early and only love; here where the old days
look out on me from every cottage window, murmur to
me in every one of these old pines, whisper in the tall
evergreens (where we so often sat together), and under
the broad green sod of this quiet lawn lie buried but un-
forgotten. I cannot tell you the ineffable happiness with
which once a year I come to this place. To these placid
fields murmurous—I have no other word—with sheep-
bells; this solitary hamlet, with its Church beside the
Green, where for five years of happiest courtship I was
the ever-welcomed hero of village tattle and romance;
these silent lanes, which once were not so silent; this
dark old manor house, to me so full of sunshine, round
which the thoughts of my long absences used to walk day
and night. Her Father lost it the year we were married,
after a lawsuit of a quarter of a century; but happily it
is still in friendly hands, and I can still sleep in the room
where she was born.

But enough of myself. Let me give you before you
are tired an abridgment of my adventures with your
four friends. In all histories one begins with Royalty,
so what shall I say of Carlyle? (I say ' one begins with
Royalty,' and, for the nonce, I follow the fashion ; but if
ever I write a History it shall be on a new scheme wherein
kings and queens shall be the accidents, the mere tinsel
caps on the flesh-and-blood head of a people.) Forgive
the long parenthesis—I must repeat, lest you forget, what
shall I say of Carlyle? Perhaps it will be childish to say
anything of *him* after no more acquaintance than an
hour's conversation. Of my impressions accept a few
words. I confess to being very much pleased and a little
disappointed. Pleased that the appearance of the man
was so much more *loveable*, and disappointed that it
was rather less *great* than I had expected. I was prepared for a face, manner and expression less tender but
more profound. Not in the vulgar sense of mystic al-
chemical fakir profundity, I don't mean that. If there be
any truth in his theory of ' Wudtan '—if there be divinity
in *movement*—then is Carlyle divine. Body, hands, eyes,
lips, eyebrows—almost cheeks, for even they seem mutable
—did you ever see such a personification of motion ? I felt,
in seeing and hearing, that I could love the man as few
men can be loved ; but I went away hoping and trusting
less—though I never trusted much—in *the sage.* We
had a long talk (he was very kind to me), and if I had
been blindfold and heard it in the street I could have
sworn at once to the speaker. But it made me melancholy
to see how hopeless—no affectation of despair, but heartfelt

black hopelessness—he is of himself and all mankind.
We had a tough argument whether it were better to have
learned to make shoes or to have written 'Sartor Resar-
tus.' He delighted me at parting with a promise to
come and stay at Coxhorne some day. From Chelsea I
went to Leigh Hunt's. He was too ill to be seen (had
the doctor with him then), but sent a kind message and
invitation. I mean to call on him again *en route* for
home. His son Vincent and I had a long gossip . . .
Marston was out. After a chat with Mrs. Marston, I
promised to see him on my return from Cambridgeshire . . .

It may be interesting, at this time—when, with
the publication of 'The Roman,' a new phase of
life was about to begin—to know in what spirit he
looked upon the life behind.

In a long and serious letter, to his eldest sister,
he says :

You think I am improved lately. As a moral and intellectual whole, perhaps I am. But I shall never cease to
look back on the four or five years preceding my illness with
a kind of self-reverence—as to an impossible saintdom,
to which I would not return, but which I can never equal
on this side death. I see that I have a wider mission and a
rougher excellence before me ; but I cannot look back
without a melancholy interest to the years when I never
thought a thought or said a word but under the very
eyes of God.

CHAPTER IV.

PUBLICATION OF 'THE ROMAN.' TOUR IN NORTH
WALES. 1850.

IN March 1850, Mr. Dobell senior writes of his son
as living at Coxhorne, and going up to business with
him three or four times a week ; and as having a
poem in the press—'The Roman'—of which he
says, 'the Rev. George Gilfillan (having seen great
portion of it in MS.) has spoken, in his second
Gallery of Literary Portraits, in the highest terms.'
He then adds, 'Two months ago, fearing Gilfillan's
praise &c. would hurt him, I wrote and urged him
to enter into the *Wilderness of Trial,* and there
resolve at the outset of public life to abase himself,
&c., &c. I think he did. He is a curious mixture
of innocent pugnacity with childlike gentleness,
but so pure and good.'

Combativeness in regard to his father's correc-
tions and amendments of his poetry was probably
the chief form in which this ' pugnacity' manifested
itself. Except from a very few, Sydney Dobell was

always, as has been said of him, singularly unamenable to literary criticism.   That he was
reverent and patient in his reception of advice
from what he considered competent authority is
abundantly proved, by his tone, not only towards
his earliest literary friend and critic ; but, according
to the creed of his mature life, the making of
poetry, as of prayer, was a thing between a man
and his God, a thing, like the deeper sorrows and
joys of the heart, with which the stranger inter-
meddleth not.

Carlyle says, ' The science of Criticism as the
Germans practise it is no study of an hour.'   To
the dicta of such a science as Carlyle then eloquently expounds, Sydney Dobell would have been
amenable, recognising in it a voice speaking with
power and authority : and for such a voice the
highest among us listen, ready to give heed to
what may be accepted as even its echo.

But to that more ordinary criticism, by those
who know less of those who know more, which is
founded on the ' hypothesis that the ultimate object
of the poet is to please,' to which hypothesis, Carlyle
goes on to say, ' there is on all hands no truce
given'—he was not attentive.

Less familiar with German Literature than is

usual to men of his culture, the accord between
the views of the position and duties of the literary
man held by Schiller and by Fichte, and those
which all intimate with Sydney Dobell must have
heard him express, is remarkable.

'The artist,' says Schiller, 'it is true is the son
of his age, but pity for him if he is its pupil, or
even its favourite.'

'How,' he asks, 'is the artist to guard himself
from the corruptions of his time, which on every
side assail him?' In Schiller's answer may be
heard Sydney Dobell's (with a difference, which the
readers of his Lecture on Poetry will easily find):

By despising its decisions. Let him look upwards to
his dignity and the law, not downwards to his happiness
and his wants. Free alike from the vain activity that
longs to impress its traces on the fleeting instant, and
from the garrulous spirit of enthusiasm that measures by
the scale of perfection the meagre product of reality, let
him leave to mere understanding, which is here at home,
the province of the actual; while *he* strives, by uniting
the possible with the necessary, to produce the ideal.

The first edition of 'The Roman' was published,
by Mr. Bentley, at the beginning of April, 1850.
The book, doubtless, owed something of its
popularity to its subject. It is not too much to

say that since Byron 'woke one morning to find himself famous,' no young poet of this century had achieved so great and so unexpected a success. His wife collected, as they appeared, all the critiques of the poem, and the volume into which they are gathered testifies to the accuracy of this statement.

This sudden notoriety had no disturbing effect on Sydney Dobell: not that he cared for none of those things; he did care, and keenly: power over the minds of other men was a thing he valued and desired, for the sake of the good it might enable him to do. But life was now and always for him so much of a 'wilderness of trial'—a wilderness, however, which he declared 'blossomed as the rose'—that there was little danger of his suffering from the 'intoxication of success;' more danger of his feeling crushed by the sense of responsibility laid upon him to realize something of the hope and prophecy of which he was the object, and by which he felt humbled, and filled, as he wrote to a friend, with an irresistible tendency to doubt his own powers.

In August of this year a visit to North Wales, accompanied by a cousin who subsequently became a brother-in-law, between whom and himself a brotherly affection always subsisted—Mr. A. J.

Mott, whose name is not unknown either in the literary or in the scientific world—made an epoch in Sydney Dobell's life.

This was his first experience of anything wild or grand in nature: up to this time—he was now six-and-twenty—he had seen less variety of natural beauty than most children are familiar with in these days. Something of the way the mountain scenery impressed him can be gathered from his letters. But it was always remarkable that he, with his universally acknowledged great gift of language,[1] had more than most of us a sense of its impotence at any crisis of emotion.

He had spoken some time before to his correspondent, the Rev. G. Gilfillan, of beginning to feel the want of some knowledge of the sublime in natural beauty. After saying how strange an experience it was to find oneself stretching out the right-hand of equality, or even looking back upon, as on a landmark unconsciously passed, some passage in literature which was of mountainous sublimity to one's youth; he went on:

---

[1] Of which an eminent modern poet and critic has said: 'I have always thought that for deep derived far-reaching phraseology, and for the power of wielding such with perfect mastery in an atmosphere of passion, the highest mood of Dobell is closely akin to Shakespeare and Shelley.'

Was there not some goddess who conceived by the force of her own wishes? I think there is some such process in the mind; and that perhaps the philosopher himself has yet to learn all the significance of that sentence 'to labour and to wait.' Something of this unconscious elevation, this unknown and unsuspected expansion—something I mean of the same kind, for it is different in species—I feel with regard to my own hills and valley. I love, worship, reverence, but—to a certain extent, am mastering them.

August the 4th, he wrote to his father and mother of his route:

Wolverhampton—than which I never heard nor imagined of a place more utterly damnable. Such fierce squalid wretchedness, such unusual degradation of taste, such unvarying brutality of look and morals. Walking about, half frightened, in this hell, for a short time, we were soon glad to take refuge in the station and wait for the Chester train. Shrewsbury is well worth the journey; the Severn there is the very ideal of a limpid stream, and winds under a ruin. Chester we had no time to see. But the Vale of Llangollen—I shall never forget that one glimpse. Opposite Llangollen station were some undulating hills about like Charlton, and I thought to myself 'I suppose there must be something behind them.' So thinking, I looked down. 'Look now,' said a man at my elbow, nudging me. I looked up: we were in the midst of the valley. I gasped for breath, the tears rushed to my eyes . . . A moment more—and it was out of sight.

To the same.

Llanberis: August 7.

. . . Leaving Liverpool on Monday, we came (stopping at Conway Castle) by rail to Bangor—-by the coast, the sea on one side, the mountains on the other. Stayed Monday night at Bangor, with the Menai Straits and Anglesea before us and Penmaen Mawr on our right. Started yesterday in a car for Lake Ogwen, walked thence to Lake Idwal; passing, in our way to Ogwen, up the Vale of Llanfranken. I give names and not feelings, for no thought can measure them. No imagination can picture these mountains. We walked to Capel Curig through the mountains, and thence took a car to Llanberis, passing by Snowdon through the Pass of Llanberis, with Glydder on one side overhanging us and Snowdon perpendicular on the other. Nothing in heaven or earth that ever I pictured can come up to the reality of the Pass of Llanberis. I sat speechless the whole way. All my brain made chaos, heaving over and over. Too great for tears or any quick emotions. All that I hoped and wished in this search for new impressions has already been far more than accomplished. Every moment is absorption.

After his return home, his desired experience realised, he wrote to the Rev. G. Gilfillan :

I should have written from Wales, or from Liverpool (where I have been staying *en route* for home), but that I could say nothing in the presence of those mountains (except perhaps their names), and that I was ill during the greater part of my stay in that great city which ruleth— or deserveth to rule—over the kings of the earth.

I loathe all towns, small and great; but of all the cities I have seen Liverpool is the most glorious abomination. The flood of life that ebbs and flows there is sublime. To stand on the banks of the Mersey and feel the pulse of Empire, day by day, reconciled me to a fortnight of city din. Nowhere in the haunts of men have I seen so much of the raw material of grandeur. And I must confess to a savage love of raw material . . . Dining with a friend one day at the Liverpool Exchange rooms, I was puzzled to know what becomes of the fine faces I saw about me, and how such a legion of intellects dies out of the world unknown. In no similar batch of the ‘ twenty-seven millions, mostly fools,’ that ever I met have I counted half so many striking features and noble heads. A few days’ experience solved the riddle. The ledgers of these men have enough poetry in them to wing a yearly flight of poets. But you have seen Liverpool, and know all this.

What shall I say of the mountains—that ocean of mountains on which my soul tossed like a boat for six memorable days? That stone tempest—it almost wrecked me. Thrown to inconceivable heights and depths, I had neither thoughts, words, nor emotions. Only a great anthem, heard once in a cathedral, and forgotten till the mountains recalled it, floated constantly through me.

But for this my brain seemed to stand still . . . When, leaving the rail at Bangor, we fairly and slowly entered the mountain country, all vivid feeling seemed oppressed out of me and for the next five days I went silent and stupefied. My whole being seemed occupied in receiving; all the other faculties seemed lent to perception. Those mountains—all my looking felt unable to take them in: and even now they seem too great to be remembered . . . I thought it would be a glorious thing to see the sea again; but the roll of the waves was child's play after those eternal billows which I beheld for the first time.

We climbed Snowdon. And for an hour we had an unclouded expanse below and above us. Then the storms boiled up from a thousand cauldrons, and we had the most wonderful sight of all. I will not try to describe it . . .

To the same correspondent he wrote, a little later, that he had delayed ' till lazier days ' answering his letter, intending that the answer should contain that ' confession of faith,' so often procrastinated, for which his friend had asked. ' The fact is,' he goes on, ' that I have just taken Newman's " Phases " in hand, and I expect that, in order to do justice to the subject, my faith will have to appear as a leading personage in the review. I see the matter must be dealt with as a whole. I must oppose one theory by another. Mere hacking at the limbs of the German giant will not do.

I must essay a statue of Christianity; and, setting
the one by the other, repeat the world-old question,
" Choose now whom ye will serve." '

Some time after he says—having had to speak
of illness:

You will readily fancy that my review of Newman
has not much progressed. However, I have done something, but shall not have a paper ready by November I
fear.[1] The symmetry of the series of papers I contem-
plate is gradually growing in my brain, and I will not risk
the success of the whole by hurrying the formation of
parts. I never can do anything without time . . .
Thank you heartily for your warning about Scripture
texts and Scotch prejudices thereanent. You say they
have a ' foolish fondness for the letter.' It is my ' foolish
fondness for the letter' which has ' bound it upon the
brow' of my style. I once learnt the New Testament by
rote, and I cannot unlearn the beauty of those sweet old
Saxon phrases in which I have thought so long. Full of
the light that never was on sea or shore—the light of the
holiest, happiest and best of recollections—I feel, in using
them, to mingle a new element with earthly speech, and
relieve, in some sort, with their glory the dreary lifeless-
ness of words.

To the same.

. . . I have now read part of ' The Covenanters '—not

---

[1] The introductory paper was published in 'The Palladium' for
January, 1851, but the series was never completed.

all yet, but enough to have an idea of it—I was more
than satisfied. The book bears, I think, certain unimportant marks of haste, as compared with your more polished
productions; but it has a freshness, an earnest sledge-
hammer purpose, a highland covenanting heartiness of
will, which look perhaps the more truthful for an occasional roughness—which is the differentiæ of rock and
masonry. Moreover (and this I think very important),
there is an increase of calm throughout the general style,
which throws out the energetic portions finely. I rejoice
from my heart at this growing calm, for it seems to me
the desideratum of your manner . . .

 . . . I think that of the chapters on the Prophets I
like 'Ezekiel' best. But of this I will speak more at
large and at leisure. Impatient to see 'the Dream,' I read,
a day since, that golden chapter. Surely you wrote it
and the introduction much later than the rest. There is
a something of superiority about them for which I have
no words. I am conscious of it as of the balm of morning, the solace of twilight, or that invisible but efficient
breath of life which distinguishes the living features from
the dead. But I should be at a loss to lay my finger on
the definite excellence: and I am pleased that it is so,
because the improvement looks more thoroughly like
growth. At one thing I particularly rejoiced. With all
the glorious eloquence of your other works, there is to my
sense, a certain lack or inequality of *instinct,* which makes
the flights uncertain and prevents their taking rank as
works of art. Now in this chapter of the 'Destiny,' and

in everything that you have lately written, I recognise so much more completely the Poet and the Poem.

Towards the end of this year Mr. Dobell, the elder, wrote of having had all his ten children, with wives, husbands or lovers, gathered about him: the group, including the first grand-child, the baby-daughter of his third son—Dr. Horace Dobell. He says:

It was indeed a day of thanksgiving to me and to my dear wife . . . Dear Sydney appeared like a crown of glory to us, and acted his part with gentleness, gracefulness, and kindness to all.

CHAPTER V.

SOME OF THE CORRESPONDENCE OF 1850.

THE publication of a poem so widely popular as
' The Roman,' not only enlarged the hitherto small
circle of its writer's literary acquaintance, but
made him, henceforth, the recipient of frequent
appeals from young authors and would-be authors,
for criticism, advice, and sometimes for even more
substantial assistance.

It was against his theory and his practice to
regard literature as a legitimate bread-winning
occupation: the known fact of his not being dependent upon his pen for subsistence, no doubt, in
some quarters, gave rise to the supposition that
he had been ' born with a silver spoon in his
mouth,' was a man of what is called 'wealth and
substance.' But probably, a good deal in his own
conduct—a certain largeness and liberality in his
dealings—encouraged this belief: only those behind
the scenes could know that what was freely spent
in some deed of disinterested kindness might have

to be spared from desirable personal expenditure.
But the sacrifices thus made were light in comparison with others of a less palpable nature made
almost as freely.

His state of health already caused all but
purely spontaneous brain-work to be laborious—
to an extent only to be understood by those who
have had some kindred experience: yet the care,
the patience, the conscience with which he attended
to the affairs of others, the heartiness and thoroughness with which he made them his own, might be
testified to by a cloud of witnesses.

His absolute candour may have made him a
few enemies; but the generosity of his pleasure
in giving pleasure when he could praise, and the
delicacy and tenderness with which he censured,
won him the friendship of most of those who
appealed to him.

The following letters and extracts from letters
may, for the most part, be left to tell their own
story. There were many reasons why the friendship with Dr. Samuel Brown, begun about this
time, was hailed with peculiar pleasure; but, all
his life, friendship was more to Sydney Dobell than
is common in these days.

It has been said, and with truth, that he was

apt to over-estimate his friends. The reason may
have been, not only that he was disposed to
generosity of judgment, but that under his genial
influence what was best in those associating with
him expanded and came to the surface : of the
double nature most of us are conscious of possessing, the nobler and the fairer side was that known
to him.

In his earlier correspondence the reader will
be struck with the contrast between maturity of
thought in some directions and extreme youthful-
ness in others. In what may be learned from
within, he was mature ; in what must be learnt
from without, singularly the reverse.

That enthusiasm which has been said to be
' the fundamental quality of strong souls ; the true
nobility of blood, in which all greatness of thought
or action has its rise,' he possessed in large measure.
His unreservedness in expressing it, his transparent
simplicity and candour, unlimited trust in the
goodwill and good faith of his friends, and largeness of expectation, both from himself and others,
are characteristic of a man with small experience
of the world, who, knowing no evil—almost ignorant of the meaning of envy, malice, and uncharit-
ableness—dreads none ; and, while harmless as the

dove, for want of the wisdom of the serpent lays himself open to misconstruction. Had he been more self-conscious, he would often have appeared less so. He freely uttered thoughts which a wary man would have hidden, and sometimes by his unwonted frankness drew upon himself the charge of unwonted egotism.

In the records of his early manhood, as in those of his youth, there is little trace of that brightness, almost joyousness of temperament, and that appreciation of fun and humour, so memorable to all who had personal intercourse with him in his. maturer years. Things without and things within combined to suppress his natural elasticity, and he was beset with an unremitting and over-strained sense of responsibility. During the last phase of his life, when he was laid aside by an Authority against which there was no appeal, he was more open than ever before to the gayer aspects of things : as if then first licensed to relax the bow, conscious that his hand was Divinely held—

And all the tedious taxèd toil of the difficult long endeavour

Divinely suspended.

To the Rev. George Gilfillan.

May 1850.

. . . You will partly see why I disagree with you on
Dawsonian matters. I think you expect too much and
give too little. You try him by a test for the gods, and
do not allow that he does the work of a man. It seems
to me that in your Gallery you have conceded too much
and too little. You assume that he aspires to replace
apostles and admit that he is received as a prophet: and
naturally enough laugh him to scorn. Now (apart from
the amiable foibles of that little clique of worshippers
which every 'man preaching' is sure to be tried and
tempted with) I think nobody in England either accepts
him as a prophet, or would be inclined to believe in his
apostolic aspirations. I admire and respect him as a
voice crying in the wilderness, and believe him to be too
shrewd to dream he is anything greater. I frankly agree
with you that there is a dash of quackery in his manner
and matter; but less than one would expect from the
child of an age of quacks. His mission seems to be to
set the middle classes *thinking,* and I have seen and heard
of no man so gifted, naturally, educationally, experientially,
for the important work. His lectures are not lectures
for an auditory of genius or of sustained cultivation; and,
of course, on such hearers would fall dead enough. But
I honour him as a strong-hearted, ready-handed man,
standing on his solitary stump—the only solid footing in
the swamp that divides the monetary from the intellectual

power of this country—and translating (with an aptitude
which almost rises to originality) what he hears from the
one party into the dialect which the other can understand.
At the same time I have little doubt that in a purer
atmosphere than that of Birmingham, freed from the
incessant temptations of the platform, and addressing
himself to a higher range of intellects, he has the power
to command almost as much respect from a loftier audience
as he has obtained, on easier but hardly less useful terms,
from that middle-class rising-mind with whom in many
parts of England his word is already law. With regard
to his clerical attributes I can say nothing, for I never
heard him preach. His idea of a Church seems to me an
amiable chimera, a benevolent impossibility, ludicrously
unscriptural, and equally at variance with Divine dispensation and human nature. That his moral hospital does
unspeakable good to those outlying sick who have no
other refuge, I have no doubt; but I shall never dignify
an unorganised crowd with the title of ἐκκλησία, whether
they meet in Chapel, Cathedral, or on Kensington Green.

George Dawson is a personal friend of mine, and I
have had some opportunities of studying him. You
would be charmed with the unaffected humility of his
private life, with the earnestness of his own convictions
as to the present path of his duty, and with a certain
generous chivalry of feeling with regard to antagonists,
which I was not prepared to find. . . . I expect nothing
great from him in the way of creative genius or calm
life-long induction; but I do expect that in the practical
workings of the coming time, his strong hand will be felt

right and left. He has a wonderful faculty for making
the concrete out of the abstract, governing men of the
masses, and getting through work.

To the Rev. Richard Glover.

Coxhorne House, near Cheltenham: May 21, 1850.

I am not going to thank you for that warm-hearted
prophecy which was put into my hands the other day.
Whoever publishes a book, and wishes to retain power to
write another, must send it into the world to fight its own
battles—drive it like a full-fledged nestling from the
home which the new brood will claim. . . .

If I held myself bound in gratitude to acknowledge
all the kind things that have been said and written of me
for the last two months, I should have little chance of
accomplishing the oracles, or giving occasion to a repetition of the verdicts. You will look upon this note, therefore, as the expression of an earnest latent interest in
yourself, and your pursuits, which you have, at length,
very good-naturedly given me an excuse for expressing.
Meeting your worthy Father in the railway the other day,
I learned from him your change of profession and abode ;
and the fact that you had a leaning towards poetry. I
suppose that very few minds of more than ordinary power
have not stepped at first in measure ; though in nine cases
out of ten they have broken with maturing strength and
growing instincts into a rougher gait. The child dances,
the man strides. Whether you will go the way of all
flesh in this matter, remains to be seen.

Fear not, in this case, to tread it : 'tis a glorious ' way.'
Glory, like heaven, has a short cut to it from every place,
and few of those royal roads are, in my eyes, holier or
more honoured than that broad firm Via Sacra, paved
with rock and umbraged with oaks, fit for gods and
accessible to all men, which we call *prose.* Don't suppose
I see no poetic power in your verses. There are some fine
lines. . . .

But my own belief is that the very highest poetry may
be written in prose; and I would give you, in all friendship, the advice and standard which I administered to
myself: Don't make poetry—commonly so called—an
object unless you *can't help it* : and if you admit it for an
object, by all means abstain from it as a *pursuit.*

Poetry should roll from the heart as tears from the
eye—unbidden; and only then. I am glad to see you in
blank verse. Rhyme is the curse of our language and
literature. . . . Pray let me hear from you now and then,
but you will not, I know, expect long or speedy answers.
I am obliged, as a matter of duty, to deny myself much
epistolary pleasure. We shall not agree, I dare say, on
many points, *cui malo ?*

From a later letter to the same correspondent :

Verse is an incantation with dominion over ' the powers
of the air.' Prose is a sword at one's side to hew a path
upon earth. May you ever use it for truth and right,
' sans peur et sans reproche ! '

To the same.

Many thanks for your letter and your poem. I scribble a line now to say two things. First, that in consequence of the severe illness of my wife and of the presence of friends at Coxhorne, I have not had a moment to give to your poetry. And, secondly, I stipulate for the withdrawal of that clause in your letter which stakes your future devotion to poetry on my verdict upon the lines you now send me. I have one advice, offered from my heart, to every young *littérateur*, and I give it with the more confidence because being young myself I know its value. I offer it utterly irrespective of the value or complexion of any past achievements of the candidate. Have nothing to do with poetry, if you can help it. 'If you can help it.' And if you can't help it, care nothing for my judgment, nor for any man's, but—writing as little as you can (in verse)—bide your time. I write this before forming an opinion on the Poem you send me, that you may see how utterly impersonal my counsel is. I hope soon to read and re-read your lines ; and shall have a great deal of pleasure in giving my opinion on them, and in assisting you at any time in any way that I am able. Never scruple to write to me from any fancy that you give me trouble.

To the same.

October, 1850.

I shall only send you a line to-day, but it will be *in tempore quod* &c. I must congratulate twice ; and both times heartily. Once on your successful examination : and once on what is hardly less important to your future— the brave and manly spirit in which you received my short critique of your poem. Take my plain-speaking as a testimony to my opinion of you. 'Strong meat is not for babes.' And recollect that before I consented to criticise, I warned you, in poetic matters, to 'call no man master.' If you are to write poetry you will write it, though your work be printed in your blood and bound with the sod of your grave. But I would still say to you, rebuff your muse; give her rough welcome and spare diet; flout her to her face as an impostor. Send away your Sibyl not three times but three times thirty—and if she come back to you at last buy of her though you pawn your life for the purchase-money. I confess to you that I think well of some of the symptoms you tell me of. Of the impulsive items I think *the least* (as diagnostic), and never could understand the convulsive movements which so many take as inspiration. It was the Pythia of old, you remember, whose oracle came in paroxysms. I dare be sworn Apollo had no fits. Don't place too much faith therefore in midnight 'tormentors,' for in these things, my dear friend, we must 'believe not every spirit.' With regard to the possibility of gradations in the poetic heaven, within certain limits I agree with you. But there is one essential condition with all these stars— that they *be* in heaven. In conclusion, I am right sorry to have caused you 'sadness'—even a temporary sadness. And should be still more sorry, but for the confidence that you are a perennial, and will spring but the more vigor-

ously for pruning. Of one thing I feel a certainty, which
I forget whether I expressed—that whatever be your
poetical fate your mind is so thoroughly poetical (but
this is not enough for a poet) that you can hardly fail to
enrich us with some magnificent prose. Don't think this
a paradox.

To Dr. Samuel Brown.

Coxhorne House, near Cheltenham : November 22.

Sunt delicta quibus ignovisse velimus—and among
them I must ask you to count the fact that I have allowed
seven silent days to elapse since the receipt of your
letter . . .

Hating all affectations, and having an especial contempt
for prudery—masculine and feminine—I tell you frankly
that your letter rejoiced me to my heart. I had felt a
fraternal tendency towards you long before 'The Roman'
gave me an opportunity of holding out a hand which I was
disappointed that you did not grasp. I tell you plainly that
your 'I like it not' rang in my ears. And these are not
everyday matters with me : for I am slow to love, and
care one jot for the literary opinions of the very fewest.

And now comes your letter ; a portrait—in photo-
graph—of the man I had pre-ordained you to be in head
and heart, face and fashion, and with a glow of hope and
health about him which I had hardly dared to expect, and
feel almost a brother's pleasure to look upon. (Our noble
friend Gilfillan has spoken with much tender anxiety of
you). Nay more, that letter of yours is the very genius

of good fortune, for in welcoming it and you whom I took to be *friends*, I find I have reaped the reward of him who entertains strangers.   Did you ever feel the eloquence of a stone in a strange churchyard with nothing but the *name* engraved ?   So with your one word ' Helen.'

I am thoroughly interested in what you say of—— . . . I have not read —— yet, but was much struck with the ' Athenæum' extracts. Remarking nevertheless, I well remember, to my wife as I read, on a certain artificial tone and Hyde Park prestige about them which I regretted to see in an author evidently young.   She has a feeling for the beautiful ; but her suns set on Kew Gardens and all her green lanes are macadamized.   A few years doubtless will change all that, for in her case I think those ' starts theatric ' are the wind upon the shallows of a great deep . . . .

Of larger calibre and metal more ' tried in the fire ' is Currer Bell.   You would have been charmed with a letter of hers, which her friend Miss Martineau sent me the other day.   A noble letter, simple and strong ; but tender all over with amenities that showed like ripple on a wave.

I was amused with her playful suspicion that ' if Mr. Dobell could see her, sometimes darning a stocking, or making a pie, in the kitchen of an old parsonage in the obscurest of Yorkshire villages,' he might recall his sentence.[1]   A fig for Mr. D.'s discernment, if he did not

---

[1] Allusion to an article on Currer Bell, which had appeared in ' The Palladium' for September of this year. For which see Appendix to this Book.

confirm it—with costs. But despite these pleasant
little episodes in reviewing, of which in my short experience I have already several, I had resolved long
before your letter reached me to give up criticism, except
as a very occasional exercise. I find that reviews take
up time and energy which I cannot spare; and (I think)
instead of forwarding, retard, or, at best, divert the great
work of literary culture and preparation. With every
intention to be scrupulously honest, I feel a perpetual
difficulty to avoid special pleading.

In poetry one's soul lies out like a broad impartial
lake before the heavens and the earth, reflecting at once
the sky and the cloud, the mountain and the mountain
goat—aye, and the very grass blade he crops. In criticism
the lake is for ever running to a river, and the river forced
as by a water-wheel into perpetual and unheard-of mean-
derings. A critique once or twice a year is therefore all
I shall allow myself. A thousand thanks for your kind
invitation. I fear I should not have waited for it if fate
had sent me to the Highlands . . . In the meantime my
wife joins me in hoping most heartily that when her
strength is a little more confirmed you and Mrs. Brown
will come and try the air of Coxhorne. We are in a
lovely valley, beautiful in winter and summer, within a
quarter of an hour of the hill-tops and of a view of fifty
miles by seventy . . .

Dr. Samuel Brown to Sydney Dobell.

Portobello : November 26, 1850.

Dear Friend,—Your long and flowing letter ran through my heart yesterday morning like a purifying stream, filling me with a sense of woodland laughter, the voice of singing birds, the million-headed caressing of country breezes, the upholding of hill-tops, and the freedom produced by the very thought of a rich expanse of *Merrie Englande,* ' 50 miles by 70!' Truth to tell, I am right glad you have received my late response to your kindly gift of 'The Roman' so frankly, so unreservedly, so brotherly, so manly. But, mind you, I *did* grasp your proferred hand last May. I only did it in silence. I said nothing ; but ' speech is silver,' you know, ' while silence is golden.'

When I read ' The Roman' the first time, I was dull and ill, as I have told you. It disapppointed me. It seemed to want body. It appeared to be sheer spirit, not clothed upon with corporeal semblance in any degree commensurate with its rich and varied meanings. It looked like a vast intention. The persons wanted human character. The drama was not ' drenched in flesh and blood,' to use a phrase of the second Bacon's. I could not seize it ; and it did not seize me. But it provoked me infinitely. It excited in me a wish to be possessed by it. It stood before me like a noble spirit evoked from the unburied past, or come forward from the unborn future : it beckoned to me with its shadowy arms ; it

spoke to me with its ineffectual lips, ineffectual for they
moved and I almost understood what they were saying,
but I could not be sure, for no sound came from them!
Such was the sort of impression your fine poem made
upon my sick mind. I said something like this in a
hasty note to Aird. He wrongfully, most wrongfully, published it. Gilfillan told me you were hurt by my so hasty
judgment. Can you not understand how I should feel
a new barrier erected between us, additional (I mean)
to ordinary diffidence? But my letter has over-leapt it
now ; and you have over-leapt it too.

A word or too about 'The Roman' though. I confess
with pride and joy that I was not long of discovering that
it requires a second and a third reading. That true
mark of a work of real art it has. Men who had read it
cursorily have been amazed when I bade them listen and
then read them passages out of it. It grows and grows on
the reader. It bears and demands study. I will read it
many years hence. I do not know how to commend it
more highly.

Yet it seems to me to be imperfect as a work of
art, to want unity and compactness, to want visible form,
to want the ruddy glow of our proper humanity. It is
an atmosphere of poetry, not a river of song. It is over-
spiritual. Heaven and earth are not welded and wedded
into one in it. It cannot move the people. It can touch
but one segment even of the cultivated classes. It fills
one with more admiration for its author than for itself.
He is a greater poet than it is a poem.

But, good God! what am I saying? Shall a man be

a poet in a day, in a year, in a paltry lustrum? Genius cannot do all. It is only the condition of all things being done. It needs also patience, perseverance, immense practice, enormously cultivated talent, all knowledges, all arts, all helps.

The reason why I ventured to dissuade you from criticism was simply this. Science which is critical and Poetry which is creative are the opposites of each other in their methods, although they have a common soul when science is great enough to know and show it. It is impossible for a poet to be a critic. It is impossible for a man of science to be a poet. Born and bred an investigator, a critic of God, I could never, never become a poet. It seems to me you are a poet born on the other hand. It will be only harmful for you to criticise, for me to poetise. You may easily attain excellence of a kind in critical writing; I might reach a quasi-poetic utterance. But both of us should (would?) lose our distinctive and native and undeniable characteristics. We should cease to be ourselves. The critical habit will impair your powers as a maker; you will grow less poetic. The poetic effort would weaken me as a discoverer; I should grow less capable of finding.

It is the part of art to clothe the idea with its symbols. It is the part of science to eliminate the idea from its symbol. The poet should know nothing of analysis and synthesis: the man of science is nothing without an absolute mastery over these instruments. The poet must move altogether, like Wordsworth's cloud, if he move at all: the man of science must move in parts, and that

knowingly. But let me stop, else I shall never have done !
I remember how Humphry Davy begged Coleridge not to
study Chemistry (he meant elaborately, as Coleridge proposed doing), because it would spoil him for his art. Now
the *method* of Chemistry is just that of the true scientific
criticism of literature.

To Dr. Samuel Brown.

The very hour to write to you, my dear friend. I
know that behind this mist that hides me from the East
an ' awful rose of dawn ' is wreathed with the golden lilies
of morning. So you and I are brightening towards each
other with a fog of ignorance between us. But alack for
this *frost*—it shall have no part in our hieroglyphs.

I wish you could see all that is before me at this
moment—the tall cypresses and 'trees of life,' to whose
heads I must look up even from this upstairs window, the
two old rookery firs far above, with the rooks sailing
through the fog like indefinite dark thoughts, the orchard
trees beyond (all of wild pear, with every branch a line of
beauty) stretching away to the base of the hills and to
certain visionary woods, groves, and great outlines, which
I am rather conscious of than see through this wide morning mist. A bitter frost spent all last night in swaddling
the twigs in a thick rime. You might fancy it all a white
coral country under the sea.

I was interrupted at the last sentence a week ago, and
have since found no opportunity to continue. And now,
taking out your noble letter, and running it through again,

the re-reading at once tempts and forbids me to throw down my pen. . . .

Whether we were ever fellow-passengers in the Stygian ferry boat and exchanged a password in Hades, whether we were unconsciously struck from the same flint, kneaded of the same 'red earth,' plucked from the self-same twig of Igdrasil, radiated from the same star, exhaled from the same petal of the eternal Lotus, or twanged off in chords upon the seven-stringed lyre of this Universe, or by what means, contrivances, and appliances soever our mutual 'being' was 'struck into bounds,' certain it is that you and I know more of each other than we think.

I find with some amusement and surprise that at this second letter we have already got beyond 'writing-point,' that I would substitute a squeeze of the hand for 'thank you,' and would rather walk with you in silence than read the most eloquent epistle of even your eloquent pen. . . . I have a lingering hope that a stroll of this kind (up the hills) is not so far off perhaps as you imagine. The President of the Literary Institution applied to me the other day to recommend him some lecturers. I asked him if he had heard (amongst others) Gilfillan or yourself. . . . I promised to mention the matter—caring therein (I fear) profoundly little for the President and diabolically much for myself. Is it possible that you could lecture here about the middle of January?

I was right heartily pleased with your quaint description of your *élite* of Portobello, and could sympathise in it from my soul.

Explaining the home-keeping nature of his own life, he adds :

Translating, however, that dear word 'home' rather widely : for we often spend whole summer days together on the hill-tops hereabouts. Don't fancy this babbling of 'hills' an affectation. And don't fancy me a cynic—real or (still worse) pretended. When anyone invites me to Cheltenham I accompany the refusal by a hearty welcome to Coxhorne : and I find this no bad test. . . .

. I need not tell you that I thoroughly enjoyed your graduated opinion of 'The Roman.' . . . In all the exceptions you took and take to it I earnestly join you: and though Gilfillan says well that I was hurt when your letter to Aird appeared it was more at the publication than the sentence. I was grieved with the jury rather than the verdict. Thanks for your eloquent antithesis of Poetry and Science. I admire from my heart the masterly estimate of your own intellect, and still more the philosopher who could make it.

In a matter of self-knowledge I will not dispute the superiority of so cherubic an eye ; but you must allow me, nevertheless, to believe the author of 'Galileo' a poet. . . . I believe you are thoroughly right about criticism, and when I have finished Newman, the 'Bards,' and one other book (a Novel by a cousin), trust me, I throw away a cudgel which already wrings my hand.

Your picture of our silent quartett by the fireside is delicious. It is not the only portrait of which the original must remain admired, but not possessed. I fear it will be

impossible for us to go to Scotland next year.   We mean,
if practicable, to see Switzerland.

Blindness, disease, poverty, every dark possibility, calls
out to me from the future to fill my whole being with the
present.   To crowd my sense with great images while I
can yet see, to school my ear while it is yet open to the
separate notes I must afterwards combine, to dye every
fibre of my brain with beauty while I can still feel.

These things oppress me with the weight of moral
duties.

Will you go with us—you and your ' Helen ?'   It
would perfect the tour.   At present our companions are to
be (I hope), the novelist cousin I spoke of just now, and a
young brother of mine.

Answering his correspondent's enquiries as to his
wife's health, he says :

She both ' suffers' and 'droops ;' but, I thank God
from my soul, her worst appears to be over.   I fell in love
with her at ten, we were engaged at fifteen, and married
at twenty. . . . While weak from a long illness she set
to work at the Classics (in the midst of other studies),
and acquired at once the Latin grammar and such severe
nervous derangement as never left her, for years afterwards,
an hour without pain.   Two years after our marriage I
was confined to my room for four months with rheumatic
fever. . . .

This completed her overthrow—the fatigue and the
unbounded anxiety. . . .

CHAPTER VI.

NOTES AND MEMORANDA.

THE following Notes and Memoranda will, it is thought, be of interest as giving something of the intellectual history of the period. Inside the cover of the book from which they have, with two or three exceptions, been extracted,[1] is written :

In this book I mean by Nuclei, my own thoughts (set down in the rough as nuclei for after additions) as they have occurred to me from time to time, without regard to their consistency with each other, and, indeed, by their frequent inconsistency marking the ages of my mind. They were begun in 1848.

The writer was then twenty-four.

The book contains, besides these Nuclei, sentences, and short passages with which he had been struck in his readings of Carlyle, Ruskin, Schlegel, Kant, Fichte, the older poets, and some curious and little known writers on abstruse

---

[1] This book had not been found when the volume of ' Thoughts on Art, Philosophy and Religion ' was prepared for publication.

subjects, classical quotations, comments on specialities in the use of Greek words occurring in important Biblical texts—(a small Greek Testament was for many years his constant pocket companion), out-of-the-way bits of historical, antiquarian, mythological and etymological information, and observations of facts connected with the natural sciences.

NOTES AND MEMORANDA.

We want a King of the World.

Many things in the Old Testament indisputably show God specially at work among that people. Prove that, and it prepares you for the rest.

Concerning Evidence of Resurrection.

The calm brevity of the record an evidence of truth. The work of men over conscious of the fact they recorded. Christ's prediction of more weight than any exoteric evidence, because it virtually brings to bear all the evidence of his life.

The anxiety of Paul to rest the whole value of his preaching on the Resurrection a grand evidence. It makes the brain of Paul an evidence. He is surety for a world of unknown facts. So of the other Apostles. And the unbelief of the Apostles, compared with their after belief and selection of the Resurrection as the master fact, inestimable testimony also to unknown evidential facts.

CHAPTER VI

NOTES AND MEMORANDA

The following Notes and Memoranda will ... be of interest as giving something ... history of the period. Inside the ... ... book from which they have, with ... ... has been extracted,[1] is written ...

In the book I mean by Nuclei, my own thou... ... in the rough as nuclei for after additions ... ... occurred to me from time to time, witho... ... consistency with each other, and, indeed ... ... inconsistency marking the ages of ... They were begun in 1848.

The writer was then twenty-four.

The book contains, besides these ... sentences and short passages with which ... been struck in his readings of Carlyle ... ... Kant, Fichte, the older poets, ... and little known writers or ...

[1] These notes and are ... found when the volume of ... ... Philosophy and Religion was prepared for public...

...mments on special
... recurring in im
... Greek Testament
... pocket companion),
... rical, antiquarian,
... al information, and
... nected with the natural

NOTES AND MEMORANDA.

ng of the World.
the Old Testament indisputably show
ork among that people. Prove that,
for the rest.

g Evidence of Resurrection.

of the record an evidence of truth
conscious of the fact they recorded
more weight than any custom
ly brings to bear a the ...

to res the ... of his
... It makes
H... for a world
... And the
... belief

re sight,

re teach-
monious
abstract
express
d are not
which she
rcibly the
hilosopher
her, in any
te his own
blasphemy
e dilemma,
refusing to
kened glasses.

dge. Because
; and, through
upward train of
g beyond reason
instinct) therefore,
ies, is after all the

mankind only the verbal
certain truths of mental
or personifications of objec-

Peter and Paul, types of utterly distinct characters, equally convinced.

When once reason is engaged in the work of stern demonstration, the belief in God is the prerequisite of every other. Believe your eye? cries the philosopher, it is the father of lies! Believe your touch? Believe your eyes first! One stands motionless, as in a dark night, fearing to strike against some terrible truth, which he lacks senses to discern. Who shall gainsay the impressions of disease? How do I know that the jaundiced eye is not clearer vision? The minority have the truth elsewhere, why not here?

No thought can measure 'the height and length and breadth and depth' of the first evangel of Resurrection. It was the spell that changed the moral universe, and transformed the feeblest spirit to a Prometheus looking unmoved on time and circumstance, fate and eternity, and saying to the thunders of the heaven and the earthquakes of the earth—τί δ' ἂν φοβοίμην ᾧ θανεῖν ὂν μόρσιμον.

To say that Nature is a sufficient revelation, is to declare the miracles of Christ to be Christianity. Let us see what a Gospel could be educed from the miracles of a silent Christ and dumb Apostles. Still less may we expect from the ever-visible miracle, Nature, because in this the wonder-worker is unseen. Fancy that suddenly in Palestine, by different road-sides and in diverse villages, the lame walk, the dead arise, and the blind receive sight, no man knowing the cause or seeing the Healer.

One evidence to me of the Divinity of Scripture teaching is the fact, that it is always and at once harmonious with the most concrete and familiar, and the most abstract and recondite truth. The words of Scripture express Truth as she is to the most ordinary capacity, and are not incompatible with those other aspects of her which she affords to a diviner beholder. To understand forcibly the wonderful difficulty of this adaptation, let the philosopher speak to a *lower* intellect of Truth *as he sees her*, in any but Scriptural words. He must either violate his own consciousness or teach what would practically be blasphemy and ruin. Scripture rescues him from the dilemma, neither contradicting his celestial truths, nor refusing to the weakness of human eyes the veil and darkened glasses.

Genius after all is the basis of all knowledge. Because reasoning is but a conclusion from premises; and, through however many syllogisms you conduct the upward train of thought, there must always be something beyond reason to prove the first premises. Genius (instinct) therefore, in some of its lower or higher varieties, is after all the ' *ultima ratio.* '

Some see in the religions of mankind only the verbal or visible representations of certain truths of mental structure—subjective truths—or personifications of objective facts.

Such might find in Aaron's rod that budded, and in
Christ arisen, no more than the metaphor of seasonal life
and death, and the rising and setting of the sun and stars.
But once admit that the mind of man and the eternal
processes of Nature are themselves but the visible and
sensible representations of a Pre-existing Spirit, and then
it becomes likely that what seemed reflections of them
are in truth equally facts and co-reflections of God.

The existence of any wide-spread form of religion is
an evidence that something in the human nature responds
to it. Whichever part of that nature may be the respon-
sive, that part is elevated by that form of religion to
the keystone of the human edifice, the central sun of
the human system. Hence the infinite importance of
the truest possible form of religion, in order to the
proper construction of the human mental scheme. And
hence fundamental truth in a religious system is essential
to the proper appreciation of all the subsidiary truths.

While God is infinite and man eternal, who, in this
day-dream of our first blind life, shall compass ' the end '
of any of God's institutions ?

Religion is Philosophy made human. That statement
of absolute universal truths which makes them coincide
with a system of perceptions which has human consciousness for its centre. It is the carrying of the humanizing
principle, which, applied to the materials of which we are
made, makes a human being, as distinct from other being,

into the regions beyond those materials, *i.e.* the applying
the principles on which we are made to everything that
is not we.

Religion is the humanisation of the super-human
truth : the bringing it under such conditions as are intelligible to human nature, and as may be combined into
a consistent system, without in any part of it trans-
gressing the bounds of the intelligible ; and which, in
every part, will work well with the other truths of the
universe.

Christ is that form in which God governs mankind.
The sun is that form in which He governs the planets.
Christ is God manifest in the flesh. Every ideal thing is
God manifest in its substance. There will be a time when
mankind, the race, will be God manifest in the flesh. The
sun is the sensible expression of ' the Father of Lights,'
God manifest in solar substance. Christ is the sensible
expression of the Father of Men, God manifest in the
flesh.

All sciences and knowledges have relation to an ideal
man. True morality is that which an utterly ideal man
would spontaneously feel and do. True religion is that
set of truths which he would voluntarily select out of all
existing ideas. Beauty is that which he would spontaneously love. All moralities &c. for the individual have
reference to the moralities &c. of the ideal individual : so
all social ethics have reference to the social ideal.

In proportion as the individuals approach the ideal individuals, will the social ideal become more and more necessary and natural.

A thing is not virtuous *because* it is disagreeable. A thing to be virtuous *need* not be disagreeable. ' Oh how I love Thy law.' If a virtuous action be *more* virtuous when disagreeable: *why?* Because the action then represents the sum of combined virtues. The direct faculty which induces the action itself, and the additional self-denial which induces performance under the circumstances. Doubtless the performance of a virtuous action under easy circumstances, *requires* less virtue, but does not prove *per se* the possession of less than the same action under the reverse. Why? Because a less amount of direct faculty suffices to produce the action, and there is no necessity for indirect.

Virtue is that phenomenon which precedes another, which we call reward; when the one occurs we may know that, in the system of things, the other is somewhere and some when to succeed, and be related to it. So of vice and punishment. So of motive and action, and all the mental facts. . . . Those conditions which we call ' the idea of reward ' in a well-constituted mind are usually the signs that those conditions which we call the results of the idea of reward in a well-constituted mind are about to take place; in other words, that one set of conditions are the usual antecedents of the other. Or that fact which we call ' an earnest sense of duty,' is usually followed by those facts which we call 'the results of an earnest sense of duty;' and that 'earnest sense of duty' is usually preceded by those facts which we call 'the causes of an earnest sense of duty,' but which are merely the signs that an ' earnest sense of duty ' is about to appear. When we say ' a sense of duty is necessary to those results,' we only say, in other words, ' happy he in whom appears a " sense of duty," for in him will soon appear the results.' When we exhort him to read, that he may learn the sense of duty, our exhortation, his hearing it, his reading, the ideas following thereon, and the sense sequent to them are all, with their many minor intercalations, a series of facts each predicting the other.

Let us judge the character of all, and the criminality of none.

Every comparison we make is an unconscious testimony to the unity of God.

What we call causes are but signs of things to come: symptoms by which we know what God will do next.

Facts which we ought to take only for evidence of the identity of the Creator we are apt to take as proof of the relationship of the created. Apply this to the Transmutationers.

Pallas could not spring forth even from the head of Jove till Vulcan had cleft it with the axe of labour.

One of the fundamental errors of all philosophers, is the mistaking *a* characteristic for *the* characteristic of a thing.

I cannot agree with Goethe's idea of reverence, (see Carlyle on Goethe) and yet I cannot contradict it. In reverence for 'things below us,' (as evil, injury, &c.), we revere not the things, but the Hand of God which they conceal. Reverence is therefore, nevertheless, only for things above us. In reverence for 'things around us,' or beneath us, we revere either the abstraction of the good *in* them, or the idea of duty, which are divine.

Our language has been a vineyard wherein an undue irruption of labourers raised tools to a premium, and the zeal of the workman induced unnatural applications of the utensil. We therefore often dispute for an age about the precise meaning and value of words which should in calmer or better-furnished time have been discarded altogether. We have made vernacular phrases stand for arbitrary distinctions of science, and then sought to determine the scientific distinction by historic researches into the genealogy of the vernacular . . .

Every poet knows that all language was invented by the common of the earth. What would he not give to have been born without a language and with a thousand years' life to think one for himself! Every theologian in these days must feel the same. Our beliefs are the victims to distortions more odious than the worst Chinese or Karib fashion that ever made man for his garments.

We are too apt to confound words with language. Are not visible images or the ideas of them the only language in its highest sense? Words are the outward noises by which we recall the inward shape. The charm, or conjuring rod, by which language is evoked. See this in the fact that where no ideas are raised by words the soul remains uninstructed. Hence one grand reason for the choice of this earth as man's abode. Its sights and sounds are the language of his abstractions and his feelings. While a cherry-tree blooms he cannot fail to understand fragile immaculate purity. And in its sudden shedding he knows all the unspeakable sentiments which meet in 'the fall of blossom from the tree.'

I have said that Art concrete is the only art which we really know of. A poet, a painter contain the true and only possible human answers to what is Poetry, what is Painting.

This truth is of larger application and may perhaps embrace all human virtues and qualities. In examining it, we must be careful to distinguish between two classes of adjectives existing in every language: one, primitive or direct, anterior to the formation of abstract ideas; the other, secondary or reflective, and arising out of abstract ideas. 'A virtuous man' is not a primitive phrase; for it presupposes the abstract idea of virtue. 'A good man' is a primitive phrase, and out of that special fact came the genereal idea of 'virtue.' *Vir bonus est quis—qui leges et jura observat.*

Our names of qualities are really the husks or clothes of a forgotten poetical concrete (Impersonation). Truth, Goodness, &c., &c., were poetical impersonations. The impersonations having fallen out of the names, we keep the empty names and puzzle ourselves to describe the abstract idea which, because we see nothing else, we believe to be in them. Moreover, when these names of forgotten things got into frequent use, other verbal quasi-abstractions which had never had any poetical concrete were manufactured on mere principles of language, and so our tongue became full of qualities. The poetical concrete (Impersonation) of a quality is an existence, but the quality apart from such concrete is a nonentity and has no other but a nominal being.

We ought to have generalisations, but not abstractions—*i.e.* the idea of Dog universal as derived from various species of dog, the idea of a true thing as derived from many species of true things, but not the idea of doghood or the idea of Truth. We have the idea of a soft thing as derived from many species of soft things, but not the idea of Softness. We have the idea of a beautiful thing, but not the idea of Beauty. A beautiful thing is that which in a particular kind of mind produces a particular kind of feeling. So of Virtue, Vice, Safety, Hardness, &c., &c., in all which we are verbally separating the qualities of things from the things. (Virtue is the abstraction of an abstraction—the quality of '*the* virtues,' which are the qualities of good things.) Since we cannot

know qualities, let us not name them. Let us speak not
of Virtue, but of good things; not of Beauty, but of
beautiful things; not of Truth, but of true things.

Good things are what the ideal man will approve—
will do or be. True things are what he will believe.
Beautiful things what he will love, &c. &c.

What if the visible universe stand in the relation to
the Divine of the brain to the human soul: Humanity
upon its surface answering to the cineritious matter ; these
past six thousand years a passing illness of the Eternal
Nature and its scheme of salvation and ultimate golden
issue a process of Divine physiology ?

The body is probably the counterpart of the mind in
a lower sphere. Exercising my mental senses, I say ' this
is good,' ' that evil.' Exercising my physical senses, I say
' this is to be avoided,' 'that acquired,' ' this is desirable,'
' that disgusting,' &c. &c. But analysing the good and
bad of my physical sense, I resolve them all into the self-
same elements, all equally good and beautiful. Would it
not be so with whatever analysis could act upon the higher
good and evil ? Nay, that which is physically poison to
me has a place and recipient somewhere to whom it is
wholesome and sweet, even without dissolution or analysis.

There is something higher than gratitude ; and the
love by which we acknowledge beauty is higher than that
which we return for benefits.

There are two false moralities, the one deduced from
the date of our present imperfect humanity,—Positivism
and all its allies; the other in which the *actions* of the
ideal man are imposed upon the unideal, the immature—
Modern Law, ecclesiastical and civil.   The third and true
morality is when the *principles* of the ideal mind are
required in the unideal : and thus morality scientifically
worked out will be found to coincide with Christianity.

Ideal morals the spontaneous manners of the ideal
mind.

Good morals the congruous application by a given
mind of the essential principles of the ideal mind.   And
by a congruous application, I mean such an application as
consists with its given stage of development : and, of
course, (since every state of mind can ring many changes
on itself) with the best phasis of that stage.

Good law the formularisation of good morals.

Hence that Legislature is best in which an aristocracy
(etymologically speaking) originate laws, but require the
popular assent for their enactment.   For the best men in
a state are likely to be representative of the best phasis of
the rest ; but if this relation is not certified by the rational
consensus, it may happen that they are too far beyond the
masses, and their enactments would then be an approach
to ideal law (the formularisation of ideal morals), which is
always national hypocrisy for all but an ideal nation.

The mind of man is essentially recipient, and, in a
wide sense, auditory.   The loftiest poet is the deepest

listener. In the meanest experience, as in the most exalted metaphysic, we find ourselves powerless to create or to explain, but we have yet to find the limit which forbids us to receive. The wisest among us cannot account for the humblest of our phenomena; but for all the host of the stars we have heaven enough within us, and we rise without effort from the grasshopper to the thunder.

The mind works irksomely to discover truth with the blind ungenial labour of one who toils without tools. It goes into the million-headed crowd of facts, and, questioning face by face, in much ado, after great inward strife, with strange changes, counterchanges, and perplexities of judgment, in sore vexation of spirit and weariness of flesh, it finds, by pitiable patience, and draws painfully by main force, certain unwilling some of these slow-footed facts, which yield with the tardy grace of a Russian conscript, and have everyone of them the ten thousand objections of a militia-man, into such a phalanx as may escort Truth. How heart-sickening the conscription, how soul-wearing the anxiety, how life-killing the unceasing hesitations!

But behold it receiving a dictum of infallibility. How as at a trumpet-note the wild motley tumult fall into rank and file. Given the truth, the principle, and the daily way of the soul blossoms at every step with unsought evidences; what signs, capabilities, connexions, connexities, indications, confirmations, beauties, objects, uses, harmonies start into sight.

Given the followers, and we were puzzled as to the standard. Given the standard, and we recognise every follower by the light in his eye.

All men are alike sent into the great universe of facts,
but how few have wrung from them their hidden lessons !
Every new step in philosophy erases the old foot-mark,
and may, therefore in its turn be erased.   But where is
the assumption so wild that, once declared, has not found
eloquent defenders ?   Where is the system so unworthy of
God and of man that it has not its orators and Fathers ?

Nay, what proposition can a man realize to his fancy
for which, when once presented, he himself could not find
something to say.

The life of a little man by a great man is more valuable than that of a great man by a little one, for every
man who describes the life of another gives, if you look for
it, more or less of his own.[1]

Biographies, other than of the less by the greater or of
equals by equals, are really not biographies at all, and
resemble those huts which the Achaian cottar builds with
the broken pillars of a Grecian temple.

The nightingale sings embowered, but let a starling
hawk, smutch, clutter, and screech, and be sure he chooses
the top twig of the highest tree in the parish.

Spring and Fall—what words for what things !   They
contain a whole lecture on expression,—that kind of expression which is in itself poetry, though not poems—the
hewn stones of the Temple.   Express *Nature the whole*

---

[1] Boswell's ' Johnson ;' Carlyle's ' Stirling ;' will, perhaps, occur
to the reader, in contradiction of the above.

as we here express *Nature the part,* and you have the poem.

To the common man, the harvest of the year is the time of fruits, and the summer of beauty and flowers but the means to that end ; to the poet the harvest is the season of beauty, and the season of fruits but the necessary provision for its renewal.[1]

. . . If there be in these latter days any mute inglorious descendant of Samuel Johnson, let him step forward, for there is work to do in the land. . . . The corruption of our noble language is of more than literary importance. We are all irretrievably word-struck, and there lies our danger and our difficulty. If the rights, duties, privileges, and immunities belonging to a fact inhered in the said fact, and were inalienably attached to it, our case were less pitiable. When the name has left the fact, the fact may be rebaptized, and there an end ; except for a few wandering phantoms, our spiritual world would be no worse. But, alas for our aristocratic institutions, allegiance goes with the title even here.

We kneel to the death's head that wears a crown,

---

[1] The same thought is expressed later in one of the Lyrics in ' England in Time of War : '

> Nor well he deems who deems the rose
> Is for the roseberry, nor knows
> The roseberry is for the rose ;
>
> And Autumn's garnered treasury
> But prudent Nature's guarantee,
> That Summer evermore shall be.

though the true prince stand bareheaded a thousand years
off.   And the dictionary-maker of to-day will make a note :
' King—a death's head clad in gold.'   And the priest of
next year shall sanctify our allegiance, for is it not written
' honour the King ' ?

No doubt when the mind has realised an idea, the
faculty of language takes off a number of impressions of
it and stores them in the memory.   When reason or comparison calls for the related idea, one of these verbal
records of the idea arises, not the idea itself—and we
mistake it for the idea.   Thus are we perpetually multi-
plying the errors of words.   To reason by ideas, to compare ideas with ideas, to speak from the first-hand idea,
to call up in the hearer a picture, not a sentence, should
be our great aim.

APPENDIX TO BOOK II.

From The Palladium, *September* 1850.

CURRER BELL.

The description of things and impressions as seen and felt by a child may be drawn from memory, and indicate unusually vivid perceptions, and a recollection wonderfully complete; or it may be the result of that highest power of imaginative genius which temporarily re-organises the whole poetic mind on the scale of the character required. On whichever plan the first few chapters of that wonderful book 'Jane Eyre' were written, the ability of the writer is of the greatest excellence in its kind. These several modes of obtaining results in some cases nearly similar, these two classes of descriptive talent, the perceptive and the ideal, have been, until lately, simultaneously illustrated and opposed in the persons of our two great novelists, Thackeray and Dickens. Thackeray has drawn uniformly from without; Dickens from within. Thackeray has painted his portraits to the life, with a nicety of instinctive taste which made them infallible; but then they were portraits, and limited to the circle of the author's outward experience. Dickens has drawn principally by amplifying and pursuing ideals; and, in this highest flight of genius, he wants but his rival's intuitive and unerring taste to rise to heights which it is now useless to indicate.

As it is, his genius, strong enough to create a literature, has hitherto been too imperfect to do more than notify a name, and, communicating to its offspring at once the seeds of life

and death, will perhaps be forgotten as an individuality when
the social atmosphere it has ameliorated, the tears and sunshine with which it has broken, and the golden grain with
which it has fructified the hard soil of our English intellect—
sayings which are 'household words,' emotions which were a
nation's monthly joys and sorrows, sympathies enfranchised,
feelings restored to caste, opinions naturalised and virtues made
popular—are enriching an unthankful posterity.

There are indications in some of Thackeray's later writings
that he, also, possesses this power of working to an inward
instead of an outward image. Admiring in him a faculty of
perception amounting to genius, we have hitherto been unwilling to concede to him the possession of the higher gift. But
there is a mellow atmosphere about some of his later scenes,
a delicacy of aërial perspective, a depth and purity of tone, a
poetic handling and freshness of rosy colour, a ' light that never
was on sea or shore,' which bespeak that a new faculty is
awakening within him. If the bold and astute satirist be,
after all, a poet, that prophet must be bold indeed who shall
set a limit to his dominion. Exercising his perfect taste in
latitudes indefinitely extended and enriched, his past accom-
plishments can no more measure his future capabilities than the
achievements of the nestling rook in yonder pine-tree, hopping
with clamorous exultation from bough to nest, from nest to
bough, foretell the power of wing which next month will
explore all the fields in this valley and outcircle every hawk in
the air. If he will take his stand no longer on the platform of
experience, but on the mount of vision; look down, not on park,
palace, or kingdom, but on the microcosm; draw no more from
the cabal and the coterie, but from the race,

$$\text{Πόλλων ὀνομάτων μορφὴ μία :}$$

embodied in his single heart, it may be his to give us some
ideals which our own times may worthily study; and, so giving,
to add another to those noble galleries of human grandeur and

beauty in which, because they are full of the central truths of humanity, the men of all ages walk and wonder and love.

There are but two prose writers in the fiction of our day of whom such predictions could be said, Thackeray and Currer Bell. Both have a heavy task to do before they can be worthy of the saying. The one to unlearn, the other to learn. Thackeray has yet written nothing which will survive its age. Currer Bell has given us one work, at least, which will endure with the prose literature of our language. That work is 'Jane Eyre.' Beliefs cannot die, if they have their root in the nature of man; and this book will live, because there is no other book in modern prose which it is so absolutely impossible to disbelieve. The author has superiors in composition, in construction, in range of fancy, in delicacy of conception, in felicity of execution, in width of grasp, in height and depth of thought. She has no living rival in the faculty of imposing belief. And in proportion to her excellence in this first requisite of a narrator is her power for good and evil in a questioning age, and the consequent weight of her responsibilities to the God of Truth. And in the measure of that power and of those responsibilities must be the interest she creates in all those who look anxiously on a generation which, having thrown to the winds the folly and the wisdom of its fathers, is in the awful predicament of learning all things anew; of undergoing the discipline of the child with the powers of the man, a new Adam, but, alas, not in Eden. For this cause, we have placed at the head of this article the name, already honoured, of Currer Bell.

Who is Currer Bell? is a question which has been variously answered, and has lately, we believe, received, in well-informed quarters, a satisfactory reply. A year or two ago, we mentally solved the problem thus: Currer Bell is a woman. Every word she utters is female. Not feminine, but female. There is a sex about it which cannot be mistaken, even in its manliest attire. Though she translated the manuscript of angels—every thought neutral and every feeling cryptogamous—her *voice* would betray her. Though she spoke in thunder, and had the phrase and idiom of Achilles, she cannot *think* in a beard. Far more curious, perhaps, than anything her pen portrays, is her own involuntary revelation of the heart of woman. It is not merely improbable, but impossible, that a man has written ' Jane Eyre.' Only a woman's eye could see man as she sees him. The landscape is too near to *us* to glow with purple light. We cannot make a religion of man, for to us he has no mysteries. We cannot worship the idol whose mortality aches in all our bones. We hear no oracles—we who have so often smelt the stench under the tripod. Currer Bell is not so troubled. She thinks of the abstraction—Man, with all the blissful ignorance of a boy's dreams of woman. To her, he is a thing to be studied present, and mused upon absent. He comes, and she owns her master; departs, and leaves the air full of vision. She hangs on every word of her hero, as though it were a message from the unknown. His 'how d'ye dos' leave a track of glory behind them, and his monosyllables have an atmosphere through which they shine, the very stars of fate. For her, he cannot leave the room but on high intent, and shuts the door after him on a world of busy speculation. Her ears are open before he speaks, and the unhappy monarch eats, drinks, coughs, smiles, walks, and sits in a distressing state of unmitigated significance. Is he sullen? It is the wrath of Jove; the thunderous exhalations of a universe of cares. Point not, oh mortal, thy conducting finger, lest thou bring down the lightnings of heaven! Is he mute? With holy awe she listens to his silence, and gazes on the taciturn face, till the Memnon grows musical. He is plotting empires; he is dreaming epics; he heaves with incommunicable sorrows. Is he gay? She does not wonder that the whole world looks brighter; for, for aught she knows or doubts, he may be leagued with the powers of nature themselves. . . .

Never since—or before—the destruction of the cities, has

man looked on man with this romance of latent love. Currer
Bell, then, is a woman, and a young woman. With a heart,
when she wrote 'Jane Eyre,' as yet unengaged, though perhaps
not wholly unsmitten; with experience of little more latitude
than her home-circle and native parish (though we augur that
she has been unusually fortunate in the peculiar characteristics
of these), and with powers which have already drawn the best
eyes in England on this young

Penthesilea, mediis in millibus;

who, if she can endure the trial of early success, will work one
of the richest fields which the world ever offered to labour, and,
hand-in-hand with one or two poets, may have to carry down
to posterity the ideal literature of our day. The nature of
those powers will be a subject of this paper. The soil of that
field we shall rather indicate than analyse.

Few things are more difficult—natural philosophers to the
contrary, notwithstanding—than to deduce the image of a
creator from his works. To infer the character of the maker,
as a being—divine or human—from one or all of the things
made, is, we are convinced, as illogical as impossible. To infer
the character of the *artist*—divine or human—from his creation,
is all to which our best intellect can pretend.

It would be easy to point out the wonderful difference of
the two enterprises, and, in some regions of thought, the immeasurable consequences of any confusion as to their nature.
True of all works, these things are especially true with regard
to the creations of human thought; and every difficulty in the
task is aggravated when we have to pronounce upon the immature productions of faculties which have yet to culminate.
To judge of the picture is a comparatively easy effort; but a
new set of talents and principles are brought into play when we
would estimate the capabilities that lie upon the canvass; and
still another, when, to the analysis of those capabilities, we add
the calculation of the mediate or immediate relationship to

them of the mind to which they stand in the nearest apparent
connection. In other words, it is easy to assign a place to a
work of art. More difficult to fix the status of the powers
which produced it. More difficult still to decide whether those
powers belong to the mind which directed the hand from which
the work came, or to some higher originating mind, of which
the plastic head and hand were only the conductor and the
instrument.

If we believe, with Ruskin, that ‘ the picture which has the
nobler and more numerous ideas, however awkwardly expressed,
is a greater and better picture than that which has the less
noble and less numerous ideas, however beautifully expressed,’
we must be careful to remember (does *he* always remember?)
that ‘ the greater and better picture ’ does not prove *per se* the
greater and better artist. If the ideas are borrowed, he may be
no poet, and small painter; nevertheless, his worth can neither
enhance nor depreciate the intrinsic value of the ideas themselves.

It is one thing, therefore, to give an absolute, and another to
give a relative, judgment on any work of human intellect, and
the favourable conditions for the two kinds of judicature may
be proportionately distinct. In an inquiry into the genius of a
nation, we think an estimate should be founded on a study of
its rude and of its most perfect, but never of its transition works.
Either Cimabue and Giotto, or Angelo and Raffaelle—‘ I Canti
Populari ’ or ‘ Paesiello ’—‘ Percy's Reliques ’ or the ‘ Paradise
Lost.’ In estimating man—the race—our *examen* must be
either of a barbarism in which the reins of education have not
curbed the unbroken faculties, or of a civilisation which has worn
them so long and so well, that they but exhibit and make available the resources of nature. Who would study anthology in
the era of the Georges?

What is true of the nation and the race is, in this case, true
of the individual, and shall guide us in our illustration of the
powers of Currer Bell. For her most perfect work the world is

still waiting, and will be content for some years to wait; and placing in an assumed order of production (though not of publication) the novels called 'Wuthering Heights,' 'Wildfell Hall,' 'Jane Eyre' and 'Shirley,' as the works of one author under sundry disguises, we should have deemed, a few days since, that an analysis of the first (and, by our theory, the earliest) of these was the amplest justice she could at present receive. Opening, however, the third edition of 'Jane Eyre,' published before the appearance of 'Shirley,' we find a preface in which all other works are disclaimed. A *nom de guerrist* has many privileges, and we are willing to put down to a *double entendre* all that is serious in this disclaimer. That any hand but that which shaped 'Jane Eyre' and 'Shirley' cut out the rougher earlier statues, we should require more than the evidence of our senses to believe. That the author of 'Jane Eyre' need fear nothing in acknowledging these yet more immature creations of one of the most vigorous of modern idiosyncrasies, we think we shall shortly demonstrate.

Laying aside 'Wildfell Hall,' we open 'Wuthering Heights,' as at once the earlier in date and ruder in execution. We look upon it as the flight of an impatient fancy fluttering in the very exultation of young wings; sometimes beating against its solitary bars, but turning, rather to exhaust, in a circumscribed space, the energy and agility which it may not yet spend in the heavens—a youthful story, written for oneself in solitude, and thrown aside till other successes recall the eyes to it in hope. In this thought let the critic take up the book; lay it down in what thought he will, there are some things in it he can lay down no more.

That Catherine Earnshaw—at once so wonderfully fresh, so fearfully natural—new, 'as if brought from other spheres,' and familiar as the recollection of some woeful experience—what can surpass the strange compatibility of her simultaneous loves; the involuntary art with which her two natures are so made to co-exist, that in the very arms of her lover we dare not doubt

her purity; the inevitable belief with which we watch the os-
cillations of the old and new elements in her mind, and the
exquisite truth of the last victory of nature over education,
when the past returns to her as a flood, sweeping every modern
landmark from within her, and the soul of the child, expanding,
fills the woman?

Found at last, by her husband, insensible on the breast of
her lover, and dying of the agony of their parting, one looks
back upon her, like that husband, without one thought of
accusation or absolution; her memory is chaste as the loyalty
of love, pure as the air of the Heights on which she dwelt.

Heathcliff *might* have been as unique a creation. The conception in his case was as wonderfully strong and original, but
he is spoilt in detail. The authoress has too often disgusted,
where she should have terrified, and has allowed us a familiarity
with her fiend which had ended in unequivocal contempt. If
'Wuthering Heights' had been written as lately as 'Jane Eyre,'
the figure of Heathcliff, symmetrised and elevated, might have
been one of the most natural and most striking portraits in the
gallery of fiction.

Not a subordinate place or person in this novel but bears
more or less the stamp of high genius. Ellen Dean is the
ideal of the peasant playmate and servant of 'the family.' The
substratum in which her mind moves is finely preserved.
Joseph, as a specimen of the sixty years' servitor of 'the house,'
is worthy a museum case. We feel that if Catherine Earnshaw
bore her husband a child, it must be that Cathy Linton, and no
other. The very Jane Eyre, of quiet satire, peeps out in such a
paragraph as this :—' He told me to put on my cloak, and run
to Gimmerton for the doctor and the parson. I went through
wind and rain, and brought one, the doctor, back with me : the
other said, *he would come in the morning.*' What terrible
truth, what nicety of touch, what 'uncanny' capacity for
mental aberration in the first symptoms of Catherine's delirium.
' I'm not wandering; you're mistaken, or else I should believe

you really *were* that withered hag, and I should think I *was* under Penistone Crags : and I'm conscious it's night, and there are two candles on the table making the black press shine like jet.' What an unobtrusive, unexpected sense of *keeping* in the hanging of Isabella's dog.

The book abounds in such things. But one looks back at the whole story as to a world of brilliant figures in an atmosphere of mist; shapes that come out upon the eye, and burn their colours into the brain, and depart into the enveloping fog. It is the unformed writing of a giant's hand : the 'large utterance' of a baby god. In the sprawling of the infant Hercules, however, there must have been attitudes from which the statuary might model. In the early efforts of unusual genius, there are not seldom unconscious felicities which maturer years may look back upon with envy. The child's hand wanders over the strings. It cannot combine them in the chords and melodies of manhood; but its separate notes are perfect in themselves, and perhaps sound all the sweeter for the Æolian discords from which they come.

We repeat, that there are passages in this book of 'Wuthering Heights' of which any novelist, past or present, might be proud. Open the first volume at the fourteenth page, and read to the sixty-first. There are few things in modern prose to surpass these pages for native power. We cannot praise too warmly the brave simplicity, the unaffected air of intense belief, the admirable combination of extreme likelihood with the rarest originality, the nice provision of the possible even in the highest effects of the supernatural, the easy strength and instinct of keeping with which the accessory circumstances are grouped, the exquisite but unconscious art with which the chiaro-scuro of the whole is managed, and the ungenial frigidity of place, time, weather, and persons, is made to heighten the unspeakable pathos of one ungovernable outburst.

The *thinking out* of some of these pages—of pp. 52, 53, and 60—is the masterpiece of a poet, rather than the hybrid creation of the novelist. The mass of readers will probably yawn over the whole; but, in the memory of those whose remembrance makes *fame*, the images in these pages will live—when every word that conveyed them is forgotten—as a recollection of *things heard and seen*. This is the highest triumph of description; and perhaps every creation of the fancy is more or less faulty, so long as, in a mind fitted to reproduce them, the images co-exist only with the words that called them up. The spiritual structure is not complete till the scaffolding can be safely struck away. That which thou sowest is not quickened except it die. This mortal must put on the immortality of the mind. Ideas should be permanent, words evanescent. Whoever has watched a trowel in the hands of a skilful mason, has seen an example of a very high excellence of authorship. The mortar is laid, but the trowel is already withdrawn. So an image should rather be thrown upon the brain than carried into it. We should oftenest drink our ideas by the Amystis. Words are but the hocus-pocus of incantation, and add little to the dignity of the spirits they evoke. We have to deal with things without, and the images of things within; and so long as the images are produced, the less we hear of those noises, which, by the strange mechanism of our being, excite them, the better for us and for them. As little of the means as possible; as much of the end. True, there are words which one does well to set in the soul like fragrant plants, sweetening all winds; words which it is wise to keep like relics, that our thoughts may touch them and be whole; words which are the wires of the batteries of feeling, and will not thrill us unless they be held. But these are exceptions, even in poetry: and the *curiosa felicitas* of poetic expression is that which is remembered in its effects. So far does this hold, that much of our best poetry has results which there is apparently no word in it to justify. Many of Tennyson's broken lines, for instance, are odorous as Indian spice-wood at the fracture. True, there are images so much out of the experience of some minds, and so far above the sphere of others, that, like certain chemical inks, they appear and vanish with the stimulus which made them visible. But the critic is supposed to be an *ex officio* cosmopolite, never out of element or latitude, and everywhere 'seeking whom he may devour,' with an indomitable eupepsia, to which nothing comes amiss. Any such constitutional disabilities are, with him, out of the question; and with him, therefore, to decide on the merit of a prose description is very much a work of time. The fire shall reveal it, of what sort it is. Give us time to forget the words, and 'if any man's work remain, he shall receive a reward,' though all the critics under heaven cry shame on him. He has shown himself a magician and true master of spirits; and while they obey him, is answerable to no man for the method of his spells.

Tried by this test, we have said that the thinking of pp. 52, 53 and 60, is a masterpiece. We are at a loss to find anywhere in modern prose a less residuum from the fiery ordeal; or to discover, in the same space, such wealth and such economy, such apparent ease, such instinctive art. *Instinctive* art; for to the imaginative writer, all art that is not instinctive is dangerous. All art that is the application of principles, however astutely those principles be applied—though it be even *ars celare artem*—smacks not of the artist, but the artisan. Let no man think to improve in his working by any knowledge that can be taken up or laid down at will, any means or appliances from without. All improvement in the creation must first exist in the creator. Say not to the artist, write, paint, play, by such and such a rule, but *grow* by it. Have you literary principles?—write them in your leisure hours on the fleshly tables of the heart. Have you theories of taste?—set your brain in idle time to their tune. Is there a virtue you would emulate, or a fault you would discard?—gaze on spare days upon the one till your soul has risen under it as the tide under the moon, or scourge the other in the sight of all your faculties till every internal sense recoils from its company. Then, when your error is no longer a trespass to be condemned by judgment, but an impiety at which feeling revolts—when your virtue is no more obedience to a formula, but the natural action of a re-constructed soul—strike off the clay mould from the bronze Apollo, throw your critics to one wind and their sermons to the other, let Self be made absolute as you take up your pen and write, like a god, in a sublime egotism, to which your own likes and dislikes are unquestioned law. 'L'état c'est moi,' is the poet's motto; 'Αρίσχομαι sums up his literary morality. If at any given time the one saying is arrogant and the other im-pious, he will wait and work in silence till they are not—know·ing that, until he can say these things innocently and truly, he is not full grown. What is true of the poet, the creator, the intellectual vicegerent of God, is true, in different degrees, of all who in any grade share the creative spirit—of every one of the apostlehood and priesthood through whom genius evan-gelises, sanctifies, and regenerates the world. And the higher in the scale, the more imperative is the duty of autocracy, and the more fatal any ' tempering of the iron with the clay.'

These truths supply us with the great secret of success and failure in the works of Currer Bell; and there is no admission we could make which could be a higher testimony to her powers as a creative artist. If this authoress had *published* any novel before 'Jane Eyre,' 'Jane Eyre' would not have been the moral wonder which it is, and will for many years remain. If 'Jane Eyre' had met with a less triumphant *furore* of review, 'Shirley' would have been a worthier successor.

To say that an artist is *spoilt* by criticism, is to disprove his right to the title; to say that he is, for the present, maimed and disabled by it, may be to bear the highest witness to his intrinsic genius—and this witness we bear to Currer Bell. When Currer Bell writes her next novel, let her remember, as far as possible, the frame of mind in which she sat down to her first. She cannot now commit the faults of that early effort; it will be well for her if she be still capable of the virtues. She

will never sin so much against consistent keeping as to draw
another Heathcliff; she is too much *au fait* of her profession to
make again those sacrifices to machinery which deprive her
early picture of any claim to be ranked as a work of art.
Happy she, if her next book demonstrate the unimpaired possession of those powers of insight, that instinctive obedience to
the nature within her, and those occurrences of infallible inspiration which astound the critic in the young author of
'Wuthering Heights.' She will not let her next dark-haired
hero babble away the respect of her reader and the awe of his
antecedents; nor will she find another housekeeper who remembers two volumes *literatim*. Let her rejoice if she can
again give us such an elaboration of a rare and fearful form of
mental disease—so terribly strong, so exquisitely subtle—with
such nicety in its transitions, such intimate symptomatic truth
in its details, as to be at once a psychological and medical study.
It has been said of Shakespeare, that he drew cases which the
physician might study; Currer Bell has done no less. She will
not, again, employ her wonderful pencil on a picture so destitute
of moral beauty and human worth. Let her exult, if she can
still invest such a picture with such interest. We stand painfully before her portraits; but our eyes are drawn towards
them by the irresistible ties of blood relationship. Let her
exult, if she can still make us weep with the simple pathos of
that fading face, which looked from the golden crocuses on her
pillow to the hills which concealed the old home and the churchyard of Gimmerton. 'These are the earliest flowers at the
Heights,' she exclaimed. 'They remind me of thaw-winds, and
warm sunshine, and nearly-melted snow. Edgar, is there not
a south wind, and is not the snow almost gone?'—'The snow
is quite gone down here, darling,' replied her husband; 'and I
only see two white spots on the whole range of moors. The
sky is blue, and the larks are singing, and the becks and brooks
are all brimful. Catherine, last spring, at this time, I was
longing to have you under this roof; now, I wish you were a

mile or two up those hills : the air blows so sweetly, I feel that
it would cure you.'—'I shall never be there but once more,'
said the invalid, 'and then you'll leave me, and I shall remain
for ever. Next spring, you'll long again to have me under this
roof, and you'll look back, and think you were happy to-day.'

Let Currer Bell prize the young intuition of character which
dictated Cathy's speech to Ellen : page 223. There is a deep,
unconscious philosophy in it. There are minds whose crimes
and sorrows are not so much the result of intrinsic evil as of a
false position in the scheme of things, which clashes their
energies with the arrangements of surrounding life. It is
difficult to cure such a soul from *within*. The point of view,
not the eye or the landscape, is in fault. Move *that*, and as at
the changing of a stop, the mental machine assumes its proper
relative place, and the powers of discord become, in the same
measure, the instruments of harmony. It was a fine instinct
which saw this. Let Currer Bell be passing glad if it is as
vigorous now as then ; and let her thank God if she can now
draw the apparition of the ' Wanderer of the Moor.'

Any attempt to give, in a review, a notion of ' Jane Eyre '
would be injustice both to author and reviewer ; and, fortu-
nately for both, is now unnecessary. Few books have been,
and have deserved to be, so universally read, and so well remembered. We shall not now essay even an analysis of the
work itself, because we have in this article fixed our eyes rather
upon the author than the reader ; and whatever absolute superiority we may discover in ' Jane Eyre,' we find in it only
further evidence of the same producing qualities to which
' Wuthering Heights' bears testimony. Those qualities, indu-
rated by time, armed by experience, and harmonised by the
natural growth of a maturing brain, have here exhibited, in a
more favourable field, and under stronger guidance, the same
virtues and the same faults. In ' Shirley,' on the other hand,
we see the same qualities—with feebler health, and under
auspices for the time infelicitous—labouring on an exhausted

soil. Israel is at work, indeed; but there is a grievous want
of straw, and the groan of the people is perceptible. The book
is misnamed 'Shirley.' Caroline Helstone, the child of nature,
should yield no pre-eminence to Shirley Keeldar, the daughter
of circumstance.

The character of the one is born of womanhood; that of the
other of 'Fieldhead, and a thousand a year.' Kant's formula,
inefficient in morals, is sometimes useful in criticism. 'Canst
thou will thy maxim to be law universal?' Place Caroline
Helstone where you will, she is still exquisitely sweet, and, in
element, universally true. To make Shirley Keeldar repulsive,
you have only to fancy her poor. This absence of intrinsic
heroism in the heroine, and some shortcomings on the part of
the authoress—a consciousness of the reader, an evident effort,
and an apparent disposition to rest contented with present
powers, opinions, and mental status—would do much to damp
the hopes of a critic, were they not the mere indications of over-
work, and of a brain not yet subsided from success. One
eloquent and noble characteristic remains to her unimpaired.
Her mission is perpetually remembered. In that reconstruction
of society—that redistribution of the elements of our conventional systems, which all eyes can see already at work, and
which, by that law of moral gravitation by which matter is
heavier than spirit, must inevitably transpose as many relative
positions as have grown no longer consistent with the law, and
make such a transfer of visible signs as shall worthily indicate
the unseen mutations of reality—in that sure and silent social
revolution, which is to give us a new and perpetually renewing
aristocracy, and with it a reorganisation of so many popular
forms of thought—there will be needed, and will arise, some
great novelist as a chief apostle. There is much work here
which the poets cannot do, and which the ungifted *may* not do.
The poets, when they are prophets, should speak only to the
highest minds. The giftless should not speak to any. They
have a better duty and privilege—to work out the thoughts of

the highest. But here is a doctrine and practice affecting every
man—wise and foolish, rich and poor, young and old, the
highest genius and the lowest drudge. And the evangelist, like
the evangel, must be cosmopolitan. We believe that, among
other high callings, this evangelism has fallen to Currer Bell;
and we bid her God speed in her grand work, because we
believe that in attempting to return to social reality—to harmonise the outward and the inward—to stamp the invisible
character on the visible face of the age—we shall solve unconsciously many troublesome problems, and shall be preparing
the way for Him, who, alone knowing the secrets of men, can
alone construct and exhibit for us in its full perfection the ideal
of society. But we cannot help thinking, with all admiration
for Currer Bell, and all respect for her artistic competence, that
on those ram's horns she has blown so vigorously before walls
that must surely come down (those grim old feudal bastions of
prejudice, and those arabesque barriers of fashion, which will
fall in the wind of them), there are other tunes possible than
that one of which she has already given us the air and variations—that to repeal the test and corporation acts of extinct
castes, and to reconstruct society on the theory of an order of
merit, something more is needed than a perpetual *pas de deux*
between master and governess, mistress and tutor. True, the
temptation was strong, and perhaps she has hitherto done well
to yield to it. It is difficult to find in other positions than
those she has drawn the precise ideal of the two classes she
would invert in situations where the machinery of inversion
would be so natural and easy, and where she could exhibit, at so
little cost of skill, the conventional rank of outward circumstance bowing before the absolute rank of intrinsic superiority.
Nevertheless, other cases exist, and it must be Currer Bell's to
find them.

We have said, that in 'Shirley' we see the qualities of the
author of 'Jane Eyre' labouring on an exhausted soil. The
fat kine and the lean are a fair emblem of the two books. Jane

is in high condition; her 'soul runneth over with marrow and fatness;' in her sorriest plight she is instinct with superfluous life; all her 'little limbs' are warm, all her veins pulsate; she is full of unction; the *oleum vitæ* lubricates her brain day and night. The other book gives one the idea of a great sketch poorly filled in, or a Frankenstein skeleton finished in haste, at a proportionate economy in fat and flesh. 'Jane Eyre' is the real spar—the slow deposit which the heart of genius filters from the daily stream of time and circumstance. 'Shirley' is its companion, made to order, fair to look upon, but lacking the internal crystal. Open the earlier work where you will, this crystal sparkles in your eyes; break it up piecemeal, and every fragment glitters. Turn over the first chapter, and pause at hazard. There is no apparent consciousness of wisdom—no parading of truths or setting forth of paradoxes—no dealing in aphorisms, axioms, or generals of any kind. Yet one could preach a sermon from every sentence. Who that remembers early childhood, can read without emotion the little Jane Eyre's night journey to Lowood! How finely, yet how unconsciously, are those peculiar aspects of things which cease with childhood developed in this simple history!—that feeling of unlimited vastness in the world around—that absence of all permanent idea of the extra-visible, which leaves everything not actually seen in outer fog, wherein all things are possible—that strange absence of all habitual expectations, which makes even a new room a field of discovery, wherein the infant perceptions go, slowly struggling and enlightening, like a faint candle in a dark night. There is something intensely, almost fearfully, interesting in the diary of a child's feelings. This 'I,' that seems to have no inheritance in the earth, is an eternity with a heritage in all heavens. This 'me,' which is thrown here and there as a thing of nought—the frail, palpitating subject of a schoolboy's tyranny, almost too fragile even to make sport for him—fear not for it. It can endure. This, that trembles at the opening of a parlour-door, quails at the crushing of a china plate, droops

amid the daily cuffs and bruises of a household, and faints with
fear in a haunted room, will pass alive through portals which
the sun dare not enter, survive all kinds of temporal and spiritual wreck, move uninjured among falling worlds, meet undis-
mayed the ghosts of the whole earth, pass undestroyed through
the joys of angels—perhaps, also, through anguish which would
dissolve the stars. Is there not something awful in these 'I's'
and 'me's'? They go about the page in a kind of veiled
divinity; and when the unjust hand strikes 'me,' or 'I' am
reviled by the graceless lip of vulgar arrogance, we shrink involuntarily as from sacrilege.

But pass over the striking passages in these chapters; take
some sentence which the circulating library will skip. It is
full of the moralities of nature. Little, ill-used Jane Eyre does
not hush her doll, but we are the better for it. 'I was happy,'
says she, '*believing it to be happy likewise.*' Uncurl your lip,
reader, and take this little sentence reverently, for it contains a
great psychologic truth. We read, week by week, 'it is more
blessed to give than to receive;' but how few of us recognise
the reason, that the best abiding happiness must arise from the
happiness of others. Happiness, the estate of the immortals, is
in the gift only of the Infinite. There is no subjective source of
happiness of which we cannot measure the height, breadth, and
depth; and, proving it finite, disable it as a cause of happiness.
The only good on earth which we can feel and cannot gauge, is
the good which exists in others. 'What we see, and cannot see
over, is as much as infinite.' What we feel and cannot compass,
see and cannot fathom, believe and cannot comprehend, is as
near the infinite as humanity can go, and proportionately near
to the fountain of happiness. Those few words are a master-
stroke of genius. Only let Jane Eyre give you her nursery
confessions, and they shall help you to read the heart of three-
score and ten. 'When thus gentle,' writes she, 'Bessie (Bessie,
be it noted, who was "too often wont to push me about," "to
scold and task me unreasonably," and who had a "capricious

and hasty temper, and indifferent ideas of principle and justice ")
seemed to me the BEST, *prettiest*, kindest being in the
world.' Alas! for the guilt of those everyday sinners, and the
wrongs of those hourly sufferers, of whom Aunt Read and little
Jane Eyre are the types. Doubtless, there is implanted in
every unsophisticated soul of us an instinct towards true beauty—
a nerve that naturally vibrates in the presence of the beautiful.
Doubtless, a distortion of circumstances may pervert these
instincts, and so constantly wring out the homage due to
beauty for that which is not beautiful, that the function becomes
permanently degraded. He who has but one window may
learn—and for the love of light—to turn towards the east when
the sun is in the west. To how many young nursery slaves,
born with hearts which should have responded to angelic excellence, has some vulgar Bessie grown to be 'the *prettiest*,
best, kindest being in the world!' And, like the darkened
plant, which has grown even downwards for sunshine, how
many tendencies, which, in a more genial clime, would have
aspired, have strengthened and fixed in compulsory prostration!
How many tastes, which should have been excited and satisfied
by balm from heaven, have become callous to all but the coarsest
condiments of the earth! For appetites—and the appetite for
beauty among them—accustomed to unnatural satisfactions, often
return to their normal state no more. Think of this, you who
leave the selfish and the ignorant to give those first ideas round
which the thoughts of after time will crystallise, to stamp
those first impressions in which the character of a life is to be
cast. But we might multiply extracts as easily as turn the
page. We have quoted these not for the reader, but the
author; and—though it be a labour of love—must quote no
more.

We sat down to this paper with no intention of what is
ordinarily expected in a review. We look upon it as a morning
talk with that accomplished young writer, with whose name
we have graced it. Literally a half-hour *with* a best author.

We rise to take leave, strengthened in the conviction with which we entered—that the authoress of 'Jane Eyre' is the novelist of the coming time. The great poet and the great novelist are members of the same intellectual group. They are both poetical creators, but they differ widely in their relationship to those above and below them. Both a little lower than the angels, and a little higher than men, the hand of the one links his glorious group to the superior, that of the other to the subordinate intelligence. The one, being lifted up, draws all men unto him. The other speaks among us, in thick thoroughfares of our Lystras, till we cry the gods are come down to us, indeed, but it is in the likeness of men. We raise our eyes to the one, we lean upon the other. The great poet gives us his work, saying 'That is high art. I set it there for you to wonder at, learn by, and work to.' The great novelist says, 'This is human life—a strange, misshapen thing, not to be spoken of in music, or drawn in the proportions of the Apollo —the concrete elements of the poet's abstract. I know that *these* you love, *in* these you work, *for* these you rejoice and weep. Hear my *Novelli* of the history of the world.' Phidias chisels out a perfect thought. Callicrates and Ictinus build a temple to enshrine such. The Athene is still wisdom; but the Parthenon was hewn in the fashion of an age, and for rites that have passed away. Nevertheless, it bore upon its front sculptures which, dispersed, are helping to civilise the world. So of the poem and the novel—the one for the worship, the other for the uses of men.

Whatsoever is for use must be accommodated, not only to the nature but the habits of the users. A being without parts or passions can seldom gain the ear of mankind. Hence our prophets and mediators. And even an ideal man can hardly claim the sympathies of the work-a-day world. To be received, he must come eating and drinking. It may be fortunate, therefore, for the novelist if he honestly share the failings, mistakes and prejudices of his time. But these things will

only make him popular, not great—the servant, not the master
of his age. To rise to the height of his vocation, his affinities
for the present must be equalled by his capacities for the future.
Well for him, if he can claim the citizenship which shields him
from stripes; but, under the toga of the Roman, there must
beat the heart of the Apostle.

It seems to us, that the authoress of 'Jane Eyre' combines
all the natural and accidental attributes of the novelist of her
day. In the ecclesiastical tendencies of her education and
habits—in the youthful ambiguity of her politics—in a certain
old-world air, which hangs about her pictures, we see her pass-
ports into circles which otherwise she would never reach. Into
them she is carrying, unperceived, the elements of infallible
disruption and revolution. In the specialties of her religious
belief, her own self-grown and glorious heterodoxies—in the
keen satiric faculty she has shown—in the exuberant and mul-
tiform vigour of her idiosyncrasy—in her unmistakeable hatred
of oppression, and determination to be free—in the onward
tendencies of a genius so indisputably original, and in the
reaction of a time on which, if she lives, she cannot fail to act
strongly, we acknowledge the best pledge that that passport,
already torn, will be one day scattered to the winds. The
peculiarities of her local position—evidently Lancashire or
Yorkshire—give her opportunity for investigating a class of
character utterly out of the latitude of the London *littérateur*—
the manufacturing classes, high and low—the Pancrates of the
future, into whose hands the ball of empire has now passed; and
in the strange combination of factory and moorland, the com-
plexities of civilisation and the simple majesty of nature, she
has before her, at one glance, the highest materials for the
philosopher and the poet—the most magnificent emblem of the
inner heart of the time. One day, with freer hands, more practised eye, an ampler horizon, an enlarged experience, she must
give us such revelations of that heart—of its joys, woes, hopes,
beliefs, duties and destinies—as shall make it leap like a dumb

man healed. But, above all other circumstantial advantages,
there is one element in her diagnosis which, alas! in these
times, is full of an ominous and solemn interest—her faith in the
Christian Record is unshaken. If this were merely a passive
faith, the ordinary accident of her youth and sex, we should
look upon it, at best, with mournful prescience, as one might see
the white plumes and unspotted braveries of a host in full march
for a field of blood. But in Currer Bell this faith is evidently
positive and energic. Self-supporting, also; for it is united
with a vigour of private judgment, without which there is
nothing for it but famine in these days. He alone who wears
these two talismans, of faith and reason, will bear a charmed life
in the strife that is before us. Him alone we count upon as a
standard-bearer in the spiritual conflict wherein all Europe is
engaging, or engaged. All the old signs and quarterings will
soon be in the dust. The proudest banners of the earth are
already tripping up their clansmen, or are bound in shreds
round wounds they cannot stanch. Meantime, the great wild
multitude heaves to and fro, without leader or watchword, and
suffocation does the work of the enemy. If God would send us
some young brave spirits to spur bareheaded into the stifling
tumult, with a cross displayed on a fair white field! Ἐν τούτῳ
νίκη might again subdue the world.

In bidding, for a while, farewell to an author towards
whom we cannot feel too warmly, and of whom it is difficult,
in the space of a review, to say enough, we would give one
parting word of an advice which, for her, comprehends all
others—*Wait*. Having learned that you have the power to
labour, let that tremendous knowledge beget in you an un-
conquerable patience; stand and grow under the weight of your
responsibilities; get accustomed to the knowledge of your
powers. As yet, like the Lacedemonian, 'every step will put
you in mind of your glory.' Reconnoitre your age; and view,
but be in no hurry to select, your enemies. The van may look
like foes to those who are in the rear. And there be guerilla

bands, that, in the perspective of life, seem mightier than those terrible hordes which, though they blacken the horizon, the rose-trees in your garden are high enough to hide; or those unearthly shapes of darkness, whereon we look in impotent amazement, because they are stretching up, like clouds, into the heaven. Go with your harp, if so it must be, into the camp of the Danes.

But, better still, (for there are giants in the camp, and you, who can scan the universe, cannot look over their heads), on some mount of attentive seclusion stand day by day, and note how 'the main battles are forming fast.' In this great estimate—in the width and terrors of the field—in the grandeur of the approaching contest—in the awful aspect of the past—in the sublime uncertainties of the future—and in sight of the solemn truths, which, as the heavens above all lands, over-arch them, you will best forget the glitter of your own newly-drawn sword, and the acclamations which greeted the tournament displays of a weapon that was given you to shape the destinies of men. Be in no haste to draw blood. To let alone is sometimes, as Thorild says, a very divine art. *Vincere et pati,* is the motto of every heroism. Remember that with time, as the Persian tells us, even the pebble will be fragrant if it lie beside the rose. Ceres, to make Triptolemus immortal, fed him from the breasts of a divinity by day, and covered him all night with fire. Learn that for gods and men there is still but one way to immortality. What I say unto you, I say unto all—*Watch.* Do not try to give largesse out of an exhausted treasury, lest you exert your prerogative to depreciate the currency, and, being conscious of the will to do wonders, take, or gain, credit for the deed. Enrich your own soul, that the alms you give us shall not be of your penury but of your abundance. Be so long bare-headed under the dews of heaven that you shall need but to nod to scatter them on the earth. Send your heart long enough into the school of life, and its daily sayings shall be wisdom for us. Every tree has in its time dropped honey-dew: it is the happiness of genius that culture can make this a perpetual exhalation. There are few fruits which, more or less perfectly, cannot sustain the life of man; it is the prerogative of genius that its very leaves may be for the healing of the nations. There is a time in the excellence of genius, when, like the spheres, to move is music. It will be well for the possessor of genius if he can keep silence till that time. These things we commend in love to the authoress of 'Shirley.'

The strength of Currer Bell lies in her power of developing the history, more or less amplified and varied by imagination, of her own individual mind. In saying this, we are not depreciating, for we are giving her the characteristic attribute of a poet—which, nevertheless, in some senses, she is not, and will not be. Before she writes another volume of that great history, in the shape of a new novel, she should live another era of that strong, original, well-endowed mind. She must go through the hopes and fears, passions and sympathies, of her age; and by virtue of her high privilege of genius, she must take not only the colour of her time, but that complementary colour of the future which attends it; she must not only hear the voice of her day, but catch and repeat its echoes on the forward rock of ages; she must not only strike the chord which shall rouse us to the battle of the hour, but seize and embody that sympathetic note on the unseen strings of the 'To come,' which it is the attribute of genius to recognise and to renew.

CHAPTER I.

1851.

During this middle period, the outward narrative of Sydney Dobell's uneventful life can be given, together with its inner history, almost entirely by his own letters.

It will be seen that, while adhering in the main, with consistency and even enthusiasm to early instilled principles, he found himself, as has been said, at variance with some of the deductions from those principles.

The change in his political opinions, from extreme Radicalism (which had inspired him, as a boy of fifteen, to write verses, published in a Cheltenham paper, connecting a violent thunderstorm with the enormity of the Queen's calling to her aid a Tory administration! and, a little later, to take an interest, more ardent than his conscience approved, in the issue of a hotly contested election) to the views he advocated in later life,[1] may at

[1] Pamphlet on Parliamentary Reform, published in 1865.

first seem startling; but it was, in some measure,
at least, a natural sequence, the inevitable result of
culture and consequent growth, and also, of that
change in the political situation, which, for a time,
seemed likely to make oppressors of the formerly
oppressed, and might well, therefore, in the most
liberal mind have directed hatred of tyranny
against the apparently threatening tyranny of the
mob.

CORRESPONDENCE OF THE EARLY PART OF 1851.

To Dr. Samuel Brown.

January 1, 1851.

Are we not all tyrants at heart? Those Neros of
Rome and Nicholases of Russia, whom I have cursed a
thousand times in my soul, and on whom I cry again, in
passing, the Anathema Maranatha of mankind—are they
not the type of me and of everyone of us? Here have I
been wishing devoutly that the Cheltenham people had
but one neck that into the mouth thereunto appertaining
I may put the despot's bit.[1]

. . . And you really fancy that you are to come into
these waters and cast anchor in any port but mine!
What! near the enchanted island, and play chess any-

---

[1] Allusion to difficulties which had occurred in arranging for a
course of lectures, which Dr. Brown had expressed his willingness to
give on ' The Connection of the Sciences.'

where but in Prospero's cell.   Improbe! the winds and
waves should avenge me; steer as you will, the conscious
waters shall dash you on my door-step.   Babble not of
hotels and boarding-houses; the 'laws of nature' are suspended as to you.   Everyone you ask shall look askance
at you.   Every *down* bed shall give you *up*, freezing or
melting you shall be everywhere fla-gellated and re*fused*.
An *out*cast from every *Inn*, you shall pace the streets
that estreat you to me, kick at doors that, *recalcitrating*,
shall *export* you, considerably soured: ' Multum et terris
jactatus et alto,' you shall be driven southward *halting*
and *terrified*, and finally, being in the last dilemma, shall
at length choose the Coxhorne of it.   Moreover, my
Miranda shall afflict you with ' stitches,' and for me I will
quelch you in the ' knotted cleft ' of everyone of my ' Pines.'

Forgive me.   ' Venus ' is truly ' under eclipse,' but
does not pause in her orbit.   She ' moves for all that,'
Galileo. . . . I like the frank simplicity with which you
catechize me.   My answers shall be as limpid.

Something of my view of the general scheme of
Christianity you may gather from the article on Newman,
which will have appeared (in ' The Palladium ') before you
receive this.   I mean to follow up that article by others,
in which I may deal more with particulars, and in the
course of which I may say, under some such heading as
' Transmutation of Species,' something like what I am
now going to compress into two or three sentences. . . .

It seems to me that almost all truths, and especially
religious truths, must be open to two kinds of treatment:

which one may call, after the old Egyptians, *hieratic* and demotic.

If I am to reply demotically to your question, what think ye of the Trinity, original sin, expiatory sacrifice, eternal damnation, and the whole accompanying machinery —the outward visible signs of these inward spiritual deformities—to be seen, heard, and felt in the churches and chapels of the day, I answer loudly and unequivocally ' *false.*'

But, arm-in-arm in brotherly communion, you and I could easily discover that there is a hieratic language of more recondite senses, in which these things have more or less of truth.

For the Trinity I have the fewest exculpatory words to say. Yet the divinity of our Lord, Saviour, and Master, Jesus, I will uphold to my last breath. Nay, I call him Θεός, and maintain, while believing him the son of Joseph and Mary, that ' there is no other name *given* under heaven among men, whereby we can be saved.'

You and I, my friend, know enough to know that we know nothing of the mysterious line which separates man and God. As one also of their own poets has said, we are also ' His offspring.' To my eyes God is in every-one of us, but in Christ He manifested ' the *fullness* of the Godhead.' . . .

[After strongly expressing his disbelief in any commonly received interpretation of the doctrine of the Trinity]:

Nevertheless, I have few sympathies for the sect called Unitarians.

With regard to the other articles of the condemned category, there are senses in which to the philosopher they are so far true as to explain whatever faint colour they may receive from Scripture.

I believe in hereditary tendencies and originally *imperfect* conformations; but not original sin. I believe in 'καταλλαγή' and in 'at-one-ment' (as Shakespeare and our 'authorised' translators understood the word), but not in atonement. And, while believing that *all divine punishment must be emendatory*, and ultimately restorative, there is a sense, nevertheless, in which the consequences of sin are everlasting.

Thus have I answered your plain questions—baldly and poorly indeed, but frankly. We can *talk* of them at large.

In reading my Newman article, my dear friend, be sure that I am conscious of its faults. The grand crime, I think, is the want of sufficient *substance:* there is gilding enough for four times the area. Don't mistake me for a Ranter. . . .

But I must end this long-letter-luxury. I indulged myself on the plea, that it must be my last sin—in that kind—for many days. And when I send a scrap to you next time you must find the mean quantity, and forgive me both the integers. . . . With a whole New Year's carol of good-will,

I am, my dear Friend, right heartily yours,

S. Y. D.

It was found impossible to arrange for the course of lectures at any time convenient to Dr. Brown, who

did not, therefore, then come to England. The
friends first met in London in the following year.
Two or three notes written during the negotiation
are characteristic, as showing the minute care and
trouble taken by Sydney Dobell, and his jealousy
to maintain his friend's position and dignity, but,
are not, otherwise, of general interest. The following undated letter was evidently written after a
considerable interval :

Coxhorne House : Thursday.

My dear Galileo,—You wondered, I daresay, that I did
not write a letter of lamentation at the indefinite postponement of your visit. I wonder too and wonder still.
But there the fact is, I did not do it. Why, I leave to
your more philosophical investigation. Looking back at
the matter now, I suspect the truth lay somewhere here.
I was very disappointed; had no strong words to say so
that hit my taste ; didn't care to say the thing feebly ; and
so was silent. . . .

. . . I returned from —— thoroughly ill. A *séance*
at accounts—I went to arbitrate some business matters
there—gave me the rheumatism as usual : and I came
back with a drag on every wheel of my soul. I was too
stupid even to write a letter. I had hardly reconquered
my brains when a new anxiety drew off the forces. E. was
ill. . . .

You will easily forgive me, therefore, that I threw up

correspondence with a kind of quiet savagery, and at the thought of a score of unanswered letters only thrust my hands more firmly into my pockets; aye, and laughed, when post-time added to the list, with the grim humour of a convict on ticket-of-leave.

And now I have fairly sat down to scribble to you of what avail to answer a letter which you yourself have forgotten? What shall I say then? Primely this, that I should be grieved indeed if my hope of seeing you this spring were at an end; and that I believe I bore my disappointment with what philosophy I did chiefly from the fact that I had no real faith in it.

. . . You should have been here yesterday, we had a motley group. Every man and woman representative. Among them, Stansfeld, the bosom friend of Mazzini and prime mover in all Anglo-Italian matters; George Dawson (whom I was glad to hear speak with genuine warmth of *you*); and the daughter of a Scotch Chieftain. . . .

Saturday.—I was interrupted in the foregoing, and now resume. I have read your two articles in 'The Palladium' with unmitigated pleasure. . . . I like your cautious boldness, my soldier-general: the care of your reconnaissance abates nothing of the vigour of your assault. I like the width of your tactics, your well-supported lines, and carefully covered positions, but am glad at the same time to see that the trooper is not lost in the strategist. I have looked for this combination, (in matters scientific and philosophical), so often in vain, that the reading of your articles was a positive luxury.

When you come I shall be very pleased to hear you
' again of this matter.'[1] And perhaps I can give you a
few facts. At all events, some phenomena which I have
referred to other causes seem to me now to look mesmeric.
Among others these.

It has happened to me sometimes to have a mental
feeling as though something were said somewhere which I
could not quite hear ; or some thought passed, as it were,
behind the scenes, in my brain, which I instantly struggle
to apprehend. After an effort of this sort ensues a state
in which lines of thought go through me of which I in
vain endeavour to understand the whole purport, and of
whose nature, even, I cannot in my normal state of mind,
form any definite idea. I know only this, that the ideas
of that new train, (which nevertheless never seems new,
but ' welcome as if loved for years,' and only the continu-
ation of an interrupted state of mind), seem larger, warmer,
clearer, nobler, better, brighter than anything I can think
in my ordinary hours. I have a feeling that all problems
are being solved, and that I am at last in my true *seeing*
relation to all things. But on coming out of this condition, (which seizes me spontaneously) I have not the
slightest recollection beyond what I am now recounting.
I seem to grow *dim*, and am myself again. I have felt
this about half-a-dozen times—always when in weaker
health than usual. . . .

The other morning, I sat silent; so absorbed that I
had no consciousness of silence . . . with the unusual
trains of thought going through me with unusual brilliance,

[1] Mesmerism.

but on this occasion, seeming at last to branch off and
expand, till I had the most perfect consciousness of *being
in two places at once*. I would not have missed the
sensation for a great deal ; it was absolutely new. It was
not transition, however rapid. It was positive *duality*.
I was as distinctly conscious as I am now that I hold this
pen, of being, as myself, in two, and two very different,
places, at the same time. . . . I seemed to have an
equally distinct consciousness of both places while the
state lasted ; though now, except the indefinite but firmly
impressed remembrance of its superiority, I can give no
account of *one* of them. Are not these symptoms mesmeric ? . . .

Till this last occasion, on which I felt the ' *duality*,' I
had, after curiously examining these states of queer abstraction, come to the conclusion that they were an involuntary effort to remember *dreams*. An unwitting return
of the brain to the routine of sleeping thought. But I
will plague you with no more theories. Let us talk over
these matters—and a thousand other, nobler and better—in
one of many walks ; ere long. . . .

To the Rev. R. Glover : (who had asked for criticism of
a poem on Hood).

I have made a few notes which, perhaps, you may like
to see. I send them as they stand for time's sake. . . .
The novelty of the measure, and the accuracy with which
you have maintained it, makes the poem appear (I know
you ask for my frank opinion—good or bad—take it for

what it is worth and no more; that I give it so plainly is
the best compliment I can pay you) better than it is.   It
is full of noble sentiment and the aspiration with which it
closes should be the heaving hope of our time—'send us'
the Desire of all Nations, the Redeemer of the World,
our long-ago-anointed and only lawful King.   Herein is
our only hope, for we have passed the limit of human cure,
and have no refuge but in that which I believe was our
destiny from the beginning—the great purpose and design
of the creation of this world—an absolute Theocracy.
Humanity may be among, but must not and, if we look
well into it, cannot be above us.

Mr. Dobell's interest in Italy and in Italian
affairs was at this time in fullest activity.   The
meeting at Coxhorne of Mr. George Dawson, Mr.
Stansfeld and others, of which he speaks in one of
his letters to Dr. Samuel Brown, led to the formation of a society afterwards well known as the
' friends of Italy.'

His brother Clarence writes :

On the publication of 'The Roman' the friends of
Italy eagerly sought out the man who of all Englishmen
had best expressed the thoughts and aspirations of the
' oppressed nationalities ; ' but they were puzzled and dis-
mayed to find that, though he could anticipate, and
sympathise with, all their desires and hopes, he held that
even their noble mission was too political and worldly in

I write a few words in haste, but they will not be—if you will allow me to do so—my last communication.

Ever sincerely yours,
JOSEPH MAZZINI.

Later in this year there was some personal intercourse between the patriot and the poet.

To the Rev. R. Glover.

Coxhorne: May 1851.

When I tell you that your letter came in the middle of a beloved sister's wedding and that my house is still full of friends, you will take as sufficient pledges of my interest and my sympathy that I opened it then and answer it now. Be sure of my heart-deep rejoicing in your success; and that the news of it added sunshine even to the brightest of wedding-days . . . The past year has given me such varied and abundant experience that I believe there are some thoughts in my head that might help you just now. But I must leave them unsaid as yet. When I was among the mountains last year, the ever-present movement of my mind seemed to be the recollection of a Cathedral Anthem. In those heights and deeps of success which have tried me lately, I have heard, constantly and as intuitively, a still nobler Hallelujah, 'Not by might, not by power, but by Thy Spirit.' This has saved me. May it in this first triumph,[1] and every greater future, save you.

---

[1] Of having passed a highly successful examination.

The festivities connected with the wedding alluded to in the foregoing letter were held at Cox-horne. A speech made by Sydney Dobell at the breakfast was so characteristic of him at that time, that a few extracts are here given from memoranda which his wife kept.

Those who were present say that the spoken words were impressive, far beyond their written suggestiveness, from the earnestness of feeling with which they were uttered. His voice, though not powerful in mere volume, had always a penetrating, what the French mean by *navrante*, quality.

. . . Upon you, my sister, has He laid the most serious obligations: the Christian duties of obedience, long-suffering and submission. And these, not because of any female inferiority or feminine incapacity to self-government, but because He has gifted Woman with a gentler temperament, a diviner purity, a more ample moral nature, and from her therefore has He exacted a more abundant moral return. When Woman rebels at the place assigned to her in the social machine, I think it must be from a false estimate of its actual nature. If it is not enough for her that the duties set before her are divinely given and divinely beautiful, let her consult the history of the world, and satisfy her wildest ambition with their dignity and power. Who are the rulers of mankind in every age? Not the governors, princes, statesmen, legislators, warriors—no, but the teachers of the world who conquered by submission and obedience. What is the most universal and absolute power that has yet arisen over our race? Christianity, which triumphed by honouring the King till it destroyed him. And what name is that which is above every name and to whom all power is henceforth in heaven and on earth?—His who learned obedience, through the things which he suffered.

From those to whom much is given, will much be required. From the stronger intellect of man is demanded the duty of government; but let woman be sure that when she accepts the duties of reverence, submission and obedience, she is not receiving the pledge of her inferiority, but the guarantee that she is only a ' little lower than the angels.' . . .

Many modern poets have written of the love of man for woman, but I will turn from them all to the words of that great ancient poet—Paul of Tarsus. And I do so the more readily, because it has been a literary fashion lately, to decry his ideal of matrimony and the Christian status of woman.

Love her, says Paul, even as the Lord the Church.

In ancient or modern literature, I know of no sentence on love, which so nobly says so much.

Love her, says Antiquity, with the strength of thy youth.
Love her, says Poetry, as thou lovest beauty.
Love her, says Chivalry, as thou adorest honour.
Love her, says Religion, as the Lord the Church.

With that love which combined every beautiful tenderness of human nature. All that was highest in the love
of husband, father, brother, and friend; which forgave the
erring, received the prodigal, and blest the Magdalen;
which while we were yet sinners gave itself for us, and
perpetually liveth to make unceasing intercession. The
love that mourned over her in Jerusalem, washed her
weary feet in Galilee, wept over her at the grave of
Lazarus, received her, in the person of John, into his
bosom, was for her rejected of men in the land of his inheritance, prayed for her at Gethsemane, and, when it
must needs be, died for her on the hill of skulls. Love
her, my brother, as the Lord the Church. 'Greater love
hath no man than this.'

In the possession of such love, and the performance of
such duties, may you, my brother and sister, pass through
the life before you in that health for which it is my happy
task to offer you the wishes and hopes of us all. May
your love run through the future like a river of life; and
when, after long years, its earlier sources are lost in distance, may you trace its course by the rich herbage of
remembrance, and the stalwart stems of all that is good
and noble, which it has nourished by the way! May it
have been Siloah's brook that flowed fast by the Oracles,
from which the Temple of God has been served, and the
golden pitchers of daily duties have been filled by the
ministering priesthood of the heart!

What follows is written by a friend whose inti-

mate intercourse with Mr. Dobell began on this
occasion :

‘ At this time (ætat twenty-seven) he looked younger
than his years.   His appearance suggested muscular
strength and activity.   He was of good height and well
developed, though then and always spare almost to attenua-
tion.   He had accustomed himself to as large an amount
of bodily exercise as he could find time for ; and took
more pleasure in it than is at all usual with men devoted
to abstract thought.   His complexion was healthily tanned
and slightly ruddy ; he wore neither beard nor moustache,
abundant brown hair as yet (though it changed very
early), not perceptibly touched with grey, was thrown up
and brushed back, in what he afterwards condemned as a
melo-dramatic manner, giving clear prominence to the
mass of forehead.   His eyes, which were deep-set and blue,
and not large, alone suggested by their look of intense
concentration, a too consuming mental activity.   Both
head and face gave an impression of greater massiveness
and power than in later life, but were by no means so
beautiful.   The shape of the head was remarkable—the
height above the eyebrow being little less than that
below.

‘ His bearing had, even now, what one of his friends—
to whom he was only known later in life—has described as
‘a touch of lofty yet gracious mannerism, which recalled
the ideal of a Castilian knight.’

In regard to this, his brother writes :

'It was one of his distinguishing theories that
Christian effort at self-improvement should be a thing of
the outer as well as of the inner man: that beauty of
manner in doing a thing should be considered, as well as
the beauty of reason or feeling that causes it to be done.'

How exalted a thing he understood by beauty,
may be gathered from his writings, and, by im-
plication, appears significantly in the following
sentence :—

To do the useful, is the tenure by which we hold this
world.   To have done it beautifully, the condition of our
transit to a better.

While in one of his latest letters he speaks of—

A moral truth still older than formularised religion —
that relation between the charitable heart and the idealis-
ing eye, which the earliest Greeks unconsciously asserted
when they entitled the Graces the Charities.

On occasion he could be stern and austere.
He was always inexorable against argument or
entreaty to any course he judged inconsistent with
the highest right, truth, justice, duty ; but the
characteristics of his ordinary manner, were gentleness, simplicity, child-hearted affectionateness and
candour, the expression of ' that noble contentment

and serenity of soul, to lose which is to lose something better than happiness.'

'Without time I can do nothing,' he says, in
one of his already quoted letters. Haste in
mental matters became with every year more and
more impossible. For this reason, and not from
any tendency to procrastination, the minute obser-
vance of times and seasons was increasingly irksome. A train of thought, once begun, would
strike down so deep, and branch out so far, that
the hours of work, grudgingly granted by his
physicians, would often come to an end before he
felt ready to commence the task he had set
himself.

A Sonnet written, years later, under the pressure of a peculiar weight of thought and feeling,
and in the shadow of gathering illness, only
expresses an intensified form of a longing—constantly his—for

> Ten heads and twenty hearts ! so that this me
> Having more room and verge, and striking less
> The cage that galls us into consciousness,
> Might drown the rings and ripples of to be
> In the smooth deep of being.

Intense in all things, his intensity was of that
intrinsic kind which gives a largeness of calm

dignity, and inspires not only a sense of trust but of repose.

Women, and women of very different types, felt in him a perfect and absolute reliance.

His love for his mother was—in spite of all differences of taste and of opinion—of passionate strength. The tie between him and his sisters— the eldest of whom was eight years younger than himself, while the youngest might have been his daughter—was exceptionally strong. It is easily seen how high was his ideal of Love and Marriage, and his relations with his wife satisfied even that ideal. For her sake all women were dear to him : all help, all pity, all tenderness, all love, given to women, were as homage, through womanhood, to her. Strong in the loyalty of his devotion, he could, without fear and without reproach, in the finest spirit of Chivalry, be the true Squire of Dames.

CHAPTER II.

CORRESPONDENCE WITH MISS BRONTË, 1851.

SOON after the publication, in 'The Palladium,' of the article on 'Currer Bell,' which is now reprinted, Miss Brontë had written to Miss Martineau :

Do not give yourself the trouble of sending 'The Palladium,' as I have already seen that number containing the notice of 'Currer Bell,' and, while admiring, with my whole soul, the eloquence and fire of the composition, have mutely and somewhat grimly wondered what grounds have yet been given, or are ever likely to be given, by the author reviewed, for the lofty expectations here set forth in language the most shining and glowing. Did Mr. Dobell possess Prince Ali's ivory tube, and could he, with its aid, see Currer Bell sometimes mending a stocking or making a pie in the kitchen of an old Parsonage House in the obscurest of Yorkshire villages, I am afraid the young poet would 'fold his silver wings' over his offended eyes, and desire to recall his fervid words. Yet I am glad to learn by whom that article was written, for one passage in it touched a deep chord, I mean where allusion is made to my sister Emily's work, 'Wuthering Heights:' the justice there rendered comes indeed late, the wreath awarded drops on a grave, but no matter—I am grateful. . . .

'Regarding my occupations,' the same letter says, ' I have no good account to give. . . . Mr. Dobell tells me to wait—and wait I will—were I dependent on my exertions for my daily bread, I think I would rather hire myself out again as a governess than write against the grain or out of the mood. I am not like you, who have no bad days. I have bad days, bad weeks, aye ! and bad months.'

On the publication, in the late autumn of 1850, of a new edition of ' Wuthering Heights,' prefaced by the passage concerning it in ' The Palladium ' article, Miss Brontë had requested that a copy of the book, to be accompanied by a note, which she forwarded to her publishers, should be sent to her friendly reviewer. For some unexplained reason, the packet did not reach its destination for three or four months. Of the correspondence begun by Miss Brontë in this way, only three of Sydney Dobell's letters—and those the earliest—have come into the hands of the Editors.

To Miss Brontë.

Coxhorne House, near Cheltenham.

Dear Miss Brontë,—Is it possible that the packet I received from you yesterday has been lying in London

since December ; or has some unforeseen accident detained
it in Yorkshire till now ?

I hope from my heart that I may believe in the last
alternative. Wherever or however the delay has arisen,
I shall not easily forgive a misadventure which has for
three months procrastinated your letter : and if, in addition to that considerable loss, I have to reckon a mal-
representation of my own conduct and feelings, believe me
I shall set down this *contretemps* among the serious
misfortunes of life.

That you and I should one day shake hands I have
calmly taken for granted : how calmly you may perhaps
remember with anything but admiration when I tell you
that among the rising genius of the day there is none to
whom I could so warmly give, or from whom I would so
gladly receive, the grasp of sympathising friendship. But
I do not love to hurry the Fates in these matters. The
lines of natural occurrence are usually lines of beauty ;
and, never doubting that in our case they would in their
own good time intersect, I would not lessen the grace of
the meeting by precipitating opportunity. Moreover, it
is, or ought to be, a delicate matter to intrude upon the
retirements of an author's private life ; and when the
sanctity of womanhood is added to more general considerations, the mere honesty of the infringing friendship can
hardly compensate for the bad taste of the trespass.
Therefore, I have more than once laid down a pen which,
at the temptation of some new apparent occasion, I had
taken up to say to you, ' let us be friends.' But now to

find that I have misread the Oracles, and that three months ago your generous hand was held out to me—'tis a very freak of destiny!

Believe me how perfectly I honour and appreciate the dignified simplicity of your letter and of that sincere disclaimer of what, in my ignorance of yourself, I had been so audacious as to impute to you. I am not yet sure that the *double entendre* of which I ventured to accuse Currer Bell is at all inconsistent with the most sensitive truthfulness in Miss Brontë; and I am certain that if I had not felt such an illusion to be within the legitimate bounds of the masquerade she had chosen, I could not, even so long ago as last year, have inferred it in an authoress for whom my respect was so heartfelt, and in whom my interest already amounted to a personal regard.   At some other time we will, if you please, discuss this matter more fully.   May I hope that in no future case we shall be sufficiently unacquainted for any such misconceptions to be possible to your reviewer?

Surely we are marked out for friendship.   Entering so nearly at once the two adjoining provinces of Literature, both young, both unknown, both (and both in a first work) singularly fortunate, both the subject of many unexpected hopes and prophecies, and both possessing objects, energies and determinations which make us independent of applause and would have carried us superior to neglect, are there not sufficient resemblances in the general features of our affairs to leave it probable that the affinity is deeper? . . . Whatever are the powers and responsibilities of each, we may thank God that we

were born in a day wherein they cannot be so small as to
miss materials for heroic exercise, or so great as to lack
worlds to subdue. Surely never was a time when one
might be more grateful to *live*, if it were only to stand a
silent spectator among the stupendous workings of the
world. Never a time when more tolerable to be weak, or
more sacred to be strong. When the feeble might more
rejoice in the exhibition of that Strength which is made
' perfect in weakness,' and the gifted stand oftener with
downcast eyes before the rebuke which humbled Pilate.
To be vainglorious, spiritually proud, drunk with applause, giddy with power, can hardly be the dangers of
genius in these days. But though to an eye like yours
it may be, in these times, a very humbling thing to be
gifted, there never was an age perhaps in which it was
and will be more dazzling to the multitude. And even as
never yet in the history of the world has genius had the
prospect of a work so splendid, or a consecration so divine,
so never yet, I foresee, as in days which we may witness,
have mankind been so ready to cry out ' It is the voice
of a god,' and to re-enact the Lystra of old. Friendship,
therefore, among those who share the same gifts, responsibilities and dangers becomes almost a duty of self-
preservation. Truly we must keep our ears for the very
fewest; but the value of the counsel which genius may
receive is in the ratio of its rarity, and a poet among poets
will be humble indeed. Therefore, and in all humility,
I ask you to be my friend . . .

I heard, some time since, that you were in delicate health,
and I wished to beg you to try the effect of our Southern

hills . . . I waited, therefore, till E— might be well enough to be the hostess of an invalid; but her illness turning out to be more tedious than we had hoped, I wrote to Miss Martineau about you, and received her reply (with the gladness of unequivocal friendship) this morning. Nevertheless, you must promise me to come and stay with us some time this summer. I cannot tell you how lovely a place we live in: and will not essay it, that you may be tempted to explore for yourself. This garden-rookery, with its dreamy music; these tall old thirty-feet cypresses, overtopping the study-window, from which I now look up the sloping fields; and all around our house this quiet green valley, shut in everywhere by orchard-hills—you will enjoy this contrast to your Yorkshire wolds. Strolling among these things, some day or other, we will, I hope, talk of the other subjects of your letter, and of that noble introduction to the book you were so kind as to send me. We will talk over 'Wuthering Heights' together, and I will ask you to tell me everything you can remember of its wonderful author. I see how freely I may speak to you of my estimate of her genius. If I have already spoken to you too freely of other things, my dear Miss Brontë,—if what I have written seems hardly in keeping with a first letter,—recollect that I have long been a brother to you in my thoughts, and that these honest words unconsciously betray me.

To the foregoing Miss Brontë replied:

My note and parcel—which it seems you have but lately received—I requested might be forwarded to your

address four months back. For a little while I rather
expected to hear from you; but, as this did not happen, I
concluded that absorbing occupation, or some other good
reason, stood in the way of your writing; and soon—ceasing to expect—I dismissed the subject from my thoughts.

Your letter is very kind—your offered friendship is
very welcome; but first—you must understand me. You
say, I am young. No. I daresay people still call me
'young' by courtesy, but really young I am not—and
young I no longer consider myself. I feel sure you must
be some years my junior, because it is evident you still
view life from a point I have long out-travelled. I believe
there is a morning light for you on the world, a morning-
feeling of strength, enterprise and courage. I am a
journeyer at noon-tide, desirous of some rest already, and
with the dim still time of afternoon in prospect. You
think chiefly what is to be done and won in life: I—what
is to be suffered. The fullness, expanse and delight of
existence gladden your mind; its brevity and uncertainty
impress mine.

Yet this dissimilarity need not, I think, prevent us
from being friends, and very true friends too. If ever we
meet, you must regard me as a grave sort of elder sister.

The impression made on Miss Brontë by her
correspondent's letter would have been made upon
her still more strongly by himself. With enough,
as the years went on, of care, sorrow, anxiety, and
disappointment, to have taken all brightness out of

most men's lives, it remained to the last true of
Sydney Dobell, that there was always about him a
morning atmosphere of gladness and of hope.

Coxhorne House: April 17.

My dear Miss Brontë,—Your frank and sisterly letter
was everything I could wish: and it would be difficult to
tell you how much I value it. . . . But I may say—and
you will believe—that it is with a grave and sweet satisfaction I see the indefinite relationship between us at
length take palpable and recognised shape.

Do not fear that I would impose upon our friendship
the tax of a voluminous correspondence. My last letter
was rather bulky, and this is perhaps unnecessarily prompt;
but we need not take them as precedents, and I shall look
for no return in kind. . . .

. . . That you are not 'young' I cannot believe, even
on your own testimony. The heart of Jane Eyre will
never grow old.

You are right in thinking that my ' havings in years '
are but small (I claim but twenty-seven). But I have
little faith in arithmetic. There is something in ' The
Roman' about *age*.[1] Some rule of estimate in which,
I think, death is taken as unity. Try me by my own
standard, and, some day or other, I will make you look up
to me as a very grey old man; showing you how often I

---

[1] Age is the shadow of Death,
Cast where he standeth in the radiant path
Of each man's immortality.

have been by my grave; aye, have felt myself lowered
into its shadow. And, for present proof that I am not
altogether ignorant of sorrow, I will enclose you something
which is not of the merriest.[1]

Nevertheless, you are right in thinking that I look
hopefully upon ' a morning world.'

I believe that our past few thousand years of human
history have been but little more than dawn. I think the
east is flushing with irrepressible day, but I foretell a
thunderous sunrise—the sublimest but most terrible season
of the earth—and beyond it—what 'eye hath not seen.'
And since we must needs mix with men, a short life in
such a time seems better to me than a cycle of mediocrity.

You think these the words of youth exulting in its
'strength;' but I believe that when we know each other
better, you will absolve me from 'presumptuous sins.'

Miss Brontë wrote, on May 1st:

If I have not time to write an *answer* to your last, I
must at least delay no longer to despatch an *acknowledgment*: brevity is better than (seeming) negligence.

Your letters will never indeed be at any time unac-
ceptable to me; on the contrary, whenever the spirit
moves you to write, you may be sure that what is written
will be read with pleasure; and for my part, I feel a true
satisfaction in knowing that—should I want to say anything to you—the way of access, by letter, is open.

---

[1] 'Crazed,' which appeared first in 'The Athenæum' of November
23, 1850.—Vol. I., p. 201, Collected Poems,

I like too the calm with which you speak of patiently allowing the course of things to teach us more of each other. I believe that the old adage, 'the more haste the worse speed,' may be true in friendship as in other matters. More reliable is the attachment which grows like the oak, than that which springs like the gourd.

The piece which you enclosed, and which you truly characterise as ' none of the merriest,' seems to me a piece to be kept by one and read often. It is not 'mere sound and fury—signifying nothing;' it signifies a great deal. I saw much in it the first time of reading, more the second, and still more on a third perusal. If I may—I will retain it.

To Miss Brontë.

Coxhorne : May 21st.

Lifting my eyes in the sunshine of yesterday to the flowering orchards above me, the 'summer snow' that stretches away southwards to the hills, and the very Avalon of apple trees that makes an 'awful rose of dawn' towards the east—an impulse seized me to tempt you with a description of their beauty. But I threw down my pen, guiltless of a line or a word, helpless before this unapproachable world, and able only to cry out, with the Prophet, in my heart—

'Ah, Lord God! behold, I cannot speak : for I am a child.'

I wish from my soul that you and I could see these things together.

And how seldom I say so much you will know when we

know each other better. With how many, even of the worthiest of human kind it is simply pitiable to look at such a scene as this.

. . . But if I begin to talk of spring, this valley or you, I shall not in the time which alone is possible to me to-day (for I have been hard at work all the morning) acquit myself of a mission which by love, loyalty and inclination I am bound to fulfil.   .   .   .   .

. . . I said just now I had been 'working hard,' without being conscious of how finely the confession was à propos to the complaints which had preceded it. In the proof from 'The Eclectic,' which I have been correcting, a paragraph was struck out by the sapient editor. It was this :—

'Yes, oh divine earth; oh incommunicable beauty, wearing thy crown of thorns, and having on the purple robe of immemorial sunsets, we have parted thy garments among us, and for thy vesture have we cast lots.' Poor citizen—he knew not it was written in Paradise.

One question, and I must conclude. And briefly as I put it, I could write a chapter on nothing else. Is it possible that you can spare time and money to go to Switzerland this summer? E—— and I hope to go in a month's time (it will not be an expensive journey—for that we authors and authoresses are not rich people, I need not tell Currer Bell; but we expect to see the noblest things in the land of marvels), and how glorious if you could accompany us!

If it is possible, come.

Miss Brontë to Sydney Dobell.

May 24th, 1851.

. . . Your proposal respecting a journey to Switzerland is deeply kind : it draws me with the force of a mighty temptation, but the stern Impossible holds me back. No —I cannot go to Switzerland this summer.

Why did the editor of ' The Eclectic ' erase that most powerful and pictorial passage ? He could not be insensible to its beauty; perhaps he thought it profane. Poor man !

I know nothing of such an orchard country as you describe; I have never seen such a region. Our hills only confess the coming of summer by growing green with young fern and moss in secret little hollows. Their bloom is reserved for autumn; then they burn with a kind of dark glow, different doubtless from the blush of garden blossom.

About the close of next week I expect to go to London, to pay a brief and quiet visit . . . I fear chance will not be so propitious as to bring you to town while I am there —otherwise, how glad I should be if you would call.

Miss Brontë to Sydney Dobell.

Plymouth Grove, Manchester : June 28th.

Your kind note reached me just when I was on the point of leaving town; but even had it come sooner, I could not have changed my plans without breaking sundry promises and seriously deranging the convenience of several friends.   I had already prolonged my stay in London to the furthest available minute for the sake of hearing one more lecture from Mr. Thackeray.   Nor was I disappointed; on the theme of Fielding—he put forth his great strength— and though I could not *agree*, I was forced to *admire*. You will be in time for his closing lecture (Goldsmith).— I congratulate you beforehand on the treat which I feel sure you will enjoy.   Thackeray and Rachel have been the two points of attraction for me in town: the one, being a human creature, great, interesting, and *sometimes* good and kind; the other, I know not what, I *think* a demon.   I saw her in Adrienne Lecouvreur and in Camilla —in the last character I shall *never* forget her—she will come to me in sleepless nights again and yet again. Fiends can hate, scorn, rave, wreathe, and *agonize* as she does, not mere men and women.   I neither love, esteem, nor admire this strange being; but (if I could bear the high mental stimulus so long), I would go every night for three months to watch and study its manifestations.

I thank you for ' The Eclectic Review,' and thank you twice for the beautiful and powerful article marked S. Y. D.

Wishing you and Mrs. Dobell all enjoyment and happiness in your excursion.

I am, yours sincerely,

C. BRONTË.

I am staying with Mrs. Gaskell, the authoress of ' Mary Barton,' but have but two days to give her.

A longer, and very interesting, letter of Miss
Brontë's, concerning 'Balder,' may be given at the
date to which it belongs, though it has already
been printed in Mrs. Gaskell's 'Life of Miss
Brontë.'

CHAPTER III.

JOURNEY TO SWITZERLAND, AND SOME CORRESPONDENCE OF THE LATER PART OF THE YEAR 1851.

IN July of this year, with the same 'prince of companions' who had been their guide in North Wales on the previous summer, Sydney Dobell and his wife went to Switzerland.

In spite of this helpful companionship, they did not escape lightly from the risks and fatigues of travel. A sort of sunstroke, from the fierce August heat in one of the Swiss valleys, laid him up for a few days of serious illness; and his wife from this anxiety, and from the varied and inevitable over-exertions of such a journey, suffered so much that the brotherly friend in charge was at times under some apprehension as to whether he should bring both his companions safely home. Nevertheless, they always looked back upon this expedition as on an experience for which they would willingly have paid a heavier price.

Very little record of this tour is to be found in the correspondence. He wrote hardly any letters while travelling, his friend acting as secretary.

For evidence of how the Alps and Alpine valleys impressed him, the reader should turn to the pages of ' Balder,' and read there a description of Chamouni, beginning :

If

Thou hast known anywhere amid a storm
Of thunder, when the heavens and earth were moved,
A gleam of quiet sunshine that hath saved
Thine heart : Or where the earthquake hath made wreck
Knowest a stream, that wandereth fair and sweet,
As brooks go singing through the fields of home.

.   .   .   .

The two following letters—to his father and mother—will be of some general interest.

Vevey : July 1851.

After explaining why he has been so silent :

A—— begged to be secretary to the expedition, and E—— and I have been too much knocked up at the end of each day to be fit for more than to go to sleep.

He says :

' I am sitting at an open window on the banks of Lake Leman, a short distance from Byron's Swiss home, and

from the Castle of Chillon. Seven or eight Alps are
standing about me, some of them wearing snow; orange-
trees are blossoming under my nose, and—an awful smell
of dinner fills the air. The worst of these noble scenes is
that they are all places of *resort*, and that you are perpetually reminded of it. It is horribly so on the Rhine.
Eating, or the preparation for it, fills your nostrils all day
long. You begin to eat at the Rolandseck, and mark
some ten or dozen ruins by the appearance of as many
courses. . . . We stay here for two or three days, for
E. and I are both too much knocked up to go on. . . .
A. has been so ceaselessly kind to both of us, so perpetually
careful,—such a model brother and *chef de voyage*. . . .
The scenery we have past through since entering Switzerland (we entered it at the most picturesque old border
town of Basle, the first town I ever saw which did not
seem a sin against Nature) I shan't attempt to describe.
We can talk it over when we reach dear home again, and
what little words can do we must try then: making up
in number what they want in quality. The thing that
most struck me I think was the first sight of the Alps —
sixty miles distant—through a gorge of the Jura Mountains. The gorges of the Jura through which we travelled
for a day or two are unspeakably magnificent: such
beautiful grandeur I had never seen approached. Wales
had prepared us for almost everything else. But what
overpowers you in these Swiss scenes, when compared with
Welsh or English, is their inexhaustible *extent*, incalculable
variety. You travel for days sure that to-morrow will be
better than to-day. For anyone who has seen Wales, and

the Wye, and who is not overstrong, the advisable plan
would be to *sleep* the journey till he entered Baden : just
waking up at a station or two to look at the people.   Till
you get to the Black Forest, there is nothing of importance, nothing I mean that you cannot see at home.
France, Belgium, and Prussia, struck us by their exceeding resemblance to different parts of England.   Indeed,
near Liège, where the oolite appears, we might have
believed ourselves at Charlton or Birdlip.   And everywhere one is impressed by the presence of the same
universal Nature.   The grass, flowers, trees, hedges of
dear England.   Indeed, the chief lesson I have yet learned
from these thousands of miles, through three kingdoms,
I know not how many sovereign duchies, and some three
or four cantons is the same (and only) lesson I learned
at the Exhibition : The unity of Man : the unessential
character of the differentiæ which divide race from race
and people from people.   We found, to be sure, the women
of Belgium and Prussia intolerably ugly.   But no wonder,
for with the hideous stenches of their open-drained cities,
they must have begun to turn up their noses as soon as
they were born.   But there is the same human heart
under it all.   We had a pretty little illustrative episode.
A young and rather pretty Swiss girl, who was travelling
with us, fell in love with E. ('at first sight,' as she afterwards told me), and in due course with the rest of us.
When we were at Berne, where her father (a Professor in
the College there) lived, she drove to our hotel, and took
us off to breakfast, which she had prepared on a hill, near
the town, commanding the Alps, and afterwards drove us

through the most lovely spots of the neighbourhood. Then she came back with us to the hotel, to have the last minute of our company, and the poor little thing cried when we went, as if she were a sister. Such a romantic little mortal! She travelled with us for four days. When alone with E. she managed to speak English: but to A. and me she was too modest to try. Nevertheless, we got on capitally, in French, and I had some long metaphysical talks with her on 'the sublime,' ' the beautiful,' ' Nature,' &c., (on all which she 'talked like a book') in that abominable lingo. Oh that horrible language! What a plague it has been to me. After the first two days I could not help thinking and *dreaming* in it. It haunted me like a spectre. Little Marie's father (a nice old man) was wonderfully thankful to us for the care we had taken of his little daughter, who had never travelled alone before. (We, finding she was timid, had given her a vacant seat in our voiture a good part of the way: but she more than repaid us for it by the abundant use she was, as an inter- pretess, in places where they only spoke German. . . . Pardon this long episode in my letter, I don't feel well enough to do more than chat just now.

Chamouni : July 25.

It rains just now (the first time since we have been abroad that the rain has come at the wrong time—we have been wonderfully favoured in weather, and indeed in everything but health, the sky has been cloudless nearly every day, and Mont Blanc—a wonderful occurrence—

clear from head to foot), so I will take advantage of the
delay to scribble a few lines to you.

[He speaks of how ill his wife had made herself in
nursing him at Vevey, where he had been thoroughly
knocked up.]—But I am now getting on creditably. Chamouni suits us both. I should like to live here for several
months: its variety is inexhaustible. The variety of
nature is always inexhaustible if you include the perpetual
changes of season and hour; but here you feel that if the
place were stereotyped at a given moment, you might
spend your life in discovering its wonders. Whatever
else we may see I have no hope of surpassing this ideal
of an Alpine valley. Two things may give you some idea
of the scale on which things are. One, that your eyes
become rheumatic with involuntarily looking up, because
to see the tops of the mountains without forcing your
eyes you must strain your neck backwards far more than
usual, and instead of doing this, you unconsciously stretch
up your eyes: and the other, that there are four large
hotels round you, and yet you neither see nor feel them as
excrescences—in fact, take no note of them at all. We
went yesterday about three miles up the valley to the
source of the Arveiron, a torrent which dives under the
great glacier of the Mer de Glace half way up the mountain, and comes leaping out of the lower end of the same
glacier in the midst of the valley, and goes foaming down
through a pine forest of trees, as large as our two old
rook-trees at Coxhorne, and among heaped blocks of granite
and a tumult of stones. We sat near the enormous mass
of the glacier, as it lay like some dead old preadamite

thing—battered, dirty, with such a look of intolerably lifeless weight, and bleeding water at ten thousand pores — half across the valley. It was a very hot day, and we heard the ice cracking and the avalanches falling higher up the mountain. It is most sublime to hear, but poor to see. The roar of the avalanches keeps up an underfire of musketry, and the ice-cracks are like the great guns of the battle. And they occur not all at once, but in series like a broadside of cannon. I should like to come here every year, to stretch my brains upon these mountains and by the entry of these sounds. The plan would be, not to go to these hotels, but to take a house in the valley for a month or two and live there. We heard this morning the 'Alpine horn' calling the cows to the mountain, and the other evening we met all the goats of the valley coming down for the night. Every cow wears a bell, and when you meet a herd upon the hill-side the music is wonderful. Tell C. I saw an eagle yesterday, and a dog of St. Bernard. I wanted very badly to buy the dog, but they asked sixteen pounds for it, and eight for a half-grown puppy. A. saw a marmot, high up in the rocks above the Jardin, near the top of Mont Blanc: and this, I think, sums up our zoological sights. We find, besides our dear English flowers, some very beautiful new kinds. . . . A. is indefatigable in his collectorship. He will have nothing that he does not pick himself, and his flower-book, besides being a valuable herbarium, will be beautiful as a self-illustrating journal of our tour. Tell —— it will deserve a golden binding. . . . We expect to go through the Tête Noire Pass this afternoon or to-morrow, and may therefore be considered *en route* for return, though we shall visit the Oberland on our way.

To one correspondent he wrote soon after his return:

For four days we lived in that valley (Chamouni), where I hope yet to live for months, and which seemed to me, by a strange and instantaneous naturalisation, to be the home for which I was born. With Mont Blanc immediately before us, and our view up the narrow vale shut in on either hand by a glacier, and closed perpendicularly behind by the green mass of the Brevent, with the avalanches roaring all the hot midday, and the booming—like a cannonade among musketry—of new crevasses in the 'sea of ice' overhead, with the rush of the white Arveiron at our feet, the scream of eagles in the air, and the groaning of winds among the inaccessible pines—my friend, you will not wonder that I shrank and shrink from all description. From one thing only my instincts invariably recoiled—the *whiteness* of the mountains. I feel sure it is a *lusus naturæ*, and out of the harmony of things. I was perpetually conscious of the-sublime-that-might-be. The glaciers in Chamouni are neither more nor less than an offence. Mont Blanc himself an interpolation on this world. Happily there are green mountains, grand beyond all thought, and grey rocks as sublime as human soul can bear, that seem at night to interfere with the stars, but on which the snow cannot lie. What right has the North Pole to have fallen among green Southern valleys? Why should winter be ringed round with

summer fields and heat? I knew by instinct it was
wrong, and reason afterwards justified the intuition.

To the Rev. G. Gilfillan.

From Coxhorne.

You are beginning to believe that I have 'suffered a
sea-change,' and that in crossing the Channel, like the
fabled Celtic dead, I left my flesh and blood behind. . . .
I am rather transfigured than transformed.

That new poem which, while it hung indefinite before
me, a mere hazy presence, as often repelled as attracted me,
(not certain if a god or demon stirred the air) has now
lately settled into shape, and —being a true spirit— holds my
eyes as by a spell. Every leisure morning is given up to
the trance ; every afternoon to such hard exercise as may
counteract the morning; and, if I write afterwards, it is on
penalty of such a night of dreams as finds me unfit for the
precious day-dreams of to-morrow. How, therefore, could
I write to you, though every day that I have lived I heard
a voice which said unto me, ' write '? Nay, I have sat
down to write, determined to give you an hour from the
enchanted morning, but before I could put pen to paper,
some one of the shapes among which I am living came
and beckoned me into the air.

Saturday Evening.—So much (or little) I had written
last night, when I found that I was positively writing *in
nubibus*, or at all events *not* in chartibus, and had
omitted one whole line altogether. Mentally it was
written, and hand and head were so far out of tune, that

I was unconscious of the physical omission. I get into this state now and then, and sit, not seldom in profound silence, with a distinct belief that I am energetically conversing. So I threw my pen away: but resume it this evening under conditions hardly more favourable, I fear.

The word I said about my growing book has I know awakened your affectionate anxieties. God thank you for them, dear elder brother. You know that for a year past I have brooded over a new scheme; but being 'a bad sitter,' as the henwives say, the egg had progressed but little, until within these last months. I was dissatisfied: but knew not with what. The fountains were bubbling up within me, but the channels were inadequate, though I had no knowledge where to cut in amendment. I felt that my project lacked something of completion, that it was the right but not the *whole* right, but I was all at a loss where to improve. So I waited, sure that it would *grow* into maturity; and it did. I feel at last that I have planned scope for *all* my powers.

The hero of the drama is a student, the subject his inner life: so far I had advanced months ago; but now my student is *writing an epic*, of which passages and best points, introduced in various manners, come naturally into the more subjective matter of the piece. This is what I wanted, as I now know and feel, by the perfect heartiness with which all my instincts now enter into the plan. The subject of the epic, the last Battle of Tyrants and Slaves. Not Armageddon: *that* I reserve for an episode in my own epic, if God bless me to write it. But the mere human last contest between those two forces which shall both at Armageddon succumb to a greater.

You see, therefore, that without destroying the unity of my work, I have every outlet for every variety of thought and passion.

Be so kind as not to speak of this plan, for the dew would be brushed from it if some more rapid writer, catching at the fine opening it gives, brought out, before I am ready, some wretched or mediocre (or still worse, excellent!) affair on my model. As yet, I think, it is original. I expect, if health be given me, to be ready to publish, *a year hence.* . . . I feel sure of only one thing, that it will be better than 'The Roman.'

I have said so much on this subject, that I must dismiss others with summary (in)justice.

Hearty thanks for your kind thought in sending me 'The Critic.' I admired your clever article, though I think, if we were walking arm-in-arm, I would propose a modification of it, which you could carry out far better than I. What need have we for ' isms ' at all ? Why Baconism *or* Platonism ? Why not realise that favourite maxim of mine, which I coined for my first review of you, ' In ambobus tutissimus ? ' Till the *mens sana* can exist without the *corpus sanum,* ' Welfare,' fustian clad and rustic though she be, will claim (and make good) relationship with the blood-royal of ' Virtue.' While a day's health is, for certain, a day's poetry, I must needs feel the Bacon, whose science leads me to the one, a true friend to the Plato, whom I love by virtue of the other. Let us give each his due place ; and feel them to be both but two

stars out of a golden circle yet unfilled, of different magni-
tudes, and neither perhaps essential to the system of which
the Sun and Centre is almighty: the one Power, the
single Vitality, the sole-existent Wisdom.

To the Same.

Since your last very welcome letter I have got 'The
Eclectic,' and read the article on recent poetry and (with
eagerness and admiration) the quotations from Smith.   If
they fairly represent the poem from which they are taken
(I cannot tell whether you mean them for plums or
pudding), you have certainly unearthed a new poet.   I
have seen very little poetry lately which seemed to me so
little alloyed.   But has he not published already either
in newspapers or periodicals? for, curiously enough, I
have the strongest impression of having seen the best
images before, and I am seldom mistaken in these remembrances.   By some curious brain-work every image that
has once entered me gets an indelible mark—it is ' blown
upon ' as the shepherds say, and never recovers its dew.
I hope in his anxiety to gain more time for study, he will
not give too much importance to a change of condition.
The weight of a man's circumstances are the press that
makes the wine flow.   Let him work and write his way
out of his lot, and be sure that in the struggle alone he
can have the bloody sweats which are immortal.   But
hoping that he will be too proud to be patronised, and
believing that a poet of twenty-one can have no better
discipline than three or four more years of a stern task-

master, I join right heartily with your kind heart in hoping that some less arduous toil may be found for him. Something wherein he might still work and be conscious of it, and maintain his self-respect. A clerkship in a merchant's office, for instance. The organisation and method of business, are, I am convinced, invaluable probation for a poetic mind.

In the autumn of this year Sydney Dobell again met Mr. Carlyle—at Malvern, to which place he had gone on account of his wife's health. After the meeting, an interchange of letters took place.

At Mr. Carlyle's request the articles written by Mr. Dobell on Currer Bell, on Newman, and on the Bards of the Bible, had been sent to him. What was written in acknowledgment will be read with interest. The other side of the correspondence is not forthcoming.

From Thomas Carlyle to Sydney Dobell.

Chelsea: October 17, 1851.

My dear Sir,—Thanks for those pamphlets you have now sent according to request; which are a very welcome arrival here. I have read your three articles, in the prescribed order, with real pleasure and interest: it is by no means every day one sees such a busy swift sharp-cutting brain, and such an ardent hoping heart, pouring themselves forth in the way of 'literature,' as are manifest here! Long [illegible]; and a clearer and clearer course through

that terrific jungle! Beyond question you will cut your way, and do a good turn to your generation—if you are *tough* enough, and can *endure*; but that too, as I suppose you understand, is a necessary part of the problem. Happy he who can hold out till the sacred *substances*, and eternal fruits, disclose themselves, amid this mad multiplicity of worthless illusive husks and hulls! I see you are full of the idea of universal revolution; which, in fact, is not to be excluded from any open mind that looks upon these years of ours: but you do not yet know how frightful a state that is for a man of real earnestness; probably you will know by and by! At any rate, we cannot help it a whit, not we: and must, at all stages of our history, study to 'abide in hope,' a deeper and sterner *Hope*, or a softer and gladder one, according to the time of day with us, or the natural temper given us. I do not quarrel with you at all on that head; nor impugn your notions about Christianity, Currer Bell, &c., &c.; but find it all very beautiful in the given time and circumstances—as the light of the sun is, through whatever media it shine.

I wish you many years, and plenty of strength, for the work that lies ahead of you; and, pray heartily you may prove *victorious* more and more, in the best sense that can be given to that word.

With many kind regards to Mrs. Dobell, whose recovery I am right glad to hear of, and whom (which is an important fact) I very well remember,

Yours always truly,

T. CARLYLE.

In a short note of March 30, 1852, Mr. Carlyle wrote :

Do not neglect to send me any readily conveyable thing you may write; whether I dissent from it or not, I shall be very glad to read it, and am seer enough to distinguish it in various essential particulars from the vague tide of semi-articulate nonsense which it is one's duty not to read in these days.

The 'recovery' spoken of in Mr. Carlyle's note must have been both partial and of short duration : but evidently gave ground for hope that a longer trial of Malvern and the water-cure might effect good.   But neither from this, from homœopathy which had been tried, nor from mesmerism which was soon—chiefly on Miss Martineau's recommend-ation—to be tried, was derived any but the most temporary appearance of benefit: and his wife's state was a cause of steadily increasing anxiety.

Writing to a sister on this subject, he mentions that the physician under whose care he had just placed Mrs. Dobell had warned him : ' as I wished to save her brain, to oblige myself to talk to her nothing but gossip, twaddle, chit-chat; not by any chance to oblige her to think upon any matters of importance, nor to reason in any way.'

In comment on some advice, inappropriate to

the circumstances, which had been offered to his
wife about this time, he wrote :

Of all kinds of slang the most intolerable is the slang
theologic. Avoid it—not as you would the devil, for he
is respectable in comparison—but as you value a true
thought. Never use one of these cant phrases without
thoroughly shaking it out, to be sure it is not a sound but
a sense.

To the Rev. R. Glover.

Because my pen has let you alone since last June, do
not suppose that my brain has been equally idle.

Perhaps it will be one privilege of a better world—I
beg pardon for the cant—a better state of things; that the
unlimited mind will be its own evangelist, and they will
have shaken hands whose thoughts have met. As it is, one
half-inch of bone and gristle is sufficient prison for a whole
world of benevolence ; the soul speaks in vain with tongues
till the tongue or the fingers will interpret, and faith,
verily, without works, is dead. The kind recollections of
you and good wishes for you which it might have rejoiced
your warm heart to know of, have therefore lived and died
here—no, not died either, for some of them are vital yet—
and actually stirred the air and troubled the consciousness
of Kent no more than if they had not been. So much for
our pride of intellect. The fact is, I have treated all my
correspondents woefully this summer. . . . Since I came
back from Switzerland my brain has so far recovered its
elasticity that I have been at work, whenever I have

worked, on my next poem. . . . I hope you sympathize
warmly in the reception of that true hero Kossuth. . . .

Since the ' Review of the Bards,' in the May or June
' Eclectic ' (I forget which), I have done nothing. Not
for want of temptation, but because I can't bear to do my
second-best, and all the first-fruits of my brain I am
giving to more permanent work. So, if God give me
health and inspiration, you may look for something this
time next year.

Of the Alps I will say nothing till we meet : to scribble
about them is something like blasphemy. . . . Be assured,
my dear fellow, that I have sympathised right heartily in
all your various prosperities and felt a real anxiety lest in
the first flush of success you should overdo the powers on
which depends your after toil.   I rejoice to see that in the
midst of temporalities you have forgotten nothing of the
claims of that better Reign to which we are both looking.
I cannot tell you how much of my confidence in your future
depends on your fidelity to that Truth of truths.   Every
year will make it more perfectly *the* Truth of the age ; the
one central fact round which all other facts, material and
spritual, must revolve ; and in the light of which alone we
can see them aright.   Ten years hence, if I live and
am blessed, I begin an Epic, the Epic of my life and of
the ripe maturity of my completed powers, on this noblest
of themes.   I don't admire your friend's taste in singing
the Reign of the Saviour to a tune which has celebrated
blockhead George Trois and blackguard George Quatre—or,
in fact, any man-made sovereignty, for they are all treason
against the one true king : but I like the sentiments of your

hymn. You will be happy to hear my wife is rather better, and that (I thank God from my heart's core to say it) her physician is *confident* of her recovery. We have been to Malvern (where, by the way, I had a charming stroll on the hills with Carlyle) since returning from abroad. . . . When are you coming here?

Before next year—that fateful '52, of which the New Year chimes will be the most awful sounds the world has yet heard.

My blood will run cold at twelve o'clock on the last day of December. The year of vengeance, the first of that last contest between kings and slaves which will probably be decided only by an Advent. 'Next year,' said Mazzini to me last summer, 'I invite you to *visit me in Rome.*' It is strange to me that your Church has not taken up the Italian cause more warmly. Its success is the doom of Popery. It is the most terribly efficacious Protestantism that Rome has yet seen. Viewed from the religious grounds a magnificent set of sermons might assist at once your Church and fallen Italy, and give a fine opening to a young preacher. Not as a *partisan*: but as pointing to those noble weapons which, in God's hands, will clear away what now cumbers the ground of Europe, and make space for the Kingdom which is to come. . . .

Recollect always that, writing or silent, I frequently remember you, and am always,

Your hearty friend,   .
SYDNEY DOBELL.

About the same time, to an expected guest, he wrote :

Come, expecting to be disappointed.   To find Coxhorne buried in dank autumn leaves ; E. faded with her long illness ; and your friend dull and stupid, with suppressed rheumatism : but these things premised, *come*, and have a brother's welcome.

CHAPTER IV.

EARLIER PART OF 1852.

EARLY in this year, Coxhorne was temporarily abandoned—for a residence of some months in the immediate neighbourhood of Malvern. During the time spent at Malvern, Mr. Tennyson, Mr. Carlyle, and Dr. Westland Marston visited the place. Friendly walks and talks with them were bright and wholesome incidents in Sydney Dobell's anxious and studious life. To his active intellect and sympathetic nature—a nature which enabled him to find good in almost any human intercourse, and to be tolerant, even respectful, towards dullness, to a degree that excited the wonder of some of his brilliant but shallower-hearted friends—the conflict of equal wits, yet more of such as he felt more than equal, was a happy and a refreshing experience.

In regard to such walks and talks, his brother writes :

His senses were as quick as those which are usually attributed to savage life. I have often accompanied him in walks taken with some scientific or literary celebrity, whom he would hold in a constant flow of argument concerning the most abstruse and knotty points of philosophy. His companion would return quite wearied with debate, and, sinking into a chair, remark upon the all-absorbing nature of his conversation. Meanwhile, Sydney, though equally interested and attentive, had also noted all the little incidents of everyday life which had beset our path, and could now report them, for the benefit of those who cared more for gossip than for philosophy.

To the Rev. G. Gilfillan.

Coxhorne: January 17, 1852.

Your 'new poet' will do you honour. That last poem of his in 'The Critic' (the Manor House) has removed whatever shade of doubt as to the class of his genius remained after the quotations of your paper. Such fresh young living throbbing gifts I know not that I have ever seen. Genius (creative and instinctive) is *about* everything he writes and *in* the most. Here and there is a weakness, which must be oversight rather than mal-intuition, for the many-sided completeness of his power is among the best marvels and perhaps (at twenty-one) its greatest. For it does not look like the unseasonable art of precocity: he is everywhere growing and to grow. Perhaps I am the more dazzled because his qualities are often not my own. Somebody—Samuel Brown, I think—said of me that I was '*mere Thought.*' Alexander is *sensuous* beyond even Keatsian intensity. Indeed, the sensuous approaches the sensual sometimes with a luscious power of passing the boundary, which makes me anxious for him.

I am right glad to see that other papers than 'The Critic' are taking him up; though such sudden appreciation at his age and circumstances will be a terrible ordeal to him. If he can pass it without growing intellectually indolent,— for he has too much genius to be morally injured by praise —he will go on, conquering and to conquer. Well for him that he has your helping hand in sailing this strait.

To Dr. Samuel Brown.

Coxhorne.

. . . I am grieved to hear of the gap between you and dear Digamma: but, to say truth, expected no less. Wide and universal as he is in his *written* estimate of character (because there he sees with the eyes of his *manhood*, and of his real intrinsic original nature), he is too apt in more personal relations to see the creed and not the man (because there he sees from nothing higher than the pulpit, and perceives with the 'esprit' not of G. G., but 'de corps'), which is all very natural and one of the many unavoidable evils of priesthood. All that astonishes me is that he can as the author rise so finely out of the surplice; and that even in the personal relations he can, as in my own case, become so transfigured even in his canonicals as to see through the heretic to the friend. Perceiving where his danger lay in these things,

I foresaw long ago that you and he might have clouds
between you : because I also foresaw, before I had read
twenty pages of 'Victorious,' that you must end in dis-
carding the speciality of Revelation.   For me, however
much it may be my misfortune to lament any intellectual
conclusions you may arrive at, I shall love you not them
as I have loved you not them—and quietly wait for better
times and developments. . . .

    . . . You must believe me always, garrulous or silent,

Affectionately yours,

S. Y. DOBELL.

To the Rev. G. Gilfillan.

It is melancholy to think that two such men as yourself and Brown should be disunited in head or heart—but
especially in heart.   I cannot notice without a mournful
feeling the evidently falling temperature of your friendship.   Why should 'diverging opinions' make 'cool
friends.'   The stars may be duller in the West than in the
East, but are they not the stars?   And which may be
nearest to the centre of the universe, alas! as yet, we know
not.   The central sun may be found after all in some
neglected Pleiad.   Few things are sweeter than to find
in a dear friend the 'unity of the spirit,' but I think we
may learn so much as this from the chivalry of our
despised 'dark ages,' that it is competent to the same
men both to live in 'courtlie gentilnesse' and knightly
loves, and to meet in deadly lists *sans peur et sans
reproche*.   I confess, with you, that I cannot understand

the state of mind which is leading Brown, and a noble
legion with him, to think that 'our present forms' of Faith
have 'become lifeless.' I cannot understand a shortcom-
ing of the 'Arm of the Lord.' I shall not believe that
'the Faith once *delivered* to the Saints' has grown old
and dead, till I see a Faith to replace it *delivered* also
and by *the same Hand.* I would not have given up
Moses till Christ, and, by God's help, I will abide by
Christ till Christ Himself shall release me. Till the veil
of the Temple is rent, I will worship there.

To the Rev. G. Gilfillan.

Malvern : February 27.

Your very interesting letter would have been acknowledged sooner, but that I have been ill. . . But I am now
better than ever, and have been feeling (and writing)
more to my satisfaction during the last day or two than
for many months. . . .

There is a time (do you know it ?) in a misty sunrise
when no ray yet sparkles in any dew or stream, but the earth
and the hills seem to glow with a light of their own, and
to be filling with a sunshine which will soon overflow
them. It is about that time in my heart. Therefore,
dear friend, rejoice with me in the blessed prospect of the
day, and sing matins for me that the night is breaking.
Since we have been here such symptoms have shown themselves for my poor sufferer as, for the first time these
many years, look like returning health. . . . Let the

opticians demonstrate the light, I feel it in my soul and thank God.

. . . You need not be told with what interest I heard of your apparition at Exeter Hall; and with what, perhaps, even deeper interest I heard your renewed confession, even under such circumstances of time, place, people and success, of the futility of lecturing and the mistake of the whole lecturing idea. . . .

I am very glad you saw ——. I agree with you about the calibre of his gift for poetical appreciation, but he has *lived* some poetry, nevertheless. His devotion to Mazzini, theoretical and practical, has been something sublime. Sublime, because of the calm *personnel* under which it has lived and wrought. The quiet, dumb, unquestioning *necessity* by which he has laboured, sacrificed, endured in that cause, as though he were born to it, and had no will or election in the matter, is a noble and curious study.

You remember my mentioning to you that grandfather of mine,[1] of whom you heard at ——'s: he on whose forehead was written ' I will be king.' I will tell you more of him another time, and of his glorious endeavour to found a Church in these days on the absolute model of the Apostolic. I fear you were not in a position to see him in his noblest aspects, for Mrs. ——'s father suffered somewhat from his ' kingly inflexibility,' and it is not to be expected that the children will give him credit for the Spartan temper that spared neither nearest nor dearest, if they stood between him and what he believed

[1] Mr. Samuel Thompson, some account of whom is given in the Appendix to Book I.

his mission. They remember only the stern leader, lopping right and left whatsoever impeded him, and forget that he struck just as inexorably when it was upon his own right hand.

I am glad of your estimate of Mazzini. I hope you saw him in his serener moments, when he is not so much Italian as man universal. When he gets excited, I hear he takes the continental gestures: when he talked to me, you might have altered his into a head of Christ.

To Dr. Samuel Brown.

Malvern.

If I leave some things in your letter unanswered, believe that the omission is no slight to it or them. That it was welcome I need not tell you, and that nothing in it passed without affectionate notice at the time, take the word of a friend. But in the hurry of leaving home, I left it behind me, having lent it to my mother, who is among your warm admirers. I remember right well, that you asked news of my poor little invalid. . . .

. . . If, after all these years, she recovers! Three centuries ago I should have gone pilgrim to Jerusalem. Further back, have built an altar. Yet further, piled up the 'unhewn stones of the brook.' And all these in this day can I do, and by God's help will I, though I neither take palmer's staff, nor cumber the dear earth with 'the work of stone and lime.' There are temples, not made with hands, invisible oratories, where but one can pray: other temples, made with hands truly, but imperishable also as

these first, where many can rejoice with me. In both, if
God please, will I burn offerings for this great joy. Unless you knew how ill she has been, and I can never write
the whole depth of her sorrow, you could not understand
the solemnity in which I see the approaching, still distant,
restoration.

After speaking of the processes of supposed
' cure,' he adds :

Though knowing nothing of medical science, I am
encouraged to believe in it because no medicines have
been employed to produce the effect : and I am inclined
to put faith in means and things in proportion as they
recede from human device into natural disposition ; not
because human device is, absolutely, less divine than
nature, but because God has so arranged that as things
appear to approach Him they should be more and more
valuable and venerable to us. What think you, oh
Pundit, to all these things? Medically, I mean.

And so, you are positively on the road to the Church
of England . . . We were so glad to hear better news of
your dear H. and of little Spring. Little tutelary goddess! may she be pure as her first snowdrop, bright as
her best primrose, musical—heart and voice—as her
mavis and nightingale, and every thought of her fragrant
as unseen violets. I can't praise enough your choice of
that name. It will be a talisman of innocence and
beauty to her.

In answering the foregoing letter, Dr. Brown wrote, among other things:

Once for all, my dear poet, do not be concerned about my theology, for it is clear (to me) that we misunderstand each other on the point. No matter, say I, a man's theology is but a poor part of him at the best. The only cause of my ever saying a word about such things was my amazement at seeing that you conceived of me as one in peril, and that Gilfillan supposed me vastly more heterodox than you, whereas I knew that I stood and stand mid-way between you!

His brother Clarence, to whom, then a boy of sixteen or seventeen, the following letters were written, says:

He was severe upon the believers in principles of Art, but he held a theory with regard to Art, which will be found in his letters: to this theory may probably be traced the failings as well as some of the virtues of his artistic creations.

He applied to Art a principle similar to that which Bishop Berkeley applied to physics. Now Berkeley's philosophy, though a very complete one, must be hateful to all painters, because it is inconsistent with the experience of all painters, and I think of all true artists. Berkeley's theory may be broadly described as one making the observer superior to the thing observed; while the experience of every painter is, that the thing observed is superior to the observer; in other words, that Art is greater than the Artist.[1]

It is *not fair* [his brother continues], to express in any words but his own what his theory was, but practically it left the artist or poet to create his own laws and to judge by them alone.[2]

Work produced on this principle would probably be original; but it would rise and fall irregularly, according to the state of mind and body in which the producer happened to find himself.[3]

Sydney Dobell to Clarence Dobell.

February 22, 1852.

. . . Not that Art can be acquired by labour, but that the *language* in which a painter's art takes expression is one of which the mechanism is only to be learnt by patient

---

[1] It seems to us that the writer of the above has lost sight of the distinction, insisted on in the following letter, between abstract and concrete art, on the latter of which alone Sydney Dobell theorises.

[2] In fact, to

> Trust the spirit,
> As sovran nature does, to make the form;
> For otherwise we only imprison spirit,
> And not embody.   Aurora Leigh.

[3] Let him take Goethe's ' good counsel ':

> Geschieht wohl, dass man einen Tag
> Weder sich noch andre leiden mag,
> Will nichts dir nach dem Herzen ein;
> Sollt's in der Kunst wohl anders seyn?
> Drum hetze dich nicht zur schlimmen Zeit,
> Denn Füll und Kraft sind nimmer weit:
> Hast in der bösen Stund' geruht,
> Ist dir die Güte doppelt gut.

study and toil, because apart from its own intrinsic (as it were, grammatical) difficulties, it is a language that by its nature is perpetually seducing him from his instinctive *art*. As Persian, for instance, among tongues, so much abounds in pleasant quibbles and mere music of sound that hardly a poet has written pure poetry in it; so the artist, except by the purgatorial influence of hard labour and incessant study of the capabilities of his language, is perpetually stopping to be pleased with the *sound*, and, therefore, never arriving at a sense; always liable to mistake painting pictures for painting ideas. And here let me fix in pen and ink a truth which you and I have sometimes talked about, but which it will be well to have definitely before you, because it is the fundamental truth on all artistic subjects.

The word 'art' is perpetually misleading us, because it stands for so many things, and is, therefore, apt to be used in one sense in the premises and another in the conclusions.

Our first step must be to throw away any connection between the word '*art*' and the idea of *skill*—which is quite another word: 'art' having nothing to do with poets and painters, or, to speak shortly, with the *poets*, for a painter, if he is anything more than a mere mechanic, is a poet in a different language—the hieroglyphic poet.

Every poet speaks in signs (or images), but the painting poet affects the brain through the eye, instead of the ear.

Next we must throw away any idea of abstract Art at all. We cannot tell what is art in the abstract any more, (for it is the same problem in other words) than we can tell what is abstract poetry. Accustom yourself, therefore, to think of the word '*art*' as meaning concrete Art, as meaning the same as written poetry, as meaning in painting, painted art, in short a *work of art.* Always think of Art, as art visible—pictures, statues, poems.

But you say ' is there no such thing as abstract *art?*' Doubtless; but equally doubtless that no human mind can discover it. Doubtless abstract art is that which when personified makes a work of art. And doubtless that is a work of art which is made on the principles on which God made the universe.

But no human reason can hope to discover all these principles (if any), and the best exertion of human reason may leave out the most essential, and is therefore quite valueless as a guide in works of *art.* Therefore God has provided a race of men born with an instinct which recognises the presence of these principles when embodied; as He provides the loadstone to point to the undiscoverable pole. In such men the presence of those principles in a work gives a peculiar sense of pleasure, or rather supplies a peculiar sense of want; and by working to the satisfaction of that feeling, changing the direction of the work when the feeling ceases to be gratified, and stopping the work altogether when the craving appears satisfied, they can produce what their reason could never have invented.

But this instinct is born in them, and can only be educated or cultivated by constantly contemplating, (devout *looking* upon, not sciolistic reasoning upon), that nature wherein is the only all-perfect embodiment, by the Great Artist, of the same divine principles.

He, looking on the work, saw that it was *good.* 'For His *pleasure* it is and was created.'

To the same.

Albert Link House, Malvern: 1852.

In the afternoon I went to the top of North Hill, and Switzerland itself could hardly have been finer. For the vapours that utterly shut out both valleys were thin enough to disclose the gorges of the hills; snow filled and shining here, and there glooming black up through the clouds because of the dark winter furze that rose above the snow. The vapours moved in a slow wind, and were continually opening into gulphs that looked unfathomable. I walked down the Herefordshire side, and found the whole valley in a dense fog, almost as dark as night. After some further wandering, I found myself on the top of one of the hills, shut into the very apex by the clouds. The hills hereabout are far finer in winter than in summer, for now they are clad from head to foot in withered fern and black and green furze—which last, in its summer livery of green and gold, has a somewhat flunkeyfied look. Nevertheless, at all seasons, there are some noble studies in them.

The perpetual offence is the Malvern 'willas.' But,

even there, the eye catches the old Abbey now and then, like music among marrow-bones and cleavers.

It struck me very much yesterday, when my eyes, aching with these houses, passed unconsciously over the Abbey and felt physically relieved. I was puzzled to account for the principles of the relief, probably no man will ever hit on them, but it was a fine lesson in a great truth. That Gothic architecture came in as a harmonious chord among the 'symphony of mountains,'—and why? The answer is, it was a work of *genius*. Genius built to *please* itself, saw it, and was pleased, not knowing why, but knowing since it was pleased that the work was finished. Therefore, I, also, seeing it am pleased, *not knowing why*, but having this only and sufficient knowledge, that it contains, though beyond my discovery, principles in common with those on which God made the universe.

In answer to a letter which acknowledged the receipt of a copy of the second edition of 'The Roman,' he wrote:

To the Rev. B. Paton.

Malvern: April 5.

When we meet, here or elsewhere, I shall have a word or two to say on the contents of your letter. . . . What you have said happens to be precisely that kind of testimony at which I cannot altogether hold my peace. To write a book which should not inconsist with the Book of Books, to dig a channel in these days which should, in however small a measure, be a conduit from the perennial spring of Truth and Beauty, is precisely the intellectual achievement for which I would the most heartily thank God.

And every fresh assertion that I am in unison with my keynote, is, as an additional voice in an important verdict, pleasant to hear. But I say I hope to chat with you on these things, because I would guard you against misapprehending my whole circle by experimenting upon an arc of it. If, therefore, my next book has less of the Christian and the Scripture, do not infer that *I* am less Christian or Scriptural. . . . In my first book I gave the Enthusiast and Apostle ; in my second I must show that I understand the doubts and sorrows of our time and nature; that I may vindicate my right to an effort, in some maturer future, at the solution of the problem I must first be known to comprehend. . . .

To the Rev. G. Gilfillan.

Malvern.

Truly there are some magnificent things in his (Alexander Smith's) contributions to ' The Critic,' but the more I see of his poetry the more I am impressed with a certain dread of plagiarism which seized me, if you remember, the first time I read your extracts.[1] Not so much plagiarism *totidem verbis* as . . . that most fatal plagiarism whose originality consists in reversing well-known medals . . . But with all this, he gives me a far greater

---

[1] See p. 234

impression of intellectual life and abundance—I said
vigour,' but it was a mistake, it is rather the upspring-
ing of a fountain, or the exuberance of a strawberry-bed—·
than any living poet.   If his *morale* is equal to some
of his intellectual powers, and will impart to them that
stern mental honesty which scorns (not from principle
only, but intuition) every success not self-achieved and
every ornament not of sterling gold; if, moreover, his
sensuous beauty be not the atmosphere of a sensual life;
and if he has (or shall learn) some high unworldly purpose, not for his poetry but for himself, I cannot imagine
any prediction too glowing for what ten or fifteen years
hence he may be and do.   At present, in the midst of his
oriental luxury, there is to me (curiously enough) a constant impression of oriental untruth.

At what is said above, Mr. Gilfillan seems to
have taken umbrage.   The following fragment was
evidently written in answer to the expression of
this feeling :

When I, as your loving friend, and interested, therefore, in your friendships, point out, in answer to your
question, what appear to my eyes as the dangers of your
protégé, you should be the last to imply offence or ill-
feeling, either by what you say or what you leave unsaid.
It would be absurd to suppose that, because you and I
love each other, all our personal fancies and special pre-
dilections are bound to be infectious; and if, therefore,
I had really formed a very contrary estimate from yours,

it could by possibility be no ground of complaint. But
the case happens to be that I have throughout thought,
felt, and spoken with an eager interest in your *trésor
trouvé*; and indeed, from the fulness of that interest, and
a consequent fear that your zealous and warm-hearted
appreciation might lead to the injury of your hopes, I
spoke—or wrote—to you in my last.

It will be noticed that these allusions to Alexander Smith were written before there was any
personal acquaintance between the two poets; and
that these fears of his tendency to be influenced by
the ideas of others were expressed from the very beginning of Smith's career: long before such charges
were brought against him by the press.

When these charges were publicly made, with
an exaggeration that, Mr. Dobell considered,
turned their partial truth to falsehood, he was
hearty and enthusiastic in defence of his friend.
They first met at Coxhorne in 1853—Alexander
Smith and the Rev. Brown Paton spending a few
days there—in the course of a walking tour. As
is well known, personal acquaintance afterwards
ripened to affectionate friendship; 'proud integrity,
strong sense, and sound unglittering manliness'
being among the qualities which commended Alexander Smith to Sydney Dobell.

CHAPTER V.

LATER PART OF 1852.

In May Mr. and Mrs. Dobell returned to Coxhorne, and at its close they were again playing host and hostess to wedding-guests; his third sister then becoming the wife of his cousin and beloved friend—Mr. A. J. Mott.

The sojourn at Coxhorne must have been short, for at the end of June he wrote home from London, whither they had gone in search of fresh advice for his wife, after speaking of the progress of his book :

Every day teaches me more thoroughly that a poet's life must be country life. I can *write* these things, under the necessity of the case, here in London, but every breath of inspiration is of Charlton air. I sit here, but *am* at home. These lodgings, however, are more 'countryfied' than you would expect from London. A robin is at this moment singing at my window.

'A long talk with Ruskin' is spoken of about this time : his great aim in which was to elicit Mr. Ruskin's opinion as to the best course, with regard to art-study, to be taken by his favourite young brother.

Of this talk he wrote to his brother:

It was delightful to find that we met at a word on many of the finest delicacies in nature and art, wherein I have often found the most gifted almost blind. In appearance he is not exactly what I expected . . . The characteristics of his mouth and eyes are a susceptible, almost tremulous, appreciation that comes and goes about a shrewd acumen that is permanent; and an earnestness, that pervades every feature, gives power to a face that would otherwise be merely lovable for its gentleness. His manner is very much an expression of all this.

Browning, whom I met beside him, is, in point of complexion, a fine contrast; dark in hair, eyebrow, and luxuriant beard as a Spaniard or Portuguese, which he very much resembles. A fine, large, expansible dark eye, and a mouth, not exactly poetic, but wonderful for its facility, arrest you at once.

In the same letter he says, it seems to him that some of the professed painters know little about true art, because art is instinctive and the exclusive fruit of genius; and many of these *soi-disant* artists are not much more than geniusy *artisans*.

In acknowledging a newspaper report of a lecture, he wrote:

To A. J. Mott, Esq.

It must have been a noble exception to the ordinary rule.   I have long been convinced that the whole lecturing system, so far as instruction and edification are concerned, is a radical mistake.   Classes, committees, clubs, &c., are the modes for acquiring knowledge or eliminating truth (and the practice of all the sciences is a tacit confirmation); but in the way of proclamation and rough suggestion, I think one can hardly over-calculate the amount of good that a strong-headed, fire-hearted, golden-tongued missionary like —— may perform just now.   And I think he is, as yet, the very man for the work.   For in these matters it requires that a man should not be too much in advance of his audience.   Nay, if he shares some of their mistakes, so much the better; they are so many hands by which he draws them to his firmer footing.   And it is the 'ordo' of the propagation of truth that it begins low down, and as it grows prepares the soil for its own nutriment.   Set five hundred minds thinking on as much truth as they can now receive, and in fifty of them your germ may, in time, grow to a tree.   Throw developed truth, pure and entire, among the same five hundred, and it will probably fall to the ground between them, or be carried off by some *one* exceptional and courageous individual, who did not bob out of its way.

.   .   .   .

You won't be sorry to hear, I know, that my book is growing very near completion.   With regard to books—

have you seen anything of Alexander Smith's Poems?
They are, after all deductions, astonishing, and would be
so from a grown poet; what then of a boy of twenty who
has been ten hours a day in business ever since he was
fourteen? He is poor, and will have to publish by subscription, unless some other way can be found for him.
I have written to him to say that if he can find four
friends to lend him ten pounds each till his first edition is
sold, I will be a fifth. Fifty pounds would do the thing
for him, independently of the humiliations, disadvantages,
and vulgar patronage of subscription.

During the time Sydney Dobell spent in London
he took an active part in the affairs of that
' Church,' founded by his grandfather, Mr. Samuel
Thompson, to which allusion has often been made,
and of which a fuller account is given elsewhere.

He regularly attended its meetings, put himself
in personal relation with its members, and soon
acquired considerable influence.

The affairs of ' The Church' occupy at this
period great space in his letters home: all connected with it being of the greatest interest to his
mother.

To his Father and Mother.

Maida Hill: September 21, 1852.

Last Sunday I went to H. J.'s, where —— had agreed
to meet us; and we had a long talk with him. He seemed

in a curious state of mind, and to be as much in the dark as anybody as to the precise nature of his own objections.[1] The nearest approach he could make to a description of them was that he felt convinced that all authority was adverse to the progress and improvement of the human mind . . . but I could see that the real difficulty was this, that he had imbibed the central doctrine of Germanism—the innate intuitive knowledge by 'the conscience' of right and wrong. We elaborately answered his objections as far as we could get him to recognize them tangibly, and each of us gave, besides, a sort of summary of the evidences of Christianity; and he has promised to meet us again. I am afraid there was no very effectual work done, but am in hope he was shaken. Nevertheless, while the central doctrine remains untouched, and indeed hardly recognised, I fear the root of the evil is as vital as ever. Sometimes he really seemed so inexpugnably stupid, in his slow misty repetitions, that I almost felt the matter hopeless, unless one could knock so thick a head against something harder, and unsettle the desiccated matter inside. But I was glad to have taken a better method when at the close, with tears on his cheeks, the rough-faced man thanked us for the kindness, patience, and trouble we had taken with him.

It was really a fine thing to hear H. J.'s talk. Such tact, facility, talent, and even depth; and language that many a cultivated man would have been glad of. It says something for the principles.

---

[1] Objections to remaining a member of 'The Church.'

To the same.

I got the two numbers of the 'Restoration of Belief'
for ——, and looked into them myself. I like them better
when viewed together than when I saw the first alone,
because they give me greater confidence in the intentions
of the writer, and justify to a certain extent the claims he
puts forward. There seems to me too much leisure in his
style, too much promise and too great certainty in his
long preludes, and too easy and confident a *petitio principii*
on some of the very points against which his antagonists
contend. But this is viewing his argument as to its effect
on disbelievers; to whom, I think he stated at the commencement, it is not addressed. All these things, irrita-
ting or ineffective with an opponent, are admirably prudent
and greatly suasive with the merely wavering, or with the
unshaken believer. And to such, I think and hope, his
book will be inestimable. Not because it discovers anything—or *many* things—new; but from the manner in
which it arranges old things, from the new side on which
it approaches the evidences, and the *reality* with which he
has the power of filling old facts, or rather those sensations
resulting from them which repetition had almost deadened.
His argument on the value of even *spurious* epistles,
scriptures, &c., as the reflexions of *true*, is very fine, and,
as far as I know, his own. But, unless he has something
yet to develope far more novel and forcible than I yet see

prospect of, his book will be no 'Restoration' to those whose disbelief comes from Germany.

That is to say to those who *really* got it from Germany; not to the ten thousand who merely picked up a German crumb from an English Unitarian or out of an infidel dish. A German idea can be thrown away; but learn to *think* like a German, and you must surrender yourself, soul and body. In this respect modern unbelief, or misbelief, beautiful, holy and lovable as it is, is far more hopeless than the old Tom Paine savagery. No one who has not gone through something considerable in German philosophy can understand the whole truth of this.

Speaking to his father and mother of the opposition he had met with at 'The Church' meetings, from a family connection who seemed to think of him as still the 'little Sydney' of former years, and to regard with jealousy his growing influence, he says, he has, he hopes, lived down the disagreeable state of things :

For several meetings it had been a mere repetition of the same routine between us—I to propose or say, Mr.——— universally to oppose or answer. . . . The meeting before last was a comical specimen. The public conversation turned on the Restoration of Belief. I drew attention to some points, and stated some opinions and expectations. . . . Mr. ——— got up and carefully dissented from each and all; though, as appeared from his arguments, he was not exactly at home in that kind of reasoning. So, in answering him, I pointed out where he was mistaken; and then showed how very right he would have been if he had not been wrong. Under which happy state of things we were of course in warm agreement.

To the same.

Maida Hill.

You will forgive so short a letter as I must send to-day, and believe I am as much disappointed to send it as you to receive. We always enjoy the notion of your having a long letter on Sunday morning, and E. calculates with elaborate precision the moment at which the postman is ascending Detmore path, reaching the garden gate, and giving in his packet. But I promised—to go with her to-day to Chelsea, to see that (to me) most uninteresting sham—the Duke's lying in state.[1] . . . Everybody seems wild about this same funeral. . . . It will have no reality of any sort—neither festal nor funeral. In the midst of that enormous ostentation of mourning not one soul will be sorry.

To the same.

Maida Hill : December 11.

It was a great relief to know that no trees are injured at Coxhorne. . . . You say nothing further of the pros-

---

[1] The reason of Mr. Dobell's failure, at this period of his life, to appreciate the qualities of 'the Great Duke,' must, we suppose, be found, at least in part, in his enthusiastic admiration of Napoleon I.

pects of the railroad, or of the projected line of it. It
will be terrible indeed if it comes through Detmore field.
Please tell us of some of these things when you write, for,
after so long an absence from country and home, one's
interest becomes positively morbid.   So even physical is
the effect of this hunger and thirst that the most unlikely
suggestions bring up visibly the outlines of the well-known
hills.   A block of houses, made indistinct by London fog,
has many a time started into Lynover or Coldsgate, or the
line of the Cotswolds, with such a strange and vivid reality
that I could hardly believe it a delusion.   But we must
all ' bide our time.' . . . I send you Alexander Smith's
letter received to-day.   He has made good terms, has he
not ? I send you also a copy of Marston's ' Monody ' on the
Duke.   The opinions of course I dissent from, and there
are one or two poor lines; but, considering the purpose for
which it was written, I think there is most masterly
writing in it.   The two lines beginning our ' Britain
bore him ' are almost unsurpassable for terse *manly* meaning.

To the same.

Maida Hill :   December 22.

. . . We intend to be by ourselves on Christmas Day
—for a day so often spent among you all we could not
bring ourselves to spend with strangers, however dear and
kind.   We shall watch the hours in the morning and see
the children[1] come up the path, and Mama and C. and the

---

[1] Children of Charlton village.

two little ones distributing the gifts. And we shall see you at dinner, and after dinner from Detmore windows watch the early winter twilight come down over Coxhorne and all the beloved scene. Oh, so much beloved! We were saying to each other what a pretty little family you have now. If B. would marry, and so clear off the first hatch, you might fancy yourselves twenty years younger and beginning a new world. Two such typical boys and such model girls—such a bright and various and all-hopeful four. And what may not be done with them and for them after all the experience of the past? I could fancy you—practised by the six foregone experiments—with theories confirmed or modified by facts, and circumstances more than ever favourable—setting yourselves to realise in this last the ideal of a family. God help and bless you in the work!

As the weeks and months, since they had come to London, passed, he had sometimes been able to hope that his wife was slowly and surely progressing under mesmeric treatment : for this reason the stay in town had been protracted. But to an intimate correspondent he wrote, at the close of the year, of the necessity that had arisen of taking a fresh opinion, when 'I can hardly hold out to you the *hope* of cure,' had been the sentence pronounced.

I look through the past weeks (he went on) as through

a lapse of London fog, wherein perspective is impossible. The cause of my silence has been sufficient indeed. I am not yet far enough from it to view it objectively. . . . All I could bring myself to do, beyond writing what was needful to my family, was to add a few passages to some parts—sorrowful enough—of my new book.

On Christmas Day, writing to his eldest sister—'in a room full of Beethoven'—he speaks of the maker of the music:

Our little friend M., who walks like a ministering angel, through all winds and weathers, four miles, two or three times a week, on purpose to play to E., and nurse her with such love and music as passes all medicine in its soothing and healing influence.

The friendship made at this time lasted, 'through all winds and weathers,' his life (as, with exceptions of the very fewest, did all his friendships), and on many a dark and anxious day, brought light and healing influences, as well as music, into his house.

In the same letter he says, after speaking of his wife:

I have a faith beyond science which forbids me to despair.

I seem to write quietly of these things, but you will not misunderstand the calm. Did you ever go through a vast machinery where a thousand great wheels whirled above, below, and about you, and all you could do was to walk silently through it and trust to come out into a safe place beyond ?

There is that safe place somewhere for all of us. God bring us to it in His time. 'I would not change the past if I might, nor all that I have suffered,' she says. Neither would I. Neither, at the end, will anyone of us. May we all be able to feel so now, before the end.

CHAPTER VI.

EARLY PART OF 1853.

THIS year began where and as the last had ended
—in London lodgings. The available correspondence of this time is slight, for reasons sufficiently
indicated in the following extract from a letter to
his eldest sister :

. . . Indeed, you must never judge us hardly with
regard to correspondence, and must always be ready to
fill up any epistolary gap with a good old text of which
we all of us have need, and especially two such rickety
folk as my darling and I,—' the spirit indeed is willing,
but the flesh is weak.' . . . I write every week volumin-
ously home, and feel that the centre ought to radiate the
circumference.   Then you won't forget that the mere
applications of one sort and another I am always receiving
from various quarters, constitute in themselves a considerable correspondence, and that these ' notes ' are obliged
to be cashed out of pocket, because I have no fund of love
and kindness, lying ready for me to draw upon, in the
hearts of the stranger-writers.   When, therefore, as in
your case and your husband's, I know I have a large

floating balance of that sort always at command, I am
naturally tempted to take long credit. . . .

To his Father and Mother.

Maida Hill : January 22.

After a good deal on matters of business, he
goes on to speak of mesmerism tried as a cure for
deafness :

I think it has done some good, and of the general
effect I can hardly give you any verbal description ; the
wonderfully subduing influence, the preternatural calm,
deeper and stranger than sleep, the curious vibratory
feeling in the head, must be 'felt to be understood.' I
wish my father would try it . . . the relief after his
heavy days of accounts would make him young again. . . .

After speaking with some detail of one of his
new-made friends, as yet unknown in his home
circle, though soon to become almost one of them,
he says :

You may think perhaps that I bestow a great deal of
superfluous care on this young girl and her fate. The
truth is, she is precisely one of those rare recruits who,
as you know, are more or less a part of the scheme of my
life and work. Good and gifted, with a most pure heart
and most high ambition, unfettered by formal creed,
panting for truth, full of all kinds of intellectual and
moral beauty, and ready to follow us through any hard

enterprise that has truth for its object and God for its reward: having neither brother nor sister, she has taken me for one and E. for the other,—and I am not inclined to eschew the responsibility.

To his Brother C—— (on his 18th birthday).

Maida Hill: February 3, 1853.

When a Knight of old was going to be dubbed, he spent the night before in prayer and fasting, devoutly watching the armour in which next day he was to be sent out to conquer; when an Arab chief is going to be married, he prays night and day for six weeks before the wedding, that the duties of the happy life he is going to enter may be seen with the purged eyes of penance and self-denial.

These outbreaks of natural instinct—this religion of Nature—are worth something as a hint even to us; and I was right glad to see from your last letter that for some time before your birthday your mind had been turned to thoughts and subjects appropriate to the commencement of a new year of life, and a new year at that season when, as you truly say, a day is almost a year in its effects upon the growing soul. I thoroughly enter into all you feel, and know precisely what you are now knowing.

I can sympathise with all my heart in that abounding sense of growth, as if a sudden Norway summer were bursting out at once, and above and below everything budded and bourgeoned; I know fully all you are witnessing within you of sudden change, instant development,

To the same.

February 5, 1853.

. . . No pursuit, no object, no pleasure is worth a
thought, except those which harmonise thoroughly, readily,
and beautifully with the pursuits, aims, happinesses and
states of mind of a divine and *eternal* existence.

Only by an abiding sense of our *eternity*, momentarily
present, and by living, thinking, speaking up to that
sense, in all things, is there any possibility of true happiness, or of that noble contentment and serenity of soul,
to lose which is to lose something better than happiness. . . .

To his Father and Mother.

February 12.

. . . The book is not yet finished, but has been
getting on satisfactorily these last few weeks. You must
not suppose, because the last scene is written, that all the
others are. On the contrary, the first is not finished yet.
But all are nearly finished, and only want filling up.
Don't fear that the —— paper will disturb me for one
moment. The thing is so cleverly said that I could not
be angry. Angry? If you want to be angry, read the
'Times' leading article yesterday on Kossuth and
Mazzini. I see the 'Times' everyday: of all the clever,
powerful, charming, prosperous, doubly-damned profligates,
I think it is the most consummate. I don't mean that
article, but the paper as a whole. Of course you are
hungry for news. There is foul play somewhere with the

telegraphs, it is said. Don't believe anything about 'suppression' till you have the best authority. When Kossuth and Mazzini declare 'the last war,' it will take a long time to 'suppress' it. You have seen, of course, their manifestoes. Don't they read like a bit of the Old Testament? . . . I was saying, not a week ago, that the present aspect of the Turkish question looked like 'the end;' and now comes the cry, 'and this is the last war.' I think the time of the outbreak is well chosen, if you calculate all the different forces, and the effects and counter-effects, here and abroad. And it has been planned with consummate preparation. I knew of Mazzini's leaving England a month ago, but was forbidden to speak of it, for a breath might have betrayed him. Nothing that has ever happened in the world is likely—politically speaking—to be so important as the issue—the real issue—for Milan is only one point in a thousand—of this outburst, for never before have men fought with the resolutions and convictions with which they will fight this time. 'No quarter' is the revolutionary watchword— and ought to have been long ago. But to us there are other reasons which make this great sign of a terrible solemnity. Never before have so many omens combined to fulfil the picture of the 'last days.' The early Christians, waiting on the mountain-tops for the sound of the horn which was to blow the fall of Jerusalem, were hardly more thoroughly in presence of a closing dispensation than we at this day; God make us ready, God help us to bear that time!

In suggestive contrast to the foregoing comes the following 'valentine' sent to 'our little friend M——,' who has been spoken of, in a letter to his eldest sister, as the maker of the music felt to be so healing and soothing an influence by his wife—— and who is spoken of in a later letter as 'now and always a light in the house':

To May.

I hear it is St. Valentine's ;
  How that is I can't say ;
One sole perpetual season's mine—
  With me 'tis always May !

You look amazement at my lot,
  Amazement at my lays ;
A-May's-meant truly ; and why not?
  My heart is all a-*May's.*

Too true, alas, a fair May-flower
  That willing heart did win,
And I can't tell you, since that hour,
  The *hawful* state I'm in !

Each science that I cultivate
  Betrays the hidden smart,
And all my favourite arts relate
  The secret of my heart.

A book of chance is all my lore,
  But 'tis enough for me,
For there I ponder o'er and o'er
  On whatsoe'er May be.

I go to the Academy,
  But, 'mid the works of mark,
The only one that takes my eye
  Is ' May in Regent's Park.'

My music's all from May-erbeer ;
  I sketch the Ma-vis glen ;
The only poet I can bear
  Is he of Hawthornden.

I sing the May Queen eve and morn,
  As sad as sad can be,
Or, fond, before a flowering thorn,
  Sigh ' Woodman, spare that Tree.'

I'm thin, for, besides wear and tear,
  I haven't eaten much,
Since *May-flour* is the only *fare*
  My dainty lips will touch.

I'm moody—ay, I've almost grown
  One great potential mood ;
I say the verb ' to love ' alone
  In *May, might, could and should.*

For me a Sweep's a sacred thing,
  For to myself I say,
Ah ! I too could dance and spring
  In memory of May.

So, if you should refuse your slave,
  I'll change my skin for spite,
And write above my Negro grave,
  ' Dis May hab killed me quite.'

Then let my sighs some pity move
  And grant the prayer I pray ;
Why shouldn't you tell me *I-May-love* ?
  I tell you *I-love-May.*

February 14, 1853.

To his Father and Mother.

I am afraid you think me a false prophet with regard
to poor Italy. But don't decide too quickly. Mazzini
has blown the trumpet, and it takes some time for
the echo to come back. Moreover, do you see that
Austria is about to invade Switzerland? and when the
Swiss rifles are at work in front, the Lombardy poignards
will be busy behind, perhaps. But I confess I have looked
day by day with confident expectations of other news from
Milan. I hear one of the London papers has extracted
the Milan song from 'The Roman' and incorporated it
with its account of the revolt. I was very much tempted
to send a letter to the editor of the 'Daily News,' on the
proper course of an English Foreign Secretary in these
days. I had part of an essay on that subject lying by me,
and I thought it might be touched up for the occasion.[1]
But on looking over it, I found a great deal would have
to be done, and I laid it aside.

Again much detail of 'Church' matters; then
he wrote:

To the same.

Maida Hill: March 12, 1853.

I must tell you that, the Sunday before last, H. J.
and I had another interview with ——. We talked for
three or four hours *with* and *at* him, and I left with a

---

[1] See Appendix to Book III.

sorrowful conviction that we might as well have talked to the chair he sat in. But how little one can tell in these matters. His son told me last Sunday that ' Father' said he had never before had his doubts so much shaken, and never before felt so hopeful of getting out of them. As usual, I sat in admiration of H. J. The tact, quickness, and instinctive accuracy with which he suited his arguments to his object and subject, and never wasted a thought or a word, renewed in me, even in a more lively manner, the surprise and respect I had felt at our former conference. I fairly held my tongue every now and then, and sat and took lessons. The art of *convincing* is one that requires some study; and this self-taught, or rather (as he is proud to confess) ' Church '-taught, hard-working hat-maker sometimes showed a mastery in it which would have puzzled many a bishop.

. . . We expect to be with you in about a fortnight ! . . . I hardly recognise it to myself as a truth yet, and can scarcely believe that I shall see the spring— the home-spring—this year. But, God helping, it will come in a few days, and I shall believe it when it comes, and perhaps enjoy it the more. What a living death is all the physical and external of this great catacomb— London. The air always smells dead. Summer and winter, morning, noon and night, it has nothing but the odour of dust . . . We intend to go to Odsey for a week, before starting home . . . My book, which I hoped to have finished before I saw you, still wants its last touches ; but I think I shall put them more rapidly, and better, under the inspiration of country air.

Have you seen in the papers of this morning the
terrible news about Mazzini and Nuremburg? Truly the
Austrians have filled up the measure of human infamy
within the last month or two. I really sometimes feel
dumb with indignation. But the Bible is a wonderful
book, and has a text for everything; and I have found
great consolation lately by saying, over and over, 'the
damnation of hell.' I spent an hour's walk in little else,
and was greatly relieved!

Knowing, he says, his father's love of a speech,
he jotted down and sent home notes of a farewell
address to ' The Church '—made on the last Sunday
of his being in town,—an extract from which may
be of interest:

I have wished for an occasion of publicly expressing
to 'The Church' how much that esteem and regard with
which I have been brought up to look upon its members
have been increased and deepened by an intercourse and
personal intimacy of nearly a year. Whatever may be
my opinions as to the efficacy of your public ministrations,
whatever may be my opinions as to the reforms which are
expedient in your public practice, I shall never forget the
lively hopes, sincere friendship, earnest esteem, ay, and
I will say affectionate admiration, with which I have come
to regard some of those who are among you.

Lively hopes and sincere friendship for some of the
young, on whom so much of the future of 'The Church '
depends, earnest esteem for those who are now bearing the

burden and heat of the day, and friendly admiration for some who have come to age in the possession of the principles, and who are themselves the best testimonials to what they have loved so well.

I cannot say how happy I am to have these sentiments towards the depositaries of those truths and principles which are doubtless dear to all of us, but which, I can never forget, came to *me* as heirlooms in the third generation, which I hold to be the noblest inheritance upon earth, and which, if God please, the energies, efforts and good or bad fortunes of my life shall be devoted to vindicate, maintain and magnify.

But I leave you not only with affectionate regard, but with the most earnest hopes and anxious interest : for I believe you are, perhaps unconsciously, entering on a new era of thought, and an era which the necessities of the next year or two will wonderfully quicken and develope. I do hope and trust that we are all beginning to feel more than we did, the very social and personal character of ' Church' union; to recognise more and more that ' the Church' is not a mere machine for theoretical religious instruction, but an association for purposes. A church, not a congregation ; a body, not a crowd; an association, and not only that, but an association for purposes. The idea of the association is that of a family—an orphan family, with the Father in heaven and the eldest Son from home. Its *purposes* are the fulfilment of the will of the absent Father. The will of that Father is the improvement of the children in every filial and fraternal duty, and that they should so be, and act, as to set a good example out of

doors. The principles on which the family moves and
works, are those of liberty, fraternity, and filial obedience.
Years ago, when the voice of the Father was fresh in their
ears, they arranged an organisation which has since proved
exquisitely adequate to every circumstance of public or
private exercise. . . .

To his Father and Mother.

Maida Hill : March 17, 1853.

If I wait till I get to Odsey before writing you my
' Sunday letter,' you will not receive it on Sunday because
of the double post; and I therefore take a spare half hour
this afternoon.

And, first, let me relieve my dear mother's anxieties
with regard to Mazzini. When I wrote I had not seen
the 'Times,' and had only heard the report by word of
mouth; which was this—that the Austrians had at last
discovered Mazzini, that he was in Nuremburg, and that
the 'hell-hounds' had drawn a cordon round the city, and
were closing in slowly, surely, inevitably, upon the game.
The account in the 'Times' was in substance the same.
However, Stansfeld came the night before last to bid us
good-bye, and dissipated all our fears. He says all the
rumours that have lately appeared, in the 'Times' and
otherwhere, are not true; that Mazzini is, he believes, quite
safe, and cannot possibly be in Nuremburg. . . . We
talked till nearly twelve o'clock. I was happy to have
direct confirmation of what I already believed—that the
Milan affair was admirably planned, and that the quietude

of the rest of Italy was not voluntary. Every town was ready to rise, and would have risen at the moment, but, four-and-twenty hours before the time Mazzini had appointed, the Austrian police got wind of the plot, and Mazzini instantly sent commands through the length and breadth of the land *not to stir.* . . .

. . . Each of these pulses of combatants was regularly pre-arranged and pre-appointed, so that every man knew his place and duty. They have plenty of arms concealed where the Austrians can't find them. Now it happened that in Milan the only detachment which did not receive Mazzini's countermand was the forlorn hope who were to begin the battle. By some fatal accident his message did not reach their chief in the hurry of the time, and they moved while all the rest, by order, were still. It is beautiful to hear that the greatest emulation was among the whole body of patriots for a place in the forlorn hope ; and the anxiety to join it was so great that they were forced to decide by lot—though death was nearly certain to every man of it.

CHAPTER VII.

LATER PART OF 1853.

' THE fourth of April—the day before my birthday
—what a birthday treat for me, if all goes well; '
he had written of the proposed home-going, and
on that day he safely reached Coxhorne.

His father, commenting on the welcome return,
says: 'He does not *seem* injured by his worldly
association in Town with artistic and literary folk,
but I can hardly expect him to have escaped
internal injury, as he has been much flattered.'

To M——.

Coxhorne: April 5, 1853.

Here in the dear home to which, God be thanked, we
came safely last night (and with less pain and injury to
E. than I feared), I sit down on my birthday morning
to answer your letter, and begin a correspondence which
shall end—where? and when? Shall it ever end?
Won't you stray away somewhere in Paradise, and shan't
I pluck a feather from an angel's wing, and send you a
letter by the penny-post of Heaven? . . .

You know what you and I have often said of Tragedy and Farce. And, to be serious, my birthday, of all days, is the one on which I would begin to write to you. It is a sacred day to me; a day on which I take account with my soul, reckon up happiness and sorrow, duties, blessings, hopes, resolutions. And to-day, in that serious estimate, I find a new happiness very dear to me—the thought of you ;—a new duty very sacred—the brotherhood I have promised you ;—and all the new hopes and resolutions which arise from these. God preserve them to me. I see that my life is to be a crowded one—that I have much to do and to bear—but I think in the thick of it I shall not forget those duties, and I am sure that the heavier the destined labour and sorrow, the more will those blessings be beautiful to me. . . .

Many kind greetings I had by post this morning; but I have no time or thought to answer them in this first day of home, country, and friends. I need not tell you the love and joy with which we were welcomed home. All our family were here to meet us. . . .

To his sister, a few days after his arrival at Coxhorne, he wrote :

Can you imagine how difficult it is to write letters with this eloquent spring about one ? They say that caged birds grow silent after the sound of a trumpet, and I have no heart to talk, in sight of the regained heavens and earth. So this is merely to tell you that I can't thank you for your right welcome birthday letter. . . .

You may guess what it is, after nearly a year of London, to come back where the air is really alive, where the sun seems in place and the wind good, and where you see not trees, or hills, or fields only, but Nature.

The rest at Coxhorne was a brief one. Death changed its proprietorship. Its new owner, returning from abroad, wished to occupy it, and in a few months, having been held for five years, it had to be given up.

It was not till after many *Wander-jahre*, not till near the close of his life, that the poet had again a real *home*; though he found and made pleasant enough temporary resting-places for summer or winter.

Up to this time, in spite of many occasional but illusive encouragements, his wife's health had not derived permanent benefit from any advice taken or treatment pursued ; and he now resolved on a journey to Edinburgh—to consult its great medical authority, Professor Simpson.

In the double hope of seeing the invalid somewhat strengthened by bracing air before starting, and of finishing his poem, they went, on leaving Coxhorne, to a hill-side cottage lodging, on the edge of one of those wide expanses of common

frequent among the Cotswolds.   Here 'Balder'
was, at last, finished.

To M——.

Amberley: July 1853.

Do you remember a day at Odsey, when, feeling but
little necessity to talk to you as we walked, I inferred
how much my affection for you had increased?' Something of the same kind I feel about letters, and think I
could be more content to send you a rose than any form
or number of written words.   These silent communicants
bear somewhat the same relation to letter-writing as a
look to spoken intercourse.   But when I come to ask
myself, if I would be satisfied to *receive* only this floral
eloquence, I begin to understand how insufficient it is.
Moreover, the *look* pre-supposes a *presence*, which is
answer to so many questions,—but now——

So I sit down to write you another letter.   That
strange quasi-humanity, a letter !   It would be an interesting task to anatomise the theory and practice of
letter-writing.   Some day, perhaps, I will do it for you,
and try to find out what should be an ideal letter.   I have
no hope of incarnating the principle, whatever it may be ;
but shall merely try to discover the plan on which some
one else may build.   To-day I have no time for plans or
buildings, and shall only give you some of the bricks as
they come to hand. . . .

    . . . I enclose you a sea-song[1] (to precede a descrip-

---

[1] 'The Betsy-Jane.'

tion of Tyranny), absolutely blown into me by the wind
of Hampton Common.   That glorious hill-top!   I walk
there sometimes, by twilight, when it seems positively
held up as on a hand into the sky, and leaning on my
Alp-stick, and looking for a long time upwards, it feels as
if, with hardly an effort, one could 'push off' among the
stars. . . .

To his eldest Sister, on the birth of her first son.

You will easily believe that for a long time past, you
have been in our daily thoughts, solicitudes and prayers,
and that for a long time to come you will be in our thanks
to God.   It must be something like a foretaste of death
to enter and pass through those hours of shadow: and
now to find yourself, brighter and richer, on the other side
of the eclipse.

Truly it is not only the baby that is born.   But you,
like Adam, enter your new life full-grown.   God consecrate
and glorify it. . . .

That wonderful small person!   Do you not cross yourself as you look on him?   This child, who, if he live, must
out-live a dispensation; this little red hand, that may
strike a blow at Armageddon.   God help you to rear him
as He helped the mothers of old.   May he be as Samuel
and as David unto you, for like them 'his eyes shall see
the King in His beauty.'   Thirty years hence, if the good
fight last so long, when I am an old man of sixty, shall I
look with pride and hope upon ——?   I think so, dear
sister, for you do not come of a stock that is used to sur-

render. As Shakespeare's Henry says to his Queen : 'Thou must needs prove a good soldier-breeder.'

Of his criticisms on the MSS. of a very young writer—one among the many who appealed to him, and never in vain, for advice and guidance—it may be interesting to give a few specimens, belonging to this time, as showing the painstaking thoroughness with which such help was given.

Of the first MS. of the series submitted to him, he wrote :

Your story has some good points—a fine moral, a true and pure tone, and a style of quiet terseness which gives promise of strength. But then there is no novelty in the plot, no originality in the characters, and nothing particularly attractive in the mode of handling. Still I have a feeling of promise in reading it, which makes me auger well of the powers of the author. There is a calm adherence to nature, and repose upon nature, which makes · me think that when you have something to say, you will say it well. By 'something to say,' I mean 'something' peculiarly your own, and something you have learnt in your own heart, soul and life, and which must therefore be given for the instruction of your fellows. And by what you have ' *learnt*,' I don't mean any principle, or didactic lesson, you may have been able to draw from experience, but the actual experience itself. If there is anything wherein it has happened to you to suffer deeply, or to feel

acutely, or to perceive vividly, take that phasis of your
life, disguise it, by altering place, time and costume, and
I think and believe you can write a valuable story. It is
not necessary that the events be the same, (indeed it is
better they should not, for many reasons), but it is easy to
invent circumstances and cases wherein our own experience
would be appropriate, and where we may embody it without its being recognised.

In another letter:

Depend upon it, whatever is to live on paper, must
have lived in flesh and blood. There is but one Creator ;
all we can do is to collect and combine His creations.

Imagination only selects, compounds, magnifies, and
diminishes. Originality is not the conception of something that does not exist, but the perception in existence
of now existing truths and beauties.

Of another attempt:

All that is not purely fiction in your story, is good
and valuable. Coming evidently from a human heart and
experience, it cannot fail to be interesting to many another
such heart, and to chord with many another such experience. This is the vital secret of success.

In criticising some verses:

The whole of this is inexcusably distorted and difficult
in expression. One is only justified in giving a reader
trouble when the sense conveyed *demands* (in order to the
perfect congruity of soul with body, idea with expression),

a form of words, or a kind of words, that is not readily understood.

Every poet is bound to put his idea in precisely those words which most perfectly express it, by most exquisitely and intimately agreeing with its deepest and most essential characteristics.

It often happens, from the slovenly and superficial way in which people are accustomed to think and speak, that such perfect expression appears 'obscure' to the general reader: but this ·obscurity is unavoidable.   No other obscurity is, however, to be tolerated in poetry, one of whose prime conditions is, that it be the ideal of language, the very transfiguration of human speech.   Now the verse in question is unnecessarily and awkwardly obscure, as if something else than the idea had decided the words and phrases.

The following, to the same correspondent, though written some months later, may most appropriately be given here:

Comparing your story in memory with the tales you first sent me, it strikes me—time and circumstances considered—as the greatest advance I ever remember to have seen.   My best expectations would not have looked for so much improvement within such limits. . . . I have of course not been able to make a written criticism of the whole of so lengthy a MS., but I could not resist the pleasure of going very carefully through the first seven folios, and noting such principles of improvement as are applicable to them. Those principles, carried out, would rectify what is amiss in the literature of the rest of the story, and it was unnecessary therefore that I should analyse it as elaborately. . . . The faults extra-literary are those which growth and experience will amend.

I am particularly pleased with the easy power of drawing distinct characters, without insipidity or caricature, and of sustaining them consistently and naturally, which is shown in this present story: for this is a rare quality, and one which I by no means felt sure you would possess.

As to the characters themselves, to say that some of them are hardly up to the mark, is only to say that you have not yet succeeded in one of the most difficult triumphs of Art. I am thinking at this moment of G——, who, well as, for so young a hand, you have depicted her, is not in fact or word what she is by description and assertion. Nothing which she says gives evidence or hint of the transcendant abilities which she assumes to possess, and which her literary success implies. Indeed, except a treatise on mathematics, one is puzzled to know what extraordinary book such a raw upstart school-girl could have written. . .

. . . I must say, even in this hurry, that I saw your Sonnet, and admired it. There was an image—appropriating and vivifying the beautiful Scripture figure of the 'door of hope,'—which was really exquisite. Alexander Smith liked it a great deal. I think you will succeed in sonnets; and there is room for some success in that way, for good English sonnets are few, and there is a ladyhood about the simplicity, unity and *completeness*, which ought to characterise that kind of poem, which fits it for feminine

thought. . . . You must be content with nothing less than
the very best thought in the very best words that the
whole force of your nature can yield.

To his Father.

Amberley : September, 1853.

. . . I did not finish telling you about the name
Balder. Balder is the abstraction of the natural good,
temporarily overcome by circumstances; but the legend
goes on to say, that in after ages Balder shall return
transfigured and glorified to restore and bless the world.
I propose to call my present book ' Balder : Part the
First.' Thus indicating the intention of a second part, in
which I hope to develope the idea of the Christian Balder.
' Balder,' will be a strong and simple title ; and the full-
length name of my hero—Balder Sorgivin, signifies
' Balder in the strife of Sorrow.' I sent off the book
yesterday. It has cost me three years of thought. . . .
On calm consideration (and nobody knows my own faults
as well as I do), I feel it is a permanent work.

To the Rev. Brown Paton.

Amberley, nr. Nailsworth : October, 25, 1853.

' To live the doctrine,' there indeed you have arrived
at the great secret of power. . . . My own belief is, that
argument, however excellent, will never cure the evil
of the age. All argument upon evidence pre-requires
a judicial state of the mind which is to receive it ; and it

is just this state which our rising doubters (beautiful, good, interesting, as many of them are), require to learn as the antecedent of all further knowledge.

My hope for any great and wide-spread change in the mental state of the time is founded, (as to its human bases), on some such plan as follows.

Let half a dozen growing men of unusual gifts and character cut their way to English eminence in their various mental departments; an eminence irrespective of theology, and acknowledged therefore by all parties and opinions. Having gained this public position and made it sure, let each come forward, with the New Testament in his hand, and say, practically or verbally, somewhat thus : 'Tried by the intellectual standards you yourselves set up, my fellow-men, you consent to acknowledge me your superior. Measured by yourselves, I am stronger, higher, and wiser than you. Behold this Book which is not good enough for you : it is sufficient for me.' The egotism—or egoism—which perhaps deforms these *words*, deforms them only *because* they are words. Put the pronunciamento into a life, and the self-assertion disappears.

Till something of this kind can be done I believe all direct polemics will be of little avail. Infidelity[1] just now

---

[1] 'Infidelity.' This term, often misused because recklessly applied, needs some comment. Sydney Dobell's own belief in Christ as the Way, the Truth, the Life, grew only more clear and profound as he grew in years. But he would have been the last to stigmatise as infidelity any earnest faith, however divergent from, or falling short of, what he held to be the truth. With the commoner forms of scepti-

is an *intellectual* fashion (last century it was a drawing-room fashion, and below contempt), it is a spiritual epidemic, and not to be touched by logic. But I believe and trust in God that we are near a better day. The first and great object which must be, each in his own manner, our first aim, is to procure acceptance of the evidence, to get the record fairly admitted in court. I think that all question of doctrine should be subponed to this. The first great belief which we have to establish is a belief in the *data* of doctrine. Let us be content as yet to make men take *the Scriptures*, and trust that God will give each man grace to read therein his own salvation.

Depend upon it ' ἡ καινὴ διαθήκη ' is the legend and bearing of the new Crusade. . . .

When ' Balder ' comes out I hope you will bear in mind that the book is but a *negative* argument for the necessity of Revelation. It is the type of the present time, struggling for noble objects, suffering, *failing*, and, in the agony of failure, demanding the superhuman.

Nine readers out of ten will not recognise the moral, but feel it unexpressed, I think. Why what a letter this looks! And I took up the pen to write a line.

---

cism, whether cynical and antagonistic, or merely idle and vacuous, he had no sympathy; but the surface formalism of so-called ortho-doxy, and indeed all phases of that indifference which is inconsistent with the vitality of any creed, appeared to him as a far deadlier evidence of ' the spiritual epidemic,' than much of what is generally scouted as unbelief.

To the Rev. R. Glover (in answer to announcement of
approaching marriage.)

Amberley.

. . . I turn to that announcement of yours which I
received with unqualified pleasure and congratulation.
Fourteen years of love—most blessed, most beautiful
—give me the right of telling you to how great a
privilege, how solemn a responsibility, how inexhaustible
and inestimable a possession—a possession at once the
rarest and most substantial, the most abundant and the
most exquisite, the most divinely universal, and most
humanly particular of all things, except the Love of God—
you, young as you are, have attained. And I say, attained in
its strictest and most literal sense—you have as yet only
reached the Land of Promise ; and in the metaphorical,
as in the actual land, the great secret of coming into and
continuing in possession, is to continue to *deserve* to
possess. I do not wonder to see husbands often less
beloved than lovers, when I see how much less loveable
they frequently become.

To Dr. Samuel Brown (of whom he had seen a good deal
during the months spent in London).

Detmore, near Cheltenham : November 23.

My dear Galileo,—Neither my silence nor yours—for
we have both been silent, you know—has, I am sure, arisen
from anything of which either friend would complain.

Mute as you were, I was as certain there were good reasons for it as if I had had an affidavit of the same ; and for my own taciturnity—*accipe hæc*, and judge if I need excuse it.

After reaching Coxhorne last April, and passing through a week of increased anxiety on E.'s account (for the journey shook her most sadly) I was taken ill myself and confined to bed, or bed-room, for more than a month. On recovering, you may easily imagine that 'the book' received every spare moment, in compensation for the month lost. But the estate and house we loved so much changed hands ; and finding that the new owner was determined to take possession of it, and that my occupation was a mere question of time, I resolved to abdicate with dignity, and to retire 'to the mountains,' where finer air might brace me to the completion of the task which I groaned to finish, and might also strengthen E. for a still greater journey on which meanwhile we had—so far as such a word can be given to mortal will—*determined.*

This journey is to Edinburgh (where we hope to be early in December), and Professor Simpson : and in pursuance of a resolve of mine, that nothing but the highest authority in Europe should set me down for life in the belief that her case is incurable. Therefore, soon after Midsummer, she, M., and I migrated to a cottage upon a hill-top six hundred feet above the level of the sea, and there I finished the three years' labour.

The book—to be called ' Balder : Part the First '—is half-way through the press. . . .

I am the less troubled at the necessary haste of this

letter, beause your new and unexpected change of place
will so soon make all letter-writing unnecessary between
us. The knowledge that you will be there has put a
soul into my fore-image of Edinburgh.

To the Rev. G. Gilfillan.

Detmore.

I thought at the date of my last letter to have placed
'Balder' in your hands before to-day, but it will be nearly
Christmas, I fear, before he sees you. However, I do
trust that he may yet be read in the light of your Yule
fire. You will see by my address that we have 'come
down out of the mountains,' and are once more in this
dear old Charlton valley, though not in that well-beloved
Coxhorne whose praises have often, I daresay, made you
smile. Happily for me, you can never convict me of
enthusiasm, for Coxhorne is no more. The past is past.
My favourite trees are felled, my old ivies, which Winter
himself might have thrown about him as a cloak, are torn
down, and the flayed house, looked down on from the
neighbouring hills—I have ventured no nearer—is worse
than naked. It looks naked, not with the nude loveliness of a statue, or a woman, but with the raw-boned
indecorum of him who runs *sans-culotte* through the
streets.

. . . I became so chronically ill that E. was too
anxious while we were so far from medical aid as Amberley,
and my father and mother besought us to come to them
during the time before our journey to Edinburgh. . . .

I have gone into these details because they best explain the fact that I am little able to write of anything important.

The two foregoing letters indicate something of the condition of health in which their writer entered on a new phase of anxiety.

On one of the last days of 1853 he wrote to Mr. A. J. Mott, at whose house near Liverpool the travellers had broken their journey to Edinburgh:

Morningside: December.

I should have given you before a historiette of our doings, but that first lodging-hunting and then, alas! nursing has kept me too incessantly employed to allow anything else not absolutely necessary. . . . After some fagging days of search, I at last procured desirable lodgings, but as they could not be had for a week, we came here to await them—in full sight of the Forth, the Pentlands, and the Fifeshire hills. But I have looked little at them. E., who had been in pain more or less with neuralgia ever since our arrival in Edinburgh, has had such a frightful aggravation of it that all my thoughts have been taken up in her endurance.

. . . Last night—the first time for nearly a week—she slept without pain. . . .

. . . Dear M. (we hope and trust) arrives to-night.

'Balder,' I fear, had not the pleasure of being by 'your fireside on Christmas-day;' for I hear he was only pub-

lished on Saturday.   Don't forget to tell me how you like
him.

As a sort of summary of this period of life, his
brother Clarence writes:

The result of experience was slow but sure. 'The
Roman,' the other poems, and the 'Essays,' of about the
same period, were written in a certain and definite faith
in a good that was to be quickly worked out before the
world—the enthusiasm of a propagandist may be seen in
every page.   But when a new work was planned the battle
with the outer world, with religious and social forms was,
for a time, given up, and an individual, personal, spiritual
campaign inaugurated, in the First Part of 'Balder.'

'It is important to mark,' his brother goes on:
that all new experience and development of ideas increased
rather than diminished his faith in God, and Christ, and
Immortality—the only difference produced was a modification of his opinions as to the outer form and expression
of belief. In his published thoughts may be found
detached passages of reiterated insistance on the true
meaning of the *Kingdom of God*—as mentioned in the
Gospel—as being that the kingdom of God is within us,
and *begins* the moment any man admits into his mind,
and endeavours to obey, the true spirit of God to be found
in Christ's teaching; and that it is not by Churches and
Societies, but by individual life and endeavour, that
Christ is to be followed and the kingdom of God attained.

So, also, in politics, that it is not so much by this or that form of government, as by the personal intercourse of man with man, that the ideal of social improvement is to be made real.

Let us all learn to behave as brethren, and the true Republic will come of itself, no matter what we call the outward establishment of the State.

For these reasons he was fervent in his hatred of tyranny, of every force that assailed or endangered liberty of conscience and freedom of private action; but was indifferent to those artificial party lines which divide political theorists; and in his last years he openly supported the Conservative party, for many strong reasons—and especially because he thought the Conservative leaders were men of wider, deeper intellectual vision, and that they perceived more clearly wherein consisted the essentials of true liberty than did the leaders of the so-called Radical party.

He held:

> Let one or thousands loose or bind,
> That land 's enslaved whose sovran mind
> Collides the conscience of mankind.
>
> And free—whoever holds the rood—
> Where might in right, and pow
> Flow each in each, like in blo
>
> If England's head an
> Where is that good b
> Her noble hands shou

APPENDIX TO BOOK III.

Fragments of Essay on 'Journalism,' and on 'The Duties of an English Foreign Secretary.' Date 1852.

Public opinion, which for some time past our statesmen have been acknowledging as a great power, will shortly become the only efficient authority.

It requires no great foresight to see that we are approaching a state of things in which our laws will not be made in Houses of Parliament ; or our home and foreign statesmanship concocted by any head in Downing Street ; or our organised system of apparent legislature have other effective occupation than to register the statutes already passed in another and invisible assembly ; or our executive have any further responsibility than the manual rescript of a policy more authoritative than their own. That, in short, we are rapidly passing, with no disruption present or prospective of monarchical forms, into the first really absolute, enduring and practicable democracy that has been known among modern or ancient men. Such a democracy, freed from the passions of great assemblies, the distractions and excitements of political organisation, the haste and intimidation of popular pressure, and forming its political will under the ordinary and congenial conditions of mental action, such a grand invisible government is possible only by the existence of a strong, high, pure, and unfettered Press. A Press in which the facts of the world and the thought of the nation could pass silently from house to house, street to street, hamlet to hamlet, homestead to homestead, and be received in faith, as notoriously the most trustworthy representation of the most honest human

perceptions and wisest English intellect of its day. A Press
which, by the exertion of every modern means and appliance,
should hold in itself 'a mirror up to nature' and collect, as with
the exactitude of scientific enquiry, the facts upon which the
national opinion is to be formed; and in its editorial *pronun-
ciamenti* upon the daily microcosm give us, not the watchword
of a party, the shibboleth of a sect, the nostrum of the monoculist,
or even the vision of the political and social prophet, but a representation (accessible to all men) of the noblest and most
gifted *class* which the Empire, for the time being, comprehends :
the best expression of the brightest talent, the bravest exposi-
tion of the most eminent virtue, the clearest dicta of the widest
experience that the body politic can boast.

Nature is nowhere more nicely graduated than in her
system of mental and physical nutrition. We have not yet
seen the naked element whose 'mobled' presence supports our
animal life, or the disembodied entity which vitalises and sanctifies what we receive for truth. The very light of heaven
would fall comparatively fruitless but for that hyaline of denser
air in which, tempered and diffused, it fructifies the year. A
fine gradation of modified recipients everywhere conducts principles to their strongest, broadest and most material exhibition :
and a neglect of the order of nature defeats her intentions and
turns her noblest blessing to a curse. The sunbeam that lights
the complex eye would blight and blind its naked nerve; and
the highest truths of solitary genius, taken up at will by the
crude mind of the multitude, may carry destruction and chaos
where they should have shone creation, order and peace. We
require, therefore, in our ideal English journal, not the solitary
foresights of the poet or the abstrusest deductions of the
philosopher, but how much of each the noblest class of existing
British men have been able to assimilate into available thought.

A solitary Mind, like an intellectual miracle, may appear in
any age and country, and bear no relation to the mental facts of

his time. But no *class* exists without both having and giving a *point d'appui.*

The pyramidal mountain of national character may bear summit, peaks, and erratic blocks which have no calculable affinity with the whole; but wherever we find a stratum it contains the *débris* of the lower and the elements of the higher, and fills its place in that rule of progressive development by virtue of which the noblest forms of the latest and the highest have their type in the rudest organisms of the earliest and the most low. Whether, therefore, the most elevated class of English mind be found up or down in the conventional scale of rank, whether it be composed of peers or peasants, masters or workmen, or, as is most possible, be mixed of all these, what-soever to that class seems theoretically good, beautiful, wise and true, is possible to be realised in the national deed, and lived in the national life. Whatsoever is, for the time being, beyond the belief, comprehension, and hearty acceptance of that class, is, for the same time, beyond the embodiment and healthy application of the main bulk of the Empire. The food may be celestial and fit for gods; but if there be as yet no digestion for it, we who had fattened upon beef may starve upon ambrosia.

In such a journal, therefore, as may assume to be the British microcosm—a diagram of the present rather than a programme of the future—this class should be authoritatively represented by competent minds, and, out of the grosser body of facts which make up the 'form and pressure' of the time, should be heard as the faithful and progressive utterance of the wide national thought.

'The faithful and *progressive* utterance;' for this class, having relations with higher individualisms, as well as with the wide gradations below it, being, so to speak, that national life-blood by which the air of heaven must vitalise the body, is by necessity perpetually absorbing from above. Itself the 'fit audience' which the poet asked, though happily less 'few' than in his 'evil days,' it is in the hearing of such a class—albeit 'a

stone's cast' removed—that the genius of an age soliloquises.
The Press thus organised, no more the fourth estate but the
realm itself, would become the actual government of the country,
and Carlyle's 'dynasty of the broad sheet' no longer a figure
of speech.

.   .   .   .   .   .

Akin to his *éclaircissements* with regard to the subordinates
of 'The Times,' are Mr. Pridham's revelations of another class
of officials, less important perhaps to the welfare of this country,
but, unfortunately, still more intimately concerned in her
political aspect and moral weight upon the Continent of Europe.
With such a British Embassy as he portrays at Vienna, there
need be little astonishment that the sympathy of the English
and German peoples has been ignored by Continental despots.
Hungary fell that Ponsonby might keep etiquette and Magenis,
like his countryman of the three jolly pigeons, 'damn' from the
great man's table 'anything that's low.' On the other hand, if
the evils our author has depicted be inseparable from diplomacy,
and the English complexion must needs get sallowed in the
absolutist climate of a foreign court, what new importance
attaches to that presiding hand at home which must work with
tools so lamentably and variably untrue? What intellect
should that be which must depend on no one of its senses,
calculate refractions for every seeing of the eye, and rectify
touch and hearing by a thousand mutable conditions? Grey
indeed should be the experience, astute indeed the serpent
wisdom, sleepless indeed the anxious industry of that unfortu-
nate statesman who must keep intact at all points a double line
of diplomatic circumvallation, defend his country not only
against her foes but her sons, and outwit his enemy by servants
who must themselves be outwitted.

Where that statesman is to be found, and by what symptoms
he may be known, is a question which recent events have in-
vested with a new and curious interest. In England just now,
otherwise not depopulated, we have the strange spectacle of an

empty Cabinet. For the locum tenens of a house 'to let' is everywhere held to be no bar to its vacancy; and the 'man in possession,' however dreadful in the terrors of the law, has never yet, that we heard of, risen to the social dignities of ownership. In this full England an empty Cabinet! In this Saxo-Norman England of genius, practical and intellectual, not a dozen men to match St. Arnaud or Nesselrode! And so the great constitutional house, which in days past so many great have gone in and out, is standing in the face of Europe dishonoured and tenantless; save, as we before said, for that 'man with a family' who keeps the building aired and holds the key. And yet in all modern days there never was a time when it might be so glorious to dwell there.

All seeing men, abroad and at home, democratic and absolutist, agree that we are in midst of a time of social trouble, 'such as was not since men were upon the earth.' That hurricane weather which in these last three years has disturbed the political ocean from its depths has only lulled a space; and the threatening roll of the waves is even more awful than the breakers. Under this wild sea of visible waters, storm-lashed and wind-ploughed, under those flaunting foam-billows, which but now were shutting out the light and making darkness horrible with wheeling birds of omen—battening gulls and shrieking cormorants, which sounded like spirits of the tempest, but were not—under all this seen and heard chaos of upper commotion, slowly, surely, as the unhasting sun under a stormy night, new mountains that shall change the aspect of the world are rising out of the mysteries of the middle deep. Mountains that shall heave the sea from their shoulders as a giant his cast lion's skin, and whose heads, even now barely beneath the waters, colour them already with the hue of things to be. Whosoever would sail in these days must launch indeed upon the sea, but woe to him if he ignore the mountains. He shall do well truly to attend the devices of present seamancraft and to look well that his vessel be such as will ride the waves; but if he will not add his wreck to the ruin, if he have a hope of

the world beyond the flood, let it also be an ark to stand upon the mountain-tops. Well if he clear the old reefs, and steer, while they last, by such charts as are still credible, but ill—ill beyond all known disaster—if amid these surges he forget the rising danger below, or pledged to the sinking lights and changing longitudes of to-day, go aground upon that great new land beneath the sea which to a wiser knowledge would have given the only anchorage of peace.

Never, so far as human foresight can discern, was there an era in the vicissitudes of our country when so great a fame has waited for that English statesman who shall have the genius to know and the power to dare the exigencies of the time. Never was there a passage in the story of the world which one great man might more utterly fill with his name. Never was there an hour when a wonderful fortune has offered so much to the statesman who is worthy of her. The high instincts of the poet, the grand attributes of the hero, the best wisdom of the sage, will be none too great for that man's career who shall pilot this dear England over the perilous waters of this present deluge and land her, laden with the past, on the Ararat to come. Doubtless no calculation can over-estimate the difficulties of the passage. For there is this grievance to a statesman in the most heroic of human times, that they are human times, and therefore not only heroic. That he, being pledged not to the heroism but the humanity of them, must be content, but too often, to wear his heroism 'with a difference.'

Your teacher or your philosopher may choose their seasons, may make to themselves wings, and, as sea birds over an inundation, alight only whereupon they find rest for the soles of their feet—good watch-cliff or commanding fishery above the rich turbulence below. But the statesman as a swimmer must needs enter the seething trouble—his whole power therein depending upon his contact. By the very conditions of his office he can ignore, omit, decline, select, nothing. No escape for him from this present scalding unmistakeable moment—

[illegible] golden shores beyond. No matter how firm a hold the present holds on him, he must clamp [illegible] keep up the support of the constitution, and [illegible] support [illegible]. Other students of this world [illegible] with peculiar "eye of news," as is [illegible], he only is, *ex officio*, professor of the [illegible] as it [illegible]; the single science in which he graduates, and "to be or not to be" for him no "question" at all. So far there is a resemblance between the statesman and the philosopher. One of the French dreamers foretells a system of nature wherein every great beast shall have his particular opposite—expatiate in the same fields of exercise with precisely counteracting powers. The lion his kata-lion, the horse his anti-horse. Some such relation ordinarily bear the statesman and the philosopher. Both occupied with indiscriminate facts; but dealing with them under opposite conditions, for opposite purposes, through opposite elaborations, to opposite results. For the philosopher, his facts are achronous. Time is no part of his universe: he may leave his ooze-bed to dry into a stratum, if he will. For the statesman, his facts are temporal, and are known to him principally as they exist in time. The one therefore is free, the other bound; and this stern necessity becomes to the statesman the mother of his whole invention. Both standing before the world of facts, with all its contained universals and particulars, the great effort of the one is to erect the first from the last, of the other to extract the last from the first. Both before a single fact, the one is conversant with its attributes, to the other the accidents are life or death;—the one straining after substance and the absolute, the other alive only to modes and relations; the one caring for its reflections in the pure crystal of genius, the other anxious for its image in the waved mirror of ordinary mind. The one sitting at the feet of God in the universe, the other of the king in the council-chamber; and each estimating all things by the power of the respective potentate. The one having the gospel of the possible, the other of

the practicable. The one mind moving on the great circle of the Divine, the other on the small of the human; the one, looking on to-day as upon his face in the eternal ocean, the other, carrying eternity as a simulacrum in the solid mirror of to-day. The one seeking to do that he may know, the other to know that he may do. The one, rich in premises—learned in thunders, whirlwinds, and still small voices from which he has not dared to draw the inference of finite intelligence; the other, with instincts seared and faculties perverted by the inexorable necessities of perpetual conclusions. The one with an intellect full of glorious imperfections—the fossil bones of things and eras yet unknown; the other with ready brain of ever-furnished ability, peopled assiduously with monstrous composites, and showing the miracles of that triumphant 'order' by which mammoth and dinornis, saurian and marsupian, redeemed from a natural and useless disagreement, may be nailed, sawn, and soldered into wholesome constituents, and do duty once more in an eclectic *status quo.* Therefore, in ordinary times statesmanship has been an employment below the ambition of great minds. Genius has been too much inspired to descend to its calculation of chances, too much absorbed to tolerate its equality of cares; and, to say sooth, diplomacy has seldom been so rash as to spread its gossamer meshes for that lion. The *entente cordiale* would have fared badly with your prophet. He must evoke what he must from 'the vasty deep,' careless whether his 'spirits' bring calm or storm. But the statesman's care is to hold that raft together on which, between past and future, the prophet stands.

The science of living dogs against dead (or unborn) lions, of to-day's atom against to-morrow's globe, of paltry success against glorious failure, of the lamp on Downing-street backstairs against another light 'that never was on sea or shore'—this elaborate littleness and learned levity has found therefore, in its average experience, no very divine gifts 'to admire the nothing of it.' Doubtless since every atom is inextricable from the universe, there is none of which the contemplation may not lead us to the infinite, no era of such mediocrity that a Secretary Milton would not have seen brooding under it the principles of the grandest times. But to common senses those are viewless influences which bind planet to planet and age to age, and transmit from one social convulsion to another the force of mankind. These volcanoes travel so long underground that eruptions become traditionary, and men build in one century round the crater of the last and above the earthquake of the next. The Foreign Office of 1752—would you thank us for it, Lord Palmerston? We trow not. The Foreign Office of 1852— would you ask a finer intellectual arena? Is there a gift of your nature, or a skill of your education which it would not tax to the uttermost? Have you a proud purpose it will not serve, a worldly ambition it may not glut, or a higher instinct it cannot satisfy? What do fame and posterity demand of you but to be a 'fellow-worker' with God in the regeneration of the world? To do safely and efficiently, from the fireside and by the pen, in the certainty of present homage and future gratitude, what the noblest of us, in darker days, have counted it glory to do at the stake, and by the axe, with no certainty on earth but the pangs in which it cast them out.

To accept by the strange felicity of concurring gifts and opportunities a glory which in the nature of things will be offered but once to any man, and comes to him, like heaven and hell, with no alternative but one.

And to add to that for which great men have already striven, this original glory as yet untried—to be the first constitutional English ruler in whom so much of the philosopher and of the statesman have been constants as to make the high and wide purpose of the one compatible with the successful practice of the other, and through whom the great thoughts of recluse speculation may find embodiment in the machinery by which States are ruled. Does not the prospect stir your nature, proud, subtle, far-sighted, large-brained Henry Temple?   then the grand humour of the divine comedy! We have seen lately, more than once, the grim *niaiserie* with which you can enjoy a terrible jest. This great Europe below and its mock kings over it—did you ever play a game so solemnly grotesque? These dozen puppets of gilt gingerbread, and these three hundred million burly school-boys a-hungered for it! These gaunt bearded masks of sapless paint and paper and those myriad hot flushed human faces behind them! The ermined effigies through which the wind already whistles, with their tinsel crowns and swords of lath, and this great continent of fighting men with a living heart in each and a wrong in the core of it! And you are to honour the gingerbread, protocol the pasteboard, take counsel with the purple rag!—and like Mahomet's saints in naked Paradise, you are forbidden to laugh!

More and harder. The hungry jaws, the flesh and blood faces and the world of fighting men—it is to *these* you must speak, for these manœuvre, with these make faith, when you bow to the gingerbread, rub noses with the mask, and hang a treaty on the bauble of Guy Fawkes; but woe to you, cries diplomatic decency, if you cast an eye in the direction of your thoughts, look but once, however much askant, upon that flesh and blood which loads your days and wakes your nights. Woe to you, cries another voice, to which your skilled ear will more readily listen, if with your inward eye you see aught else in these times. Standing under the sear forest of latter autumn, woe to him who trusts in the dead November leaves! What if there be a wind to-night? While it lay a wide, brown, homogeneous umbrage before you, have you so far been conscious of what was hid that you shall lose nothing and fear nothing and regret nothing, if it stands up to-morrow black and roaring? This is the test for a Foreign Secretary in these days.

Whomsoever it rejects, his country should reject, for she will count his hours of rule by the years of her sorrow. Whomsoever it admits, may save his nation. But whosoever, in other qualifications not inferior, shall with a larger courage, a higher

faith, a more inspired intuition evoke and direct the storms
which he might have been content but to await and weather,
may add a century to the well-being of mankind.

There is no fear that you will be found among the rejected.
You are too sagacious for that shame. You know what
manner of men they are who will write your history. You
know the coin which will pass current after you. You know
what are the heir-looms of days to come. You know which
stone of this *now* to cut your name upon—the blocks which go
to build the next era.

You know what will be fished up from the stream of time,
and which is bread, of all you cast upon the waters. The great
world is in labour, will you deliver her? If the birth could be
strangled, you might afford to stand idle; but you know that
the child cannot die, and would you have him demand the life
of his mother at your hands? The hero of a hundred protocols
is too shrewd for that!

Whether or not you are for the higher renown time has yet
to show. No man can advise you in these things. Greater
genius than your own might, by so much the more, mislead you.
It remains to be seen if to you the Eternal Providence has
given power to fix and make concrete that measure of the abstractions of such greater genius, and of the divine truths of a
higher inspiration, which is needed by the urgencies of your
time. It is for the highest genius to see and declare; to move
by intuition with certain phases of the mind of God, and reduce
to language the principles of the Divine Intelligence. Immortal,
impersonal, irrelative, without choice or object, calculation or
device, it is the verbal utterance of 'the things which do
appear,' the standing oracle of nature. Its sayings are therefore wisdom to the first man and the last, and the property of
all who in every place have to set themselves in accord with
the manifold unity of this universe. But no simony can direct
these gifts, no private interpretation monopolise this prophecy.
As in the multitude of things visible God has nowhere wholly

expressed Himself, but has chosen rather to symbolise His several attributes, so with the same wide economy is He represented in the world of mind. ' Gifts differing' receive— each in its proportion—the measure of the divine spirit in these as in earlier times. Your sun-staring eagle would starve with blindness where the meanest owl that shrieks would grow fat. Set your poet on Pisgah, and hear him : but beware of Balaam on the Treasury benches. Pull down the golden cloud from heaven, and it may be a fog in your nostrils—haply the blight and the pestilence. Dante was great when he said—

> il Veltro
> Verrà, che la farà morir di doglia,

and his old-world prophecy is swelling eleven million hearts to-day ; but when he dared to add,

> E sua nazion sarà tra Feltro e Feltro,

he was less than the stature of a lesser man.

Therefore has nature provided, scattered here and there among every age, a special order of men—as it were the Levites of genius—to whom is committed the Executive of the World ; having gifts for the particular ministry of universal truths, and standing towards a given time and occasion in the relation which genius occupies towards the sum of days and things.

Because you are of this order—how high or low in it you have yet to prove—and because you were the sole member of it among your companions-in-government, it was simply in the course of nature that the intrinsic difference between you should be made patent, and that the feeble organism in its last paroxysms should cast out the insoluble which it could not assimilate. For the same reason your return to authority is, so far as foresight can discern, a mere question of personal life and health. You can afford, therefore, to bide your time. He who has but to sit down before the city may well spare the dangers and uncertainties of assault. In truth, if this brief respite from

power shall add to that cosmopolitan experience, which friends
and foes acknowledge, a more thorough insight into the present
state of the home country than the cares of foreign business are
likely to have allowed, it may be an essential element in your
future greatness. Let Archimedes look well to his $\tau o\hat{v} \; \sigma \tau \hat{\omega}$.
You need not be told that during your long life in Downing
Street a new race of men have grown up out of doors, and that
the England of the next decade is not necessarily the England
of the last. No. That such guests as Kossuth have not been
here to teach new truths, but to receive British *sympathy*, and
that while an enthusiasm for new doctrines is, like othe intoxi-
cations, ephemeral, sympathy is the demonstration of a $\pi \acute{a} \theta v \varsigma$
already national; that the youth of this country are taking by
default, the place in popular influence which their elders do not
fill, and that the growing chivalry of young England will to a
great extent extinguish (by surviving) the selfishness of old;
that every day is more thoroughly destroying all assignable
relations between wealth and education; that this destruction
must be followed either by a fusion of classes or by a class-
warfare under new conditions, in which education will appear
for the first time as both the physical and the moral force; that
the so-called peace movement, though not to be overlooked, is
as yet almost exclusively sentimental and that sentiments
wither before awakened passions—these and a hundred other
social symptoms will have entered into your diagnosis when
considering England in her connection with democracy abroad.
But there are two other facts, more particularly visible from the
literary point of view, which may not be sufficiently conspicuous
where you stand. The first is the often-observed coincidence
that hitherto great eras of popular convulsion have been also
great eras intellectually, and marked by the up-rise of intellectual constellations. The second is that other truth—deriving
fresh significance from the first, and to which our cheapening
literature is daily giving wider and stronger application—that
' a library of books is henceforth the true university.'

The first makes it impossible to calculate what irresistible force may move at any moment the mind of the country, but lays it down as a certainty that whenever such force appears, the tendency of genius will not be towards tyranny or darkness, Hapsburgs or Romanoffs; the second, by removing education from all possibility of inspection, supervision, or control, makes it more than possible that your whole nation is in foreign schools, and that the race of British men whom a very few years will bring into the active affairs of the world may have graduated under Kinkel, passed examinations in Mazzini, gone in for honours to Victor Hugo, and received the double first at the hands of Madame Sand.

Joined to such considerations as these are a world of others which no man knows better than yourself, and which make the post of Foreign Secretary between this transition time and the final destruction of Absolutism in Europe as unparalleled in delicacy and difficulty as it may be unexampled in greatness and honour. On you, as the one public man amongst us who has already vindicated his rank in executive genius, devolves the labour and may descend the reward; if, unperverted by lesser men, you undertake it with a just confidence in your better gifts, an unshaken belief in the autopsy of your clearer perceptions, a silent determination towards ends not always to be avowed, and such a superiority to clamour, parliamentary, regal, or popular, as befits an ambition which it can neither eradicate, excite, nor define : looking to the inevitable in the faith of that genius, dealing with the present according to its wise intuitions, accepting always and in all places whatever English benefits may accrue from friend or foe, but hearing ever, above the most delusive appearance of unreal calm, the most boastful parade of re-established despotism, and the loudest manifestoes of liberty deceased, a great voice crying to all but those whom God has demented—

> The council of the brave are met
> Soon shall their swords with blood be wet
> The blood of tyranny and pride:
> On! on! this is not Regicide!

Words not inappropriate to 'Kossuth and Magyarland.'

CHAPTER I.

CONTRARY to all his expectations, when leaving England, the time spent in Scotland was of sufficient length to form a distinct era in Sydney Dobell's life, and greatly to enlarge his experience of men and things.

The letters of this period are chiefly to his own family, and are written with the frankest unreserve. Many of them, as was natural, chiefly relate to his wife's health, and only now and then contain anything of general interest.

From the beginning to the end of this sojourn the poet and his wife received the most unvarying and unwearying kindness from an ever-widening circle of friends.

One of these friends—Professor Blackie—whose first knowledge of him was acquired at this time—says, among other expressions of affectionate enthusiasm:

v   Y

His manners were not in any respect *made*; they grew, and were possible only where a highly refined social taste, and large intellectual sympathy, and an eminently generous nature acted in happy concert. That gracious nature delighted to exercise itself in deeds of public and private beneficence, which will live long in the memory of many who never dreamed of forming an estimate, and perhaps were naturally unable to appreciate, the intellectual excellencies of his work. Add to this, what those who knew him intimately might perhaps call the music of his domestic character—his devotion to his wife, his steady fidelity to his friends, and his fine sense of honour in his dealings with all men, and we have a picture before us, which, cherished in the memory, will be the best consolation for the loss of so beautiful a human presence.

'Balder' had been published so near the close of the previous year that, at the beginning of this, the writer was still ignorant of the nature of its reception by the general public. But a deeper and heavier than any literary uncertainty weighed upon him at this time. He delayed till his wife should have recovered from the evil effects of her long journey asking the opinion on her case, to obtain which had been the object of this pilgrimage, and meanwhile lived under the pressure of such suspense as is indicated in the following extract from a letter, acknowledging the new-year greeting of his brother-in-law, Mr. A. J. Mott:

How solemnly we both (you and I) have cause to look into this same new year. For me I go up into it as one of old to a certain city, 'not knowing what may befall me,' but content—nay rather striving to be content—in the confidence whereby he also was sustained. God help and bless you in it, dear brother and sister, and give you a flowery summer and a golden harvest out of that world without form and void which waits for ' His spirit to move npon the surface of the waters.' Dear M. is with us, and, as ever, a ' light in the house.'

To his Father and Mother.

No. 5 Forres Street, Edinburgh.

. . . New Year's Day in Edinburgh, and I have just returned from a turn in its overflowing streets.

God love and bless and guide you—and all our dear ones—in this year before us and in every coming year, aye and into that eternal mystery of duration when years shall be no more . . . Dear M. arrived last week and is, I need not tell you, a daily blessing to us. Your letters have come this morning and been warmly welcomed. We begin to feel less like wanderers ' in a solitary land, where no man is.' I passed this morning, in a street close at our elbows, Sir Walter Scott's Edinburgh house—the No. 39 so familiar to all readers of ' Lockhart.' Jeffrey's

house is in the Square adjoining Forres Street.   So you
see we are on classic ground. . . .

To the same.

Forres Street.

. . . I can fancy the pure white world that will surround you while you read this, for even mirky **Edinburgh**
is white to-day.   But English snow looks vital and warm
compared with the scenes beyond the town.   When once
you escape the soot of the sootiest of cities, you begin to
feel that you are indeed nearer to the north, and to think
that the Hand which spread the snows took the handful
from the Pole.   Looking on them, your mind opens to a
new sense of whiteness.   While we were at Merchiston
we had two days of snow, and I shall never forget the
effect of the far Fifeshire mountains.   They seemed as
the hills of that country whose centre is *the great white
throne.*   Whenever I write my most important poem I
should like to sit with them in view. . . . I postpone any
description of the city till I have been on some height
or other which may command it as a whole, and then I
hope to try and give you some notion of it.   At present,
it is but the disjointed elements of greatness that I see ;
passages from a grand epic, but with none of the unity
which should organise and vitalise them.   A cliff here,
a castle there, a yawning 'Norloch,' a windowed mountain
of houses beyond, these things have a strange effect of
disunion when beheld near at hand.

To the same.

Will you forgive a shorter letter than I should have liked to send to-day? I called on Samuel Brown this morning, and we talked so long that a letter to S —— I was obliged to write on returning the MS. of his play, has detained me till this minute. I found Brown well enough to be up . . . he looks very worn and ' waefu'' in point of health, and his large dark moustache makes the pale face paler. . . .

' I have some thought,' he wrote a little later,

if any of the other reviews follow the suit of ' The Athenæum,' of addressing a temperate short public letter to them, stating that I should be silent under all merely literary criticism, but wish not to be *morally* misunderstood ; and that the things they say ' Balder ' proves, viz., that vague ambitions and desires for good, unless more practically realised in the life, will not, however brilliant the gifts they are linked with, do any great work in the world, are precisely the things I wrote the book to prove.

It will appear from the above that ' Balder ' had been hostilely reviewed by the journal which had been one of the first to give a hearty and generous welcome to ' The Roman.'

Of the way the book was received, and, as to its intention, altogether misrepresented by many of

its other reviewers, the writer's own letters speak.
Even the criticisms from private friends were by
no means wholly favourable.   Nothing could have
been in greater contrast to the enthusiastic reception given to 'The Roman.'

Sydney Dobell's own opinion of the relative
merit of the two works—a deliberate judgment,
which never changed or wavered—was: There is
as much poetry in many a chapter of 'Balder' as
in the whole of 'The Roman.'   This opinion was
shared by those of his critics most competent to
judge the *poetry* of the poem; even when they
misread his design in writing it, or held it to be a
complete mistake as to constructive art.

'I have no more doubt of the work living than
I have that you live,'—wrote to him, in a letter of
far from unqualified approbation, a friend and
critic for whose poetic insight he retained all his
life a strong respect and admiration, while often at
variance with him on matters of detail.

It is as positively of poetic value as any land that
starts from ocean is physically real and a fact. . . . I
cannot over-express my admiration of the soliloquy which
precedes the catastrophe, from the point where Balder,
after the long pause, speculates on the birds feeding their
young—to the end.   It is all maintained at a sublime
level of tragic truth.

The same hand wrote to him, concerning a hostile review :

Criticism, dealing with a vital creation, has, it is true, only a transient influence either for good or evil; but even an impotent wrong vexes one, for one's own sake, and for that of the perpetrator. . . .

The notice ingenuously improves and abuses every opportunity of disparagement which the whole book affords, while it barely touches on the essential test of all in a poem—its poetry. Admitting, as I have always done, some ground in fact for the exceptions which are here so grossly exaggerated—and perverted—they do not one jot affect the conclusion, that the work which they condemn for obscurities and faults of design overflows with some of the noblest examples of imaginative power and beauty to be found in any language.

All criticism but defines the ' whereabouts ' of the critic. The Future cries 'woe,' to every *high* effort of imagination to which the Hydra the Present roars instant applause with all its consenting tongues. Genius is the Hercules who subdues, not propitiates, the monster.

Of the prefatory note prefixed to the second edition of ' Balder,' the same friend wrote :

You have explained on the ground where your reader might fairly own himself perplexed—Your philosophical intention; the cause of the difficulty being, in my mind, the absence of any character in the work to show the *author's* moral status, and so to contrast it with the aberrations of the *hero.*

What Miss Brontë wrote, in acknowledging a copy of 'Balder,' will be read with interest here. The letter has, however, already been printed in Mrs. Gaskell's Life of Miss Brontë.

Miss Brontë to Sydney Dobell.

Haworth, near Keighley: February 3rd, 1854.

My dear Sir,—I can hardly tell you how glad I am to have an opportunity of explaining that taciturnity to which you allude. Your letter came at a period of danger and care, when my father was very, very ill: and I could not leave his bedside. I answered no letters at that time, and yours was one of three or four that—when leisure returned to me and I came to consider their purport—it seemed to me such that the time was past for answering them—and I laid them finally aside. If you remember, you asked me to go to London: it was too late either to go or to decline. I was sure you had left London. One circumstance you mentioned, your wife's illness, which I have thought of many a time—and wondered whether she is better: in your present note you do not refer to her, but I trust her health has long ere now been quite restored.

'Balder' arrived safely. I looked at him, before cutting his leaves, with singular pleasure. Remembering

well his elder brother—the potent ' Roman,' it was natural to give a cordial welcome to a fresh scion of the same house and race.

I have read him. He impressed me thus. He teems with power. I found in him even a wild wealth of life ; but I thought this favourite and favoured child would bring his sire trouble ; would make his heart ache. It seemed to me that his strength and beauty were not so much those of Joseph—the pillar of Jacob's age, as of the Prodigal Son who troubled his father, though he always kept his love.

How is it that—while the first-born of genius often brings honour—the second, almost as often, proves a source rather of depression and care? I could almost prophesy that your third will atone for any anxiety inflicted by this his immediate predecessor.

There is power in that character of ' Balder ' and, to me, a certain horror. Did you mean it to embody, along with force, many of the special defects of the artistic character? It seems to me that those defects were never thrown out in stronger lines.

I did not and could not think you meant to offer him as your cherished ideal of the true great poet. I regarded him as a vividly coloured picture of inflated self-esteem, almost frantic aspiration —of a nature that has made a Moloch of the intellect—offered up in pagan fires the natural affections, sacrificed the heart to the brain.

Do we not all know that true greatness is simple, self-oblivious, prone to unambitious, unselfish attachments?

I am certain you feel this truth in your heart of hearts.

But if the critics err now (as yet I have seen none of their lucubrations) you shall one day set them right in the Second Part of ' Balder.' You shall show them that you know—better perhaps than they—that the truly great man is too sincere in his affections to grudge a sacrifice—too much absorbed in his work to talk loudly about it—too intent on finding the best way to accomplish what he undertakes to think great things of himself—the instrument. And if God places seeming impediments in his way; if his duties seem sometimes to hamper his powers—he feels keenly—perhaps writhes under the slow torture of hindrance and delay; but if that be a true man's heart in his breast, he can bear, submit, wait patiently.

Whoever speaks to me of ' Balder '—though I live too retired a life to come often in the way of comment—shall be answered according to your own suggestion and my own impression. Equity demands that you should be your own interpreter. Good-bye for the present, and believe me,

Faithfully and gratefully yours,
CHARLOTTE BRONTË.

The foregoing letter, and Miss Brontë's thorough understanding, not only of what was not, but of what was, his ideal of ' the truly great man,' it was a hearty satisfaction to him to receive. This book can hardly fail to show how much he realised his correspondent's picture of 'one who can bear, submit and wait patiently, even when, his duties seeming to hamper his powers, he writhes under the slow torture of hindrance and delay.'

At the risk of some repetition, it seems desirable to give more than one of his explanations as to his *intention* in 'Balder,' because his anxiety not to be morally misunderstood is characteristic of the sincerity of his relative estimate of moral and intellectual worth. Perhaps a few among the readers of these pages may remember his indignant disgust when—the conversation at an evening assembly having taken a turn which led him to express his views on some points of belief and conduct—one of the guests, a writer of some celebrity and, what deepened his disgust, a woman, exclaimed, with hands uplifted in incredulous surprise—'What! A poet, *and a good young man!*'

Aware that many an ambitious youth, emulous of literary distinction, might be made ashamed of such virtue as he possessed, and stimulated to vice from which he had hitherto abstained, through the desire to prove himself a poet by *not* being 'a

good young man,' he felt that such foolish words,
spoken by a person of worldly and literary experience, might work wide and deep mischief.

To the Rev. Brown Paton.

No. 5 Forres Street, Edinburgh : January 26.

. . . I am especially glad to find that you have understood so well the moral and purpose of my book. . . .

. . . I am by nature careless of literary censure, but,
on principle, I am anxious that I may not be *morally
misunderstood*. I understand from various quarters that
this strange mistake is not confined to ' The Athenæum,'
and that while the poetic merit of the book is freely
admitted, the moral purpose is constantly misconstrued.
I believe thoroughly, however, that among the real critics
of the country, now, or hereafter, some men will arise
who will comprehend and vindicate me. Your excellent
suggestion of a Preface would I am told have saved me
from this misconstruction ; and although I have a great
dislike to Prefaces (which remind me of the ' This is a
man,' or ' horse,' or ' tree ' of the ancient painters), I
should certainly have adopted the expedient could I have
foreseen that my object would have been so misread. It
seemed to me that the book expressed its moral ; that
defeat so terrible, complete, humiliating and self-confest
as Balder's could not be taken for anything but a warning. Read the 30th scene, and imagine it written as a
seduction ! I meant it for the very cry of our perplexed

and unsatisfied time.   But I am not in haste; believing
that 'the hour and the man'—perhaps many hours and
many men—will come and do me justice—moral justice,
for in matters poetical I have little to complain—and remembering in Whose service the book—well or ill—was
humbly written; and to Whom it was dedicated in the
solemnity of my soul. . . .

I regret not a little that there is no better prospect of
our meeting at the time you mention; but I have every
reason to believe that events will keep me in this noble
capital for months to come.

In the hurry of leaving England I begged—to return
to you the volumes of 'Bopp' you were so good as to lend
me.   The 'Eclipse of Faith' I retained for further reading. . . . I had expected to find great talent in the
'Eclipse,' but was unprepared for some other elements,
which explained at once the *love* with which his friends
speak of the author.

E. sends you many very kind remembrances.   Nothing
is yet ascertained as to the probability of her cure, but
the omens so far as they go are favourable.   Even these
dumb auspices are, you may readily imagine, brightening
heaven and earth to my eyes.   You say well as to the
'veiled portrait' in 'Balder.'   How falsely are Poets
called visionaries!   Did I ever give you this formula for
poetry: 'The Truth, the whole Truth, and nothing but
the Truth?'   It does not contain the whole secret, but it
is essential *to* the secret.

What a despatch I have scribbled!   Take it as the
best evidence, under these present conditions of time and

space, of the true esteem and warm regard with which I
am always,

Yours affectionately,

SYDNEY DOBELL.

To another friend he wrote, about the same
date, that knowing the writer of ' Balder,' he
would hardly fall into the error of those who took
for granted that the man Balder was held up as a
model and ideal, instead of as a *warning*.

You will see that my object was to illustrate the
fact, that no amount of ambition, aspiration, talent, and
genius, can come to anything but failure and sorrow,
unless it be complemented with much that is still better,
nobler, Diviner.   Balder, the splendid dreamer, the
philanthropic nineteenth-century pagan, with all manner
of materials for good in him, *longs* to save mankind, but
acts the misery and murder of his wife. He would re-
generate the world, but cannot bless his own hearth. I
care little, as you know, for the opinion of most men on
matters poetical, but I would not willingly be misunderstood on matters of right and wrong.

To his Father and Mother.

February 3.

Of the effects of chloroform, he says :

The strange experiences of (so to say) a dissected soul
are something which one could hardly expect in life. To
see violent emotion and all the signs of mental movement

taking place, while some of the prime faculties are evidently cut off from intercourse with this world, has an unearthly interest which would be fascinating if it related to a sufferer less beloved. . . .

Speaking of having, hitherto, avoided all social engagements, on the ground of anxiety on his wife's account, but of now feeling it necessary and right to accept some invitations—to Professor Blackie's, among others—'in return for kindnesses shown us,' he adds, that he means to continue to avoid such engagements as much as possible: 'Mrs. Blackie,' he says, 'was so winningly kind in her entreaties to be allowed to do anything for E——, that she went to my heart at once. . . .

You have seen doubtless by the papers that Alexander Smith is elected Secretary to the University. It was a hard fought contest, and you would have been amused to drop suddenly on Edinburgh, and find me one of the canvassers. Simpson came for me unexpectedly, early in the day, to use my 'influence and testimony' with the town council: and finding myself fairly in for it, I let what my hand found to do be done with my might: and did not leave off work till eight in the evening. Several influential people had got notions of Alexander's 'immorality.' I took the book with me and gave extempore lectures on the pure passages to counteract the effect of the others!

To C—— (answering a letter which criticised ' Balder ').

One word only on another branch of criticism. I recollect you comfort yourself under unfavourable reviews by the reflection that they may teach me 'humility,' and improve my character. I won't stop to smile at the notion of human castigation teaching me humility, or at the idea of such elfin-blows as those in question teaching me anything at all; but I will stop to say to my favourite brother one thing, tenderly and solemnly: ' recollect when in your boyish inexperience you would teach me " humility," that if it be humility to be as nothing before God, if it be humility, not as a dutiful theory, but as an actual involuntary consciousness, to ignore the possession of a single substantive power or quality, to live, move, speak, but as the helpless instrument of the One Omnipotent Sole Life, Sole Good, then are few humbler men alive than I.'

To his Father and Mother.

After speaking of his wife's health, he mentions an engagement to meet Samuel Brown at lunch ' at the house of a friend of his (and ours) Mrs. Stuart Menteath,' and of having met Kingsley on the previous night:

He was not in any way the man I had pre-pictured, and looked at least fifteen years older than I had supposed him.

He spoke kindly of 'Balder,' which he had read . . . particularly admires my idea of woman as shown in it. . . . He
is a slender tall man, with (I think) small head, small
eyes, a reddish weather-beaten face, and a nervous mouth.
I can believe him in domestic life very loveable, but, he
is evidently bashful (from the consciousness of his stutter)
in a large company, and tries to carry it off by an air of
impulsive nonchalance, which betrays its unreality and
does not do him justice. . . . Several other interesting
people were at the same party. Among others Dr. Hanna
and his wife, and Helen Faucit—whom I admired much.
She called here to-day. Earlier in the evening—at Lady
Agnew's—I had met another Scotch theological celebrity,
Dr. Guthrie, the eminent Free Church preacher, a grand
rugged-looking man, who might have been a soldier in
Cromwell's Ironsides, and given out the Psalm to charge.

There was also Mr. Oliphant, the author of the 'Shores
of the Black Sea,' an intelligent young man, who is going
out to Constantinople. I did not have much talk with
Dr. Guthrie, but he sat by with genial smiles, while
Lady —— and I discussed profoundly Whewell's new
book on the 'Plurality of Worlds.' She is a clever
woman, rather young, fond of literature, slightly conscious
of her Ducal blood, but only shewing it by a lively happy
complacency.

To the same.

Forres Street : March 3.

. . . You will be sorry to hear that Samuel Brown is
worse again. I told you in my last, I think, that I was

going to meet him at Mrs. Menteath's. He seemed thoroughly himself that day—what a curious, calm, subtle, conscious, various, ever-furnished 'self' it is!—but has not left his bed since. . . .

Gilfillan, who disappointed us on Friday, made his appearance last Tuesday morning and spent the day with us. He seems to me the very incarnation of force : not power, but force. . . .

. . . The night before last I went to a party at Dr. ——. A large party, with nothing very remarkable in it, except the absence of anything sectarian, or 'Scotch,' in the atmosphere. A great deal of music, some of it by professionals and most of it Italian, hardly reminded one of Kirk or Presbyters, or that it was heard under the roof of the hereditary head of the Free Church. A grand bust of Chalmers—the head of a poet-philosopher, the nose of a statesman, and the mouth of a woman—struck me a good deal.

Speaking, in another letter of Dr. Samuel Brown, he says :

There is something of a sublime pathos in the quiet silence with which he takes his four years' arrest from study and labour. He is very proud, in his calm way, of his baby ; which indeed sits in its nurse's arms with the air of a chancellor . . . This is the week of the general assembly of both churches of Scotland, and the city is so full of parsons it is enough to make one sick. Though some of the grave-looking men from Highland

Manses are interesting to look upon in the streets where
John Knox walked . . . It is a pretty good testimony to
the constancy of our love that, like Paul, I might have
a stereotyped close for every one of these family letters.
The same much much love to the same ever dear ones.

To the same.

Forres Street: March 10.

. . . I am sorry my mother seems to think that I am
always in too great a hurry to write you such letters as
you would like. I try to tell you what I think will be
interesting and, as you know, I have never yet let anything come in the way of your weekly letter. I can
hardly be set down among ' people who have nothing to
do ' and am amused at your suggesting this as a reason
for my chronic hurry. Of all hard work and all time-
consuming occupation I know nothing worse than perpetually ' seeing ' people. To be always subject to inva-
sion at any moment at home, and to be daily bound to
some ' engagement ' abroad, is as severe labour as business
itself. But my mother mistakes the tone and level on
which I am meeting these genial Edinburghers. I
thought she might have trusted my pride with regard to
' lionising.' If it be half so terrible a beast as she has
often described it, ' the lion ' would be dangerous company
forsooth ! . . .

I spent an interesting evening on Wednesday . . .
D—— was there and Alexander Smith. I was very much
pleased with D——. I had been reading his book, and,

through much that is incomplete and youthful, had detected some profound critical qualities that indicate one born to be a critic, and a universality of acquired knowledge which betokened one educated for criticism, and I was thoroughly glad to find the outward visible signs in agreement with these inferences.

I never, I think, saw such strong perceptive faculties, except in the portrait of Hazlitt, and these are united with a sensitive mouth all quivering with feminine appreciation, but capable nevertheless of settling into wide judicial quiet . . . Smith and I seem destined to be social twins . . . He seems very comfortable in his little office at the College. What do you think of me as a collegian? Blackie has invited me to attend his college lectures on the Greek Poets, and I went last Monday for the first time. It was very interesting as a study, both of him, and of his class, and I intend to go, if possible, every Monday. Blackie is beautiful in class, his genial fraternal kindness to his students—so patient, so appreciative—is rare and noble. I have no time to describe to you my half day at Craigcrook, and its lovely Charlton-like scenery, so must defer it to another letter.

To C——.

Forres Street, Edinburgh : 1854.

Send me such a description of the state of things in the dear home valley as may give me an idea of *spring*.

Here I see that the trees in the squares are bursting ; crocuses and primroses are in the prim town gardens,

rooks, that still have nests in trees long since surrounded
by tall houses, are carrying sticks, like black scavengers,
from the midst of the streets, the sparrows make unusual
noise in the dull quadrangle we see from our bedroom
window, and I know, therefore, that *somewhere else* it is
spring. Somewhere, but not here. These are but the
disjecta membra of the indescribable and unimaginable
whole, and I want not the limbs but the whole.

By passing two springs in a city, I feel that I have
missed in art, and in that divine education which is above
all human instruction, what nothing can ever restore. It
is true that from the highest places of this Edinburgh
you can see over to the surrounding country, but the view
thus had is too general to supply the defect I am now
expressing. You see Nature indeed; but not the changes
in her face—the *seasons*, in which are contained her best
lessons to the human artist. The exquisite harmonies of
each of those changing ' stops,' the delicate and complete
keeping of each of these varying expressions, the *thoroughness* of work, the cosmical wholeness of perfection in these
pictures, wherein the out-of-sight work in the rock, the
enfolded secrecies of crumpled bark, or broken turf, or
calyxed bud, the highest invisible twig, or the closest inaccessible thicket, are as appropriately finished and cared
for as the parts she blazons before the eye of man—these,
and a thousand more, are the examples which Nature only
can give, and among which the mind becomes unconsciously tuned to *her* ' principles of Art.'

The same letter speaks of a meeting of the

Royal Edinburgh Medical Society, which he had
attended, and at which he had spoken, on the subject of temperance, at the urgent request of Professor Simpson :

Speaking of Professors, (it concludes), reminds me of
an excellent joke (but I valued it as being something
better than a joke) I had with Professor Aytoun the night
before. You remember he abused me in last 'Blackwood,'
and called me 'Gander Redney,' a squib on 'Sydney
Yendys.'

He and I were at a party, but had not come in contact.
As I was bidding Mrs. —— good-bye near the door,
Aytoun came up also on his way out. Dr. Simpson
seized him, and introduced us. Aytoun looked puzzled
and amused, and was profoundly polite, but was obliged
to follow the ladies of his party, who had already left the
room. I stepped after him, and clapping him on the
shoulder, said, 'The Dr. did not introduce us perfectly
just now—he omitted some of my styles and titles—*you*
probably know me better as *Gander Redney*.' How his
eyes twinkled! and Simpson told me afterwards that at
the bottom of the stairs he told the story with roars of
laughter.

To A. J. Mott, Esq.

March 24.

. . . Dear M.'s note (enclosed) will tell you what has
happened to us within the last few days. 'What has
happened,' is, as yet, the best formula I have for it. My

heart has been so often disappointed on this vital subject
(his wife's recovery), that it refuses to look up at the
voice of promise. I know with my head the inestimable
blessing we have received; and intellectually recognise to
God and to man how exquisite and how beautiful it is.
But as yet it is a lifeless theory, that neither quickens my
pulse, nor enlightens my eye. This is natural enough:
I look on, and understand it, and know that it will soon
be otherwise. God also knows and understands.

And so you are going to Detmore, to live among the
English spring. You will see lambs and primroses, green
hedges and mossy hills, and all the swelling season of our
generous England. What a contrast to these stony straths
and unrelenting rocks—the very skull and skeleton of
Nature.

At the end of a long letter of literary and
artistic gossip, written to amuse the home-circle, a
few days later, he sends: 'Loving thanks to the
dear little girls for their picturesque letters and
flowers. Their description of the dear English
spring went to my heart of hearts. And the
violets and primroses and crow-foot from the very
fields of home!'

To his father he writes:

I see by your hint that you fear we are extravagant.
I could easily show you that under the circumstances it
is impossible to spend less than we do. . . . Be at ease
regarding this, for your very own self could not more
thoroughly desire to be prudent than we.

CHAPTER II.

EDINBURGH, 1854.

APRIL 7 he wrote to his father and mother, in acknowledgment of congratulations and admonitions received two days before, on his thirtieth birthday:

'How poor it seems to be acknowledging with this steel pen, on this cold paper, with this black ink, the birthday letters which the day before yesterday brought me. . . .

How great a blessing it is to feel that dear as you all were this time last year, to-day you are even dearer to us than then. That last birthday in that country April, with the yellow flowers by the English road-sides, the thrush in the Coxhorne oak, the primroses by the stream, the lambs in the fields.

But one could hardly have a better scene for writing of a birthday than this that I see through the window— the Forth coming into sunshine from the midst of a mystery of hills, moving for a few miles before us, grand and wide, bearing its many ships and enriching green shores, and then passing through fogs and clouds into the unknown, unlimited, unfathomable sea. What an allegory of Life !

Thanks many for the seriousness of my dear mother's letter, although I trust and think I needed no reminder of the solemnity of the time on which I enter. . . .

Thanks, too, for her frank expression of her fears for me, her opinion of my apparent inconsistency, and her advice to reconsider my principles. . . .

To the same.

April 14th.

He speaks of his wife having again suffered terribly from tic doleureux: this time in consequence of the unusual fatigue of being present at a crowded assembly, to witness some tableaux— for which Alexander Smith had written a prologue, her husband an epilogue:

C. should have seen them, (he says of the Tableaux,) they were composed with the art and thought of great pictures. Archer and Drummond had been employed for many evenings in grouping them. . . . Before I forget it, I must say a word or two more on my father's hint about expensiveness, because I should be sorry you should suppose we have grown careless. The power of spending by no means indicates the duty or liberty to spend. And I think we have sufficiently proved our appreciation of this truth by such simplicity and economy as our four or five months, at Amberley, in a cottage at fifteen shillings a week.

Here in Edinburgh there are but two places to live in, the old town and the new.

He takes trouble to explain the necessity of living in the latter, mentions the

many incidental expenses (cabs, for instance, for I can't walk to a party in an Edinburgh evening wind more than one time in ten) which swell up the gross amount.

Of an Edinburgh evening wind.—Do not suppose I speak of anything you ever felt in England. The wind here is as thick as water, and faster than the fastest hail-storm I ever felt at home. I am often obliged to stand still in crossing a street to let it go by, as one would halt on the bank of a mountain torrent.

The Prologue and Epilogue referred to in the foregoing letter seem worth preserving.

PROLOGUE.

The curtain rises on our mimic scenes.
Pale Flora, watching o'er the Prince, forlorn ;
Ruth, standing like a poppy 'mong the corn ;
And Mary, saddest, fairest of the queens,
Bending, in tumbled and dishevelled grief,
Above melodious Rizzio, stabbed and torn :
Frail Lucy, shrinking 'neath her lover's scorn,
With faith as worthless as a withered leaf
That o'er the waste by ev'ry wind is whirled.
—Another curtain, o'er a stage of gloom,

Is slowly rising : calm and pale with hate,
Two foes are closing in the tug of doom.
Upon this stage shall rise our mimic state,
But on that other stands or falls the world.

Epilogue.

Our shows are ended.   All the pictures rare
That filled the bright eyes of this brilliant crowd
Dissolved, like those strange landscapes of the air
Which sunset paints upon a coloured cloud.
Yet, gentle friends, I would not have you deem
You saw but fabrics of a faithless dream.
In changing form, but in unchanging youth,
Truth is eternal.   And we showed you *truth !*

The trembling suppliant minstrel clings no more
To the fair hand ; the husband's wrath is o'er,
And all the fatal hour.   But love, and hate,
Hope, fear and pity, are not out of date !
Treason and murder, as of old, will pass
Through to-night's shades ; suspicion's baleful breath
Is poison still ; and loveliness, alas !
Still lights the unlovely dark of horror, sin, and death.

No more our chieftain's daughter bends above
Her sleeping prince ; but still, while love is love,
By sorrow's sleep such loyal truth shall kneel !
No cot so lowly but a heart as leal
As knelt beside the monarch's slumbering head
May watch the humble woe, and guard the peasant's bed.

Malcolm no more salutes his beaming queen ;
Their thrones are empty as this vacant scene.
But, on a nobler stage, and loftier seat,

Beauty still holds her empery o'er mankind,
Power sinks subdued at virtue's sovereign feet,
And mortal might bends low before the immortal mind !

But not alone our pictures have displayed
The stuff whereof each changing age is made ;
We point the moral of the moment ! aye !
We paint the portrait of the year and day !
Fancy transports you to another clime,
And thinks she sees a mirror of the time ;
From sky to sky our rising curtain furled,
Our actors nations, and our stage the world.

Look on our bridal contract ! and behold
Far east, another freedom bought and sold
As foul a treaty and as dire a wrong,
Forced on the feeble by the guilty strong !

See our poor murdered babes, and understand
What the weak suffer at a tyrant's hand !

And in the Saxon Maude and Celtic King
Behold the wedded nations that shall fling
The despot deep in his Siberian tide
Of molten snows ; and while his howling pride
Sinks in the floods, from the calm Ararat
Of freedom, view the sanguine deluge cease.
With upturned eyes receive descending fate,
And lift with mutual hands the open book of Peace.

To a young Sister.

Abercrombie Place: April 11th, 1854.

I have not forgotten your wish you see; and I send you a kiss for it and for the way in which it was expressed.

May my letters be indeed to you like 'messages from Paradise'—except that I trust they may not be 'few and far between.'

What the Paradisical element in them can be I am at a loss to guess: but be they terrestrial and black as midnight clay, may your love, dear, little-great sister, ever as now transfigure them to the texture of that higher region wherefrom all love descends.

There's a long complicated sentence for you! Strange enough to be written to a little sister if I did not know that that young sister has already so much of the mind of a woman. 'The mind of a woman.' There indeed is a text for birthday wishes. God give you one day 'the mind of a woman.' This is a better wish than if I said even the mind of an 'angel,' for God does all things in an ordained progression, and the order of His providence is first 'woman,' then 'angel.' Therefore you will neglect nothing that completes the true character of woman, nor think anything unimportant that is a part of it, however small; conscious that the God Who created womanhood can alone know the real value of anything that He has made, and that sometimes in our human estimates 'the first may be last and the last first.' Now the ideal of a

woman's character is *Beautiful Goodness.* Not goodness
only, but beautiful goodness. You will say, perhaps, that
all goodness is beautiful; and so it is when in perfection,
but, like many other things in nature, it requires to be
complete and fully developed before you perceive all its
qualities. Summer fruit is summer fruit, even before it
is ripe; there are all the main substances present in it
which constitute a fruit—stone, skin, pulp, juice; but it is
only when warmed into perfection that it becomes flushed
with colour, tinted with bloom, sweet to the taste and
beautiful to the eye.

So with goodness. Goodness is goodness also long
before it is ripe; and many people think it the better the
sourer and bitterer it is. But you, dear sister, will be
content with nothing less than goodness sunshined into
beauty.

Never be careless of anything that is beautiful. It
may seem a trifle; but beauty is divine, you know, and
God can dwell as easily in an atom as in heaven. The
bloom on the plum, the flush on the rose, the immaculacy of
the snowdrop, the intensity of the light; these trifles sometimes make the difference between beauty and non-beauty.

You are now entering upon one of the most touching
and precious times of life, when the child begins to
blossom into the maiden—I was going to say girl, but we
have called you 'girl' a long, long while. Your birthday
comes precisely at that very age of the growing year.
May the God of goodness and beauty, Who never fails
to flower the Spring into Summer with harvest, find you
as obedient as the dutiful earth, and bless and glorify you

likewise. And long seasons hence may He gather your wheat into His garner, that you yourself, relieved from that burthen of works and duties, may burst forth again into the Spring which is everlasting !

To his Father and Mother.

Abercrombie Place : April 27.

. . . Have you seen a most interesting calculation, extracted from the London Quarterly, of the hours of greatest mortality? The hour after midnight being the minimum—the hour when Death himself sleeps. They might have increased the interest of the paper by extending the range of it. I saw, in a learned botanical work some time ago, that the hour on each side midnight is the only one in the twenty-four when no flower either opens or closes. How strange to see that the instinct of universal mankind had already perceived, and expressed in a thousand legendary forms, what science now discovers to be statistical truth.

'I am writing this evening' he says, at the end of a long letter,

because I may not have time to-morrow, as I have promised to take D—— to lunch and dine at Craigcrook. He is anxious to know Mr. Hunter, and I am pleased to have the opportunity of gratifying him . . . Alexander and I seem fated to appear together. There is hardly a week now in which we are not either abused or praised side by side, in some magazine or newspaper. Curiously enough,

while our public epiphany has been of this twin character,
our private union has been more and more complete.   He
frequently spends his evenings with us, and seems to enjoy
them thoroughly.

To his eldest Sister.

I sent you a message in my family-letter of acknowledgment of your birthday greeting; but that greeting
was so kind and so welcome that it deserves, and shall
have, a separate recognition.   God bless you, and grant
that each time you write me a birthday letter and I send
you these birthday thanks we may both love each other
better and both be worthier of love. . . .

If ever there was a time when 'happiness' itself
might pause to examine its tenure and verify its securi-
ties, surely it is that on which we are now entering, when,
as it were, the very 'fountains of the great deep' seem
about to be 'broken up' and this May-thunder that now
roars over my head is but a faint symbol of the storm that
will soon burst below.   But I think I said something of
these things in my general Detmore letter, and will not so
soon again enlarge on them.   You know what I think and
believe and, as I trust, think and believe the same; and
will need no one, therefore, to point out the signs of the
time or read for you the omens of a closing dispensation . . .
You are right in supposing my time is closely occupied—
indeed from morning till midnight I have hardly a leisure
minute just now.

To his Father and Mother.

May 5.

. . . The weather here must, I think, have been milder than at home, for vegetation is unchecked and the spring seems more forward than in those dear fields to which the very word 'spring' always transports me. E. had a threatening of tic doloureux after the little unusual excitement of Lady Agnew's evening, but, God be thanked, it did no more than threaten. We spent some pleasant and satisfactory hours with the Agnew family and Professor and Mrs. ——.

The letter then speaks of a lunch next morning with Sir George Sinclair, 'schoolfellow and friend of Byron,' and of hearing

some curious stories of Byron's Boy-and-Manhood, and of other historic matters of that day, from a fine courteous princely specimen of the old English man—one who took part in such old-world dinners as when Peel, Wellington, Burdett, Follett, Hardinge and others of that stamp made up a 'small party of eleven.' To-morrow we are to go to spend the day at Craigcrook, to introduce Alexander Smith to the Hunters, and to enable M. to bid them good-bye.

Of ' another fulmination ' in ' Blackwood,' called ' Firmilian, a Tragedy,' he writes :

I laughed more, on first reading it, than at anything I have read lately. It is wonderfully well done (by Aytoun), and professes to be a critique on a new tragedy,

of which specimens are given: said tragedy being a
happy burlesque on me and Alexander; the incidents of
' Balder ' being travestied in a style intended for his and
mine. The thing is so finely done that hardly anyone
but those in the secret will know what it means. Poor
—— entering as Apollodorus is slain by the friends whom
Balder throws from the Tower. But you must read
it. . . .

. . . We are looking forward sadly to dear M.'s de-
parture—or rather we are trying not to look forward, but
to keep our eyes upon the days in which she is still with us.
She has become so much a part of our daily life that it
seems hardly possible we are to lose her; and we can
neither of us fully recognise the approach of that great
absence which will soon be so hourly real to us.

To his Sister on her birthday.

Edinburgh : May 8.

How well I remember, on the morning you were born,
sitting with my nose almost touching my copy-book and
carefully inscribing ' Clara Elizabeth Dobell, May 9,'
having meanwhile very indefinite notions of the significa-
tion of the same, and feeling only that somewhere above—
either in heaven or upstairs—a new substantive had joined
the things wherewith I was before acquainted; but whether an angel or a baby made not the slightest difference
to my consciousness. And now you are a grown woman,
' wooed and married and a',' having passed all the experiences of childhood, girlhood, wifehood, aye, and
motherhood.

How strange to think that what was on that morning, so far as I was concerned, no more than some score of black letters has since come into the visible as such a dear and important reality—a thinking, feeling, acting, moving far-off separate and yet connected being; and that having more or less together, sometimes well-seen and sometimes out of sight, crossed the pleasant land and fair boscage of youth, we both stand together to-day, alive and strong, upon the same dark sea-line and try to look across into the impenetrable future. Never, since first human eyes looked across it, was that great ocean more tremendously ominous—more surely heaving with destructive forces, or blacker with impending thunder—than it lies to-day to your sight and to mine; and not to ours only, but to that of all but the blind—wise and simple, small and great—as the murmur of the whole earth bears witness. . . .

. . . However dark that prospect may be, dear sister, may we each live to see the other safely over it. For me, I thank God to have been born in so grand a time, and to belong to the generation upon which—perhaps—'the ends of the age are come;' but I sometimes fear it will be no idle sight-seeing, and that we had need trust and pray earnestly that none who are near and dear to us may suffer to make up the show. God grant, indeed, it may be otherwise, and that some good day in His Providence we may all meet, one by one, and two by two, upon the far further shore.

A A 2

To his Father and Mother.

May 19th, 1854.

I don't think I have given you any account of the journey we made with Alexander Smith to Craigcrook some time ago.

E., M., Smith, and I, went over in the middle of the day and stayed the afternoon and evening. The Hunters were most kind in doing all they could to prevent the day from being injurious to E.

M., Smith, Professor Henderson, who happened to be there, Mr. and Miss Hunter and I were out on the hills about the house the greater part of the afternoon. They are lovely hills, as I told you before, and always remind me of home. Smith exclaimed ' how like Coxhorne ! '

Professor Blackie and the two young Hunters came in to dinner. . . .

. . . Smith left a very favourable impression at Craig-crook. He stood with excellent gentleness and quiet strength a good deal of raillery at dinner-time on the subject of our water-drinking; but even those who laughed respected him for his firmness. . . . He spent last Sunday afternoon and evening with us, and seems to love to be here. In the course of those familiar chats some beautiful facts have accidentally escaped him. Among others, I find that for years he was the chief support of his family, and the very staff of his father who seems to have leaned on Alexander since his earliest youth. Also, that much of the money he received for his book was spent in

enabling a young friend who longed for the Ministry, but
had not the wherewithal to study, to pass through the
University. These facts are accompanied with such a
state of feeling regarding them as makes them even more
beautiful. He will probably pass next Sunday afternoon
and evening with us; and we shall have some long talks
upon Religion, in which I can see with delight that we are
gradually growing to think alike. . . .

    . . . I don't know if in my short scrawl to my father,
I said much of Dr. Emily Blackwell, the American lady.
You will be interested to hear that, by the testimony of
the physicians here who have as yet practised in her
company, she is not only skilful as a practitioner, but very
womanly as a woman. She was extremely kind to us on
Wednesday, and stayed with E. the greater part of the day,
which, alone as we are now, was a great assistance and
comfort. How we miss M.; or rather how we long for
her, for the idea of missing carries a utilitarian notion
with it. She had become so completely as a child to us
that to lose her seems out of the very nature and propriety
of things. She left us last Saturday.

The next home letter again speaks of Dr.
Emily Blackwell's very kind attention and sympathy during a serious aggravation of his wife's
illness; and adds, after naming 'plenty of kindest
volunteer help,' in this season of trouble 'I need
not tell you how we missed dear M.'

The same letter says, of Sir James, **then Pro**
fessor, Simpson:

He is certainly a very curious instance **of a man**
pursuing a single science to eminence, and yet **remaining**
cultivated in others. . . . His breakfast and **luncheon**
tables are daily levees. . . . You never can tell **whom you**
are to find there.

This man will be a lord, that an author, **that a**
painter, that some strange pilgrim from some **out–of-**
the-way land where flesh is still 'heir to ills.' **Equal to**
this liberality is the brave self-respect with which **he**
acknowledges, when needful, the rank from which **he**
sprang. . . .

. . . Edinburgh has been excited lately in **welcoming**
Prof. Forbes of London, who has been presented **to the**
Professorship of Natural Philosophy here; and of **whom**
his friends prophesy, as the 'second Cuvier.'

I met him last night at Prof. Blackie's. I was amused
when he told me he knew me well already through a
'great friend and admirer,' Professor somebody of
Dublin.

One of the most curious experiences of literature, I
think, is the constant discovery of these unknown persons
to whom one is unconsciously 'a friend.'

Then he writes of a young man in whom he is
interested, who had been studying for the Ministry,
but had just been voted a heretic by the Presby-
tery, for a sermon he had preached, on the first

page of which occurred a quotation from 'The Roman.'

He came to me the other night in much trouble of mind, .for it ' will break his mother's heart to see him rejected.'

I am going to see if I can find any literary employment, the hope of which may at once strengthen him to hold out in heresy and mollify the mother's wrath at a living lost.

About this time Mr. John Nichol—now Professor of English Literature in the University of Glasgow—wrote to ask Mr. Dobell to contribute a poem to a College Album, of which he was the editor. The poem was sent, and a frank letter from Mr. Nichol, stating his reasons for not having had it printed, called forth the following reply :

To John Nichol, Esq.

No. 25 Abercrombie Place, Edinburgh : June 10, 1854.

The opinion I have had the pleasure of forming of you from the reports of your friends, and from our brief personal communication, was strengthened not a little by the fine feeling and good taste of your frank and manly letter.

On looking into your Album—(for which will you accept these late thanks ? I had no idea till our friend Smith explained the matter the other day, that the volume was a present; I took for granted it was a subscription copy) —I saw that there were other Englishmen admitted, and inferred, therefore, that there was some unacknowledged objection to the particular poem contributed. I thank you for the friendly freedom with which you have stated the existence of the objection, and the nature of it. I daresay there is a great deal of truth in what you suggest, though on reading the returned MS. I do not perceive any obscurity. But this may merely be from the fact that the mind very readily runs in its own ruts.

Nevertheless, with a view to things much more important than this bagatelle, I will say a word or two which may incidentally explain the exception you take to it. I don't think critics sufficiently recognise the difference between an allegory and a poetical image. And as the difference is one of genesis, I will confine myself to that rather than attend to mere symptomatic distinctions. An allegory is a work of conscious calculation; but the birth of an image is somewhat in this wise. The existence in the poetic mind of any abstract notion (*e.g.* 'Truth'[1]) is attended by a certain state of feeling, (I speak untechnically), and such a mind has a power to select (or if necessary to create by combining) some visible form to correspond to the feeling; such form being precisely that which if it had preceded the feeling, would have called that feeling into existence. But the visible form is selected or created with no respect to the abstract notion; the feeling

---

[1] This had been the title of the poem sent by Mr. Dobell.

produced by that notion and capable of being produced by that form is, as it were, the common measure of both.

You see, therefore, that a poet may not be able to explain his own image; which can never happen with an allegory.

The poet's image will be as much truer than the allegory as nature is truer than man, or instinct than artifice; but it will be a higher order of truth. I was once amused by a person of literary taste, and some critical abilities, who came to me for an explanation of Tennyson's 'Vision of Sin.' I gave him my opinion of the poet's meaning, but he was disappointed and almost indignant He expected a minute rationale, and especially to know what the fountain stood for, and what was meant by the gourds as distinct from the grapes. Whether these things help in any way to a solution of the difficulties regarding the returned MS. is of no sort of importance; but I think you may like to have them as facts of experience, and, so far, useful to reason upon.

Will you be so good as to convey to Professor Nichol the expression of my high estimation, and of my thanks for his kind wishes and friendly message.

With respect to D. he will perhaps bear in mind, when writing on other subjects to either of the electors, that iteration has great effect upon us all, and that the oftener D. is mentioned by his friends the better.

Reciprocating your hope that we may see more of each other, and that our acquaintance may (I think it will), develope into something more substantial, believe me

Yours very faithfully,

SYDNEY DOBELL.

Mr. Nichol—then a young man, nine years Mr. Dobell's junior—wrote his warm thanks, for what he called the kind and generous spirit in which his objections had been received, in a tone and manner which caused this little correspondence to be the beginning of an affectionate friendship. There were many points of sympathy—among them must have been enthusiastic admiration for Kossuth—in reluctantly declining an invitation to meet whom, at the Observatory, the residence of the distinguished author of 'The Architecture of the Heavens' (the father of his correspondent), Mr. Dobell had said that he would right willingly have walked from Edinburgh to Glasgow to welcome the Hungarian Patriot: which cordial expression of 'sympathy in his idolatries' was highly valued by Mr. Nichol.

To the Rev. R. Glover.

No. 25 Abercrombie Place, Edinburgh : June 26.

I think it was about this time last year, that you wrote to me in all the 'sickness' of 'hope deferred,' and I infer from the cards that reached us the other day, that you are now in the very midsummer of happiest accomplishment. Then you were surveying—gloomily enough, I remember— the barren tract of, as it seemed, your inhospitable fortune, *now* 'the wilderness and the solitary place has been made glad, and the desert has rejoiced and blossomed as the rose.' Meanwhile the earth has been but once round the sun, and the child that was then new-born cannot yet speak. How wonderful a lesson has God given to you; and given not in the voice of rebuke, but in the paternal accents of love.

I said just now that you are at present in the ' midsummer' of your happiness. I trust the figure is imperfect, because midsummer implies a crisis and a succeeding declension.

The astronomers tell us, you know, that the 'star of love' has phases like the moon, and I hold that love itself should be a crescent moon, for ever filling, but never full. And if your love is an ideal love, your friends will congratulate you ten years hence upon a ten-times richer and ampler light. May they indeed so congratulate, and may you yourselves—as the best human guarantee of that future congratulation, remember that love is indeed a light. There are few metaphors more thoroughly true than this, and none more important for a lover to understand. Beautiful as love is in itself, it is most beautiful when it is made to fall upon other things and glorify them.

The lovers who look upon love may grow blind, for the eye will tire of the unused light, but let them turn from the dazzling splendour to the substantial world of duty which it enlightens, colours, and consecrates, or to those far celestial spaces, which its beams already penetrate and humanise, and they will know the true blessedness of loving, and the real ecstasy of love. Your imagination

will easily extend the allegory to all its various applications.   That your life may make the imagination **personal**
is the hearty wish of

Yours ever,

Sydney Dobell.

CHAPTER III.

CLERMISTON AND LASSWADE, 1854.

By the time the Midsummer had come, these months in Edinburgh streets had made the ' country souls' of both husband and wife long for green fields, with a longing that was, he says, in his wife's case, ' hunger and thirst.'

His home letters speak of search, made chiefly on foot, for country lodgings—near enough Edinburgh not to be out of easy reach of medical help :

Curiously enough (he says) the country lodgings are nearly as expensive as those in favoured parts of Edinburgh, so we are disappointed in our expectation of saving by the country. I have had some good experiences of Scotch life and populace in the course of my peregrinations. I often wanted dear C. with me as I passed the beautiful girl-children who really seem, in some places, like those of whom of old in the market-place of Rome the good Father said, 'Non angli, sed angeli.' Such perfect faces, so delicate, so harmonious, such golden hair—or rather ～ h hair of *beams*, such streaming sunshine—for it is

not dark enough for gold—such gracious legs, such feet,
'beautiful upon the mountains,' I never before saw in
childhood.   To understand the last part of my rhapsody,
you must understand, what I forgot to tell you before, that
directly summer comes, Scotland takes off its shoes and
stockings. . . . What becomes of all this juvenile beauty
is a puzzle, for the grown-up Scotch lassies are by no
means remarkable for their looks.

After speaking of a favourable review of
'Balder,' which had then lately appeared in
'Fraser,' he says:

I don't see the cogency of my father's objections to
the dicta about genius.   The hound, which he brings as
example, is a good case in point.   He says 'can I not
'*teach*' a hound?'   I answer, and the Reviewer would
answer 'You cannot teach him *to smell*;' if you could,
Nature would not have endowed him with the gift.   So
with genius.   You may teach it its letters, but you can't
teach it to do its own work.   You may teach the hound
to sit on its hind legs, but you can't teach it to know the
track of *game* from all other tracks in the world.   You
can't teach it its natural business. . . . You know the
great canon of military success, 'Maintain your ground
till the enemy has tired himself, and then pour down
upon him.'   The law holds good for every kind of earthly
warfare, and does not impede or supersede the heavenly,
but rather gives the appropriate vehicle for the sustaining
afflatus, or the descending thunderbolt.   In coming upon

this military maxim, shortly since, I was interested to find
how instinctively I have always unconsciously obeyed it
in all matters of contest.

To his Father and Mother.

Abercrombie Place : July 14.

. . . And so you are actually upon making a family
tour—a ‘ *tour de force* ’ in every sense,—for you will be
quite a little army. We had a lingering hope, not
dreaming that it was to be a migration of the clan, but
only an excursion of the chiefs—that you would have gone
to the Highlands perhaps, and taken us in your way . . .
it would have refreshened our eyes. But I would not,
even for that refreshment, interfere with your present
plan, for I can see that it may be of inconceivable satisfaction to my father. To visit, after such an interval,
and under circumstances so changed, the scenes of his
childhood—and his father’s grave. It will be a pleasant
trip for all of you, through such truly English and
historic ‘ wealds ’ and coasts, but you will all have to
remember, that you cannot see what he sees; that what
to you are trees, roads, stone-walls, and all manner of
realities, are to him

> the enchanted elements
> On a magician’s table, poor to look on,
> But things that being moved perplex the stars
> And knot the threads of nature.

Forgive the quotation, but I knew no other body’s

words—as the Scotch say—so much to the point. God
guard the voyage and bless the return.

We have at last secured country lodgings, and secured
them after all near Craigcrook. They are in a farm-
house on a hill, commanding a wonderful view of the
Pentlands, and within a stone's throw of a point from
which, standing and turning round, you see the Forth,
the City, the Pentlands, and the sea. Then we have the
use of the beautiful Craigcrook grounds, which join the
fields in which the house is. . . . Good Mr. Hunter has
exerted himself to get these lodgings for us, for the
farmer refused to let any part of the house, when I called
in the course of my peregrinations. The Hunters are
extremely kind to us, with the heartiest of good will. . . .

Although I have seen something of the country and
the people in these wanderings, which have now occupied
nearly a fortnight, I am not at all sorry to come to the
end of them. They have not been without their pleasant
and unpleasant adventures. Some of the farmeresses I
found extremely amiable, and some of their dogs uncom-
monly ferocious. One lady took me into her room and
feasted me on cream and cookies; another was so good
as to refresh me with milk, and to volunteer a walk with
me towards the next likely homestead, and all of them I
found to be wonderfully communicative, after the first
few sentences, and laudably anxious to forward my wishes
to the utmost. But nothing in the way of experience of
English farm-houses would prepare you for the barbarous
accommodation of the Scotch. I hardly found tenantable
rooms in any of them; and the sitting-room we have now

taken I shall have to re-ceil, to furnish, and to provide with a stove!

To M——.

. . . I need not tell you what to-morrow is.—[The anniversary of his wedding-day.]—But it has even an unusual significance to me as being the tenth from our wedding, the close of so large and well-defined an era in so eventful a portion of this commencement of eternity. How the Drama of Life with me has seemed cast into these ten-year acts. Three times ten years ago I was born! Ten years after I saw for the first time her who has never since left my consciousness. In half ten years more we were engaged, and at the end of the other half married. In the next half I finished my first book, in the following my second.

How at such times one can understand Napoleon when, after Waterloo, he sat in that terrible arm-chair for four-and-twenty hours motionless. If I had not somewhat divided the thought through many preparatory days, it would seem a burden too heavy to be borne. The strange wonders of the past, in happiness, in sorrow, and—whether sorrow or happiness—in blessing! The weight of the forward shadow of responsibility, and of such a future as these 'latter days.' . . .

To ——.

Abercrombie Place.

. . . Your last letter gave me a rare pleasure in testifying to the growth of your own convictions in a direction where mine have long been very strong. You will find somewhere in ' Balder' the question—' Who is our King ? ' That question I hope to devote my life to answer.

As a link in the chain of thought, I have some notion, before beginning ' Balder: Part the Second,' of writing another book, and am strongly drawn to the Maccabees as a subject. The analogues of the time and circumstances are strong in Israel now and Israel then. . . .

To his Father and Mother.

Abercrombie Place : August 4th.

So you will actually be at Hastings when you receive this letter ! . . . While you are in Sussex could you not take the boys and girls to some of the ancient places connected with the former Dobells—Street Place and Folkington Hall, or their ruins ? A chivalrous and romantic feeling with regard to family is, I feel sure, a refining and elevating thing when not overdone; and the localities at Cranbrook, though transfigured and glorified to yourselves by recollections of persons and events, are not exactly of the kind to do much good that way to the young folks, who have no such hallowing associations. It seems to me it would be admirable to let them look *through* them to a more poetic family past yet further back. . . . I don't know when we shall be able to leave Edinburgh. E. is not yet allowed to get up.

All our friends have been very kind. There has been a constant rain of flowers, grapes, and enquiries. But we are thirsting for the country, this fine hot weather.

In his first home letter from Clermiston he writes, on August 18, of his wife's delight at country sights and sounds, so long denied, so constantly desired, and of her joy to be in the fields again.

Of the 'Sonnets on the War,' a little volume, the joint production of Sydney Dobell and Alexander Smith, Mr. Dobell's share was chiefly written at Clermiston; where he remained till the approach of winter made 'the windy hill' untenable.

Trying to amuse those to whom his home letters are addressed, he speaks of having lunched in Edinburgh,

in a room full of nations; I was for an hour between a Danish Secretary of State and a Norwegian Chief Justice. It was a fine study in intonation, dialect and natural character, both speaking variations of the same language. Soon afterwards I was amused at the difference between true and would-be aristocracy. Some young fine-gentleman who was present, began to speak, with delightful languor, to the little Danish statesman, who complimented him on the extreme beauty of Edinburgh.

'Yaas,' answered the youngster, with an *ennuyé* drawl that must have cost him considerable effort, ' it is a beautiful city, but I do think the very dullest I ever was in. I'm sure you must find it so. There is no life, no—'

'Your are right, sair,' quickly interposed the little

courtier with great animation, ' it is for certain not to be compared with *Glasgow*; life! there is life indeed. The waggons, the carts, the omnibuses, the carriages, the warehouses, the merchandise—Glasgow is the city, sair, a very grand city indeed!'

You should have seen the unspeakable disgust in the face of the young exquisite. Speaking of foreigners, reminds me of a Dutchman with whom the Hunters, who have just been on a Highland tour, travelled for several days. He knew but little English, and was obliged to conjure it to his memory by a process which is the finest specimen of the law of association that I ever remember to have met with. You are to suppose him in a new hotel.

'Waitere.' 'Yes, Sir.' 'You are to call me at six o'clock to-morrow. Eef you call me, I shall wake. Eef I wake, I shall have been asleep. Eef I go to sleep, I must have a bed. Ah, that is it—I must have a bed—let me have a bed!'

Speaking of unfriendly coldness shown towards him by a man whom he had earnestly befriended —and continued to befriend—on account of a somewhat unfavourable verdict he had pronounced on a MS. submitted to him—he says:

That —— should think me mistaken is very natural and unavoidable, the absurdity is in supposing that quoting authorities will change my opinion in such a matter. . . . My verdict—condensed—was 'Good in many places, very good in some places, but masterly in no place.'

On Thursday evening, just as I had returned from Edinburgh, Alexander Smith arrived on one of his brotherly visits, and he had hardly sat down, before Professor William Thomson of Glasgow, who is staying for some days in Edinburgh, rode in. In the midst of the conversation, came my father's letter. I glanced at the contents, and seeing it was on a difficult business, put it safely aside to be studied after they were gone.

I read it before going to bed, and gave it another consideration in the morning; but before I could write a reply —— appeared to spend the day with us, and while he was here two of the Miss C.'s walked in. Under this advent of unexpected guests in a cottage room, with no one to protect E. from an undue share in the conversation, you will easily believe that I might have wished very much to write without being able to take up a pen. . . . I can fancy how exquisite must be the English summer. Last evening as, after the most beautiful day of this year, I returned down the lane from seeing —— away, and looked through the calm still wayside trees, upon the wonderful evening scene, the words came to—not through —my lips, ' holy and beautiful;' and then followed the consciousness of what it is I have looked and felt for in Scotland in vain. This was the first evening in all our eight months' sojourn in which those words could be said. The Scotch weather is always one perennial fuss : one loveless selfish agitation of unmeaning winds.

To a young Sister.

You have been such a kind and indefatigable correspondent, that I can resist no longer some more individual answer than you receive in my ' family letters.'

How welcome are the home details that fill your despatches, you, who have never been ' an exile,' can hardly tell. From the length and colour of the grass, the progress of the hay-making, or the ' whitening unto harvest,' down to the capture of the quest, and the line of grey hair upon Jeannie's back, there is not a fact great or small that we could afford to lose. I am so glad to see your love and keen perception of the facts of Nature, and trust they will continue to grow with your growth. The principles which men learn from a million facts are really contained in any one of the million, and the most stupendous occurrence in the universe is really not more marvellous than the least observed—the grey hair upon Jeannie's back is truly as wondrous as the Milky Way—who can tell *how* either came to be ? Once ask yourself in any case ' *how* ' and ' *why*,' and you begin to learn the value of that saying of Scripture about ' the sparrow ' that ' falleth to the ground.' Learn, therefore, to observe carefully the facts around you, and to think closely upon what you take note of: and whenever you have time to spare, write us a long account both of observations and thoughts.

To his Father and Mother.

South Clermiston : October 19.

Oh that I could be home with a thought, and see the silent golden English autumn!—though there are things at home that I long to see far more. In every season the difference between England and Scotland is distinct and characteristic, but in none, I think, more than in this. At home the wide, grand, calm, melancholy time dies ' like an Emperor standing,' and falls a corpse of gold. Here the perpetual flurry of the weather pulls it to pieces, like a traveller in a flock of wolves. At home every colour of leaf, and every stage and age of death may be seen together on the tree, till some November night brings them all down at once: here a ghastly green, that grows daily more spectral, carries an old-maid-like sort of horrid youth into the very jaws of the grave. Every day finds the trees thinner and thinner, but still grinning with a grisly green. The Edinburgh winds have set in, and we begin to think that our position on these heights will not be much longer tenable. You, among our kind English storms, which seem only like one who loves you in a passion, can hardly fancy—indeed, I could hardly realise them till they returned—the maniac, pitiless, senseless rabidness with which these nor'westers attack one. A charge of Cossacks—with all their noses frost-bitten— would not be so confounding. We are thinking of descending into the valley, nearer Edinburgh, and in a more protected situation; but do not propose ˊto go into the town. . . . We shall not be able to get so beautiful a place in the vale, but I feel beauty—with an invalid household—must be surrendered for comfort. A long lane of Scotch snow, three miles and a half of wintry tempest beyond it, and a house whose stone walls are *soaked* by the dry wind, are too dear a purchase even of a home whence you can every day see into the Highlands. The place is curious in its combination of Scottish advantages. From the field in which the house stands you look across the Forth—which is beautiful as the Lake of Geneva—to 'Dumferline gang,' where the king 'drank the bluid red wine;' this very Clermiston is the 'Clermiston Lea,' which in the old ballad 'rang back the trumpets of bonnie Dundee;' and, walking hence to Edinburgh, I have the Pentlands by my side—stained everywhere with Covenanting blood—and pass the old castle of Napier of Merchiston. Standing in this field, too, and looking south-west, you dive into the heart of the Highlands, and find yourself—like some wanderer at the Congress of Vienna—I beg pardon of the mountains—unawares in the company of kings. That camel-backed hill is Ben Ledi, that other camel Ben Venue, that low cone Ben More, the farther one Ben Voirlich, and the mere apex of cloud—far above yonder table land—Ben Lomond.

After speaking of various interesting visitors, past and impending, he says:

If so many people are coming out to see us as the experience of the last few weeks promises, we must in our next lodging secure more than a single sitting-room; for E. is often too ill to talk much, and sometimes even to *see* a stranger

Anxiety to work this winter, and the impossibility of doing so if, to his cares for his wife, were added crowding social engagements, was his reason for not re-entering Edinburgh.

Lasswade was fixed on as a suitable locality for the winter months; as being the most sheltered spot in the neighbourhood, and, while far enough from Edinburgh to give a sufficient reason for declining evening engagements, near enough to be accessible to the doctor. The new resting-place is described as ' a comfortable snug cottage, tolerably pretty without and wonderfully cosey within; and containing—no trifling item in its excellence—two spare bedrooms.'

The Rev. Alfred Vaughan, author of 'The Mystics,' and his wife, are first mentioned, among many other interesting people, as personally known about this time. Of another new acquaintance he speaks, as ' having all the symptoms of one who is the fragment of a genius '—'there is a distinct difference,' he adds, ' between the men who stop short of genius but have great talent, and the men who have somewhat the nature of genius but seem

fragments or dilutions of it.' Brodie, a young
Edinburgh sculptor, on a statue by whom he had
written a Sonnet, and who afterwards executed a
bust of Mrs. Dobell, is spoken of; and the starting,
by two young literary men of his acquaintance, of
a penny newspaper, called 'the War-Telegraph,' is
mentioned as 'an admirable instance of how two
young men who really are in earnest, and have not
their eyes and energies weakened by other pursuits,
will find modes of getting money.'

Though not occurring just at this time, we
may give here a short sketch of a character which
he describes as—

representative of a curious, interesting, but by no means
numerous class of mind, that which forms the *gradus*
between genius and mediocrity. . . . A mind of well
furnished and good capacity, lacking no faculties, nor over-
abounding in any, seeing clearly wherever it sees at all,
possessing a representative for all the great and good
qualities of humanity, a genius in nothing, but clever
everywhere—this is the most intolerant intellect alive. . .

To his Father and Mother.

Clermiston : November 2nd.

This day last year we left Amberley for Detmore. To-
day we are again sending off our trunks and boxes, but
not, alas, to the same destination. How tenderly we turn

to the memory of that last visit. How fondly look forward to that time to come, when it may please God that we again set out homewards. . . .

Lasswade is a village in a green valley on the banks of the small river Esk. Noble trees and grassy undulations remind me of home; and Nature no longer looks as if she had driven a hard bargain—as if she clothed the earth by contract, and was resolved to make a good thing of it. On the top of one of the hills above the stream, and looking away over a level arable country of no great beauty, to the distant Moffat hills, is the house to which we are going. . . .

. . . Did I ever mention the strange effect of this neighbourhood to the Pole, the long summer days and enormous winter nights? At midsummer we could read long past ten o'clock. At midwinter the wave of darkness will return, and the flow will be proportionate to the ebb.

. . . I am going, I trust in God, to begin to work on 'Balder: Part II.' It is to contain, among other things, three or four complete dramas, showing, as far as I have yet determined, the innate yearning of mankind for a millennial state, as shown in the mythologies, creeds, and social life of Classic, Gothic, Jewish, and Mediæval times. (I think of beginning with the Jewish, and the History of the Maccabees). . . .

The whole book, thus planned, is spoken of as the portal to that future Epic he hoped to write.

To the same.

. . . We are very much pleased with our 'wee bit housie,' as the Scotch call these parts of houses. . . .

Kind thanks to dear Pater for his anxieties about 'Balder: Part II.' I am afraid I cannot gratify him with regard to size, for I hope to make it even longer than 'Part First;' but, from the subject and construction, it will necessarily be what he wishes as to objective and cordial interest. In Part First, I wished and planned to represent the subjective and internal phasis of the character; in Part Second, faith and happiness will have changed the scene of activity. The three or four dramas, of which I spoke, will be contained, as kernels, in a shell of domestic life and story. The dramas themselves will, I hope, be full of the most vigorous human action. . . . I say '*will*,' but you know the qualifications with which that word must always be written. But I think if I can be true to so great a design, I shall live for the sake of its accomplishment.

It may, we think, be said that this feeling—that he should live to do the work he had planned—*never* left him.

To his Father and Mother.

Everything, just now, from the delay of the second edition of 'Balder,' *down to* the salvation of Europe, is

depending upon the war and Sebastopol!—[After speaking
of Alexander Smith, and their proposed companionship in
a volume of War Sonnets, he says:] '*A propos* of poetry—
what a curious crop of admiration, that little ballad of
'Ravelston'[1] has reaped.   I am receiving praises of it from
all quarters, and from critics of all sorts and sizes.   Their
enthusiasm amuses me, because it is sometimes warmest
in those in whom 'Balder' awoke little regard.   Now I
could, I believe, engage to supply 'Ravelstons' on easy
terms by the dozen, while 'Balder' was the highest effort
of my poetic faculties.   However, as successful ballad-
writing is admitted to be one of the best evidences of a
poet's completeness, (as requiring the spontaneous and
simultaneous exercise of nearly every poetic quality), I
am not at all dissatisfied with the popular satisfaction. . .

. . . You must not suppose that sonneteering has
occupied me altogether these last few days.   I have, in
addition, sketched the plan of one of my dramas satisfactorily, and have partly worked some of it in.

To the same.

Lasswade: November 24th.

. . . Yesterday evening, after a day of sleet, the large
interfering stars shone down all manner of promises of
frost.

Have I mentioned the size and splendour of these
Scottish stars?   The northern heaven seems compensation

---

[1] 'Keith of Ravelston,' afterwards entitled 'A Nuptial Eve,' and
published in 'England in Time of War,' had been printed in an Edinburgh paper.

for the sterility of the earth; and I have seen no clouds
and stars to be compared with those of Scotland. In
England, you look up for the stars; in Scotland, the stars
find you out. If during a dark night out of doors the
clouds suddenly clear off, you start as if a twinkle was at
your elbow. I mean, I should start if I were of a startish
nature; as it is I feel a start *in posse*, which, with one or
two exceptions, is the nearest approach to that exercise I
ever remember to have taken. The clouds are marvellous
studies of grandeur and colour; but the exquisite warm
melting clouds that we see in English Aprils are here unknown.

The weather overhead yesterday was not more gloomy
than the temper of the city below. Edward Forbes, the
professor and philosopher, whom I have often mentioned
in my letters, died on Saturday, and was yesterday buried.
I don't know when I have been so much shocked by the
death of one so little personally known to me. He was
still young, in the prime of mental power; and after a
long youth and early manhood of wonderful research and
discovery, he had just begun to share with mankind a
wealth of knowledge so solid, so various, so rare, and so
widely valuable that it will be very long before we see it
in one ownership again. He combined what so few
scientific men combine, the philosophic with the perceptive
qualities; and his perfect possession of all the facts of
natural science, in every one of its provinces, enabled his
philosophy to connect, identify and organise in a way that
would be impossible to any narrower range of view. Last
year he was suddenly appointed to the chair of Natural

History here; and the exertions he made to commence his Lectures instantly, and carry them on successfully, notwithstanding the disadvantages of haste, are said to have hastened his death.

. . . .

He kindly invited me to attend his Lectures, and I went to many of them: I was not more pleased with the intellectual power displayed in them, than with the sweet and gentle qualities he showed at other times.

I have seen him sit for an hour together, making paper animals for children, which he did with his fingers with a marvellous facility, *tearing* them out without scissors. He looked so strong and well and vigorous. . . . All the day after the news of his death, I heard a voice, almost supernaturally persevering, in my ears: 'Work while it is called to-day; the night cometh, when no man can work.'

To M——.

. . . Yesterday I sketched the plan of one of the dramas of my next book. I told you, I think, my intention to have three or four dramas contained in it, but I don't think I have mentioned the *ideas* of these. The whole book, you know, is, like Part I., a preparation for the future epic. As that is, if God please, to represent the ideal structure of human society—man in the state for which God created him—a Theocratic world—*this* is to illustrate the universal tendency of the race towards the estate for which they were formed. My present plan is, therefore, to have a Classic, a Jewish, a Mediæval, and

an Eighteenth-century drama, showing how, in the mythologies of old time, the dispensation of Judaism, the Romish
Church of later days, and the Communism of the French
Revolution, the great necessity displayed itself in various
shapes. That in Judaism God Himself typified it, while
the world was not yet ready for its realisation ; and that
in Papal Rome it organised itself, but failed because only
worked by fallible *agents*.

These dramas are to be surrounded by a setting of
nineteenth-century life, and, as you may easily perceive,
afford in themselves the most magnificent opportunities . . . Yesterday I sketched the plan of the Mediæval
story.

To the Rev. J. B. Paton.

Lasswade : December 21.

After speaking of the physician's hope that his
wife's cure was almost completed, he wrote:

I tell you this, but I have not yet myself come to
recognise it. I know it as a truth, but have not fully
realised it as a blessing. My heart in seasons of great
sorrow and trial becomes calm as a stone, and from that
petrifaction it is not wholly melted . . . If indeed ' this
cup might pass ' from her ! But more precious than that
alleviation is the knowledge that, whether it come or not,
she can complete, with her whole heart, the sublime saying
of her Lord.

In that book of Sonnets which I hope not many days

hence to send you, there is one which I think you will specially enjoy—that in which the volume is dedicated to *her.* You will recognise that it is by Alexander Smith; but how few of those who misjudge him from some passages in the 'Life Drama' will be prepared for its lofty beauty of holiness.

Let me, in a word—for I must not spare more to the subject just now—warn you not to expect so much from the other sonnets as your letter implies. The form of the Sonnet forbids anything like *adequacy*, though I think you will confess we have done more with that form, in some cases, than we had, perhaps, a right to anticipate. We preferred to confine ourselves to sonnets, from the feeling that till the great events of which we speak are toned down by time any mortal description of them would fall dead on the public ear, and be but candle to sunshine in the public eye.

The following passage relates to the novel of a dear friend, of which he was anxious to secure a suitable review in ' The Eclectic : '

It seems to me by no means necessary that the review should be devoted to that one story: though a critique on that single book, if preceded or followed by an excellent essay on the general subjects connected with it, would form an admirable article . . . The great secret in a review, so far as its practical use to a *book* is concerned, is, to take care that there shall be at least one or two sentences which would answer as extracts for advertisements.

This ought always to be borne in mind when the book reviewed is one we wish to advance. The advertised extracts are all that the general public sees of the article, and the most brilliant essay may be useless *to the book* from the fact that it has nothing which can thus be made universal and permanent.

To his Father and Mother.

Lasswade : December 29, 1854.

You will receive this on the last day of the year ! With what prayers from and for all of us will this strange wild year go out to God ! What dead men's bones, or what deep sea-jewels, shall the New Year bring us not out of the dark and tossing future ? What terrible vision, or what face of divine reality, shall be shown from behind ' His frowning Providence ' ? Happy for us that neither years nor sparrows fall ' without our Father,' and that God Who ' clothes the grass of the field ' can so clothe the new years that are also coming up, as that ' Solomon in all his glory was not arrayed like one of these.' But whatever is to come, dearest Father and Mother, let the old year end with loves from us both to all of you and the New Year begin with the same.

To C——.

Lasswade : December 31, 1854.

And this is the last day of the year ! Of what a wild and stormy year. Not only tempestuous in the broad sea

of the world, but on the shores and in the havens that
are so well known and so dear.

One almost lives, as at Alma or Inkermann, with a
sense that the air is full of balls and with a terrible calm
from the very fact that they are so many. You may
'duck' to a single shot, but under fire the danger is too
great to be recognised. You are content, so far as yourself is concerned, to say, with the soldier, 'Each bullet
has its billet,' and to praise God that at all events it must
be signed in heaven.

Indeed, if one had but one's single self, how fearless,
how unanimous would be the march and the battle of this
world! *Fiat voluntas*—and 'Forward!' He need fear
no weapons to whom the worst that can happen is to be
hit, and the worst hit that can be hitten but ends the
knowledge of it. But directly we begin to love, we give
hostages to fate, and are at the mercy of every wind.
Then something more than courage, higher than philosophy, wider than piety, diviner and completer than any
single human faculty, is required to say as it ought to be
said—'Thy Will be done.' To say it from any lower
reason is not virtue, but indifference.

Speaking of this era of his brother's life—
which was that of the beginning and progress of
the Crimean War—Clarence Dobell writes:

He had always felt the keenest interest in things
military; and his imagination realised the tragic details
of war, even when war was far removed. The battles on

the Sutlej were the first important engagements that occurred during his lifetime, and the noble poem of Ferozepore, called 'A Musing on a Victory,' [1] shows how his mind was stirred by the news from a battle-field so many thousand miles away : but in 1854 to 1855 he saw his country engaged in a struggle for life or death. English blood was flowing, Englishmen were suffering and dying by thousands, and the reality of the contest was brought home to the dullest and most ignorant. No wonder, therefore, that the spectacle woke in him a storm of patriotic emotion. . . .

Hitherto his love for England had been tempered by a keen appreciation of the cold, cramped and prosaic side of the national character, and he had been fond of extolling the virtues of other nations at the expense of his own. But it is only in time of danger that Englishmen appear in their true character, the Crimean War and the Indian Mutiny brought out the old virtues, and from that time Sydney was a fervid patriot, tendering his country his first allegiance in all things. Patriotism became a ruling passion that held him to the last, and finds expression in the last expiring flush of his genius, the truly called 'Saga'—'England's Day.' A poem that, despite of a tone of reckless defiance displeasing to English common sense, contains, as I think, some of the grandest lines ever sung by a war-poet, lines fired with the very spirit of the old sea-kings, and that no man who was not a Greek, or a Scandinavian, could have sung.

---

[1] Page 289, vol. I. of Collected Edition.

From reminiscences of this time sent to the Editors by Mr. Daniel Gorrie, one of those many young men friends who gathered about Sydney Dobell during his sojourn in Scotland—(and who are spoken of frequently and with cordial interest in his letters home)—we extract what follows.

After speaking of the impression received— that Mr. Dobell in completing 'Balder' planned to act in harmony with the advice given to all young poets by the author of 'Festus,' 'to work all things into their work'—as the fruit of conversations during walks in the neighbourhood of Edinburgh, the writer says:

The magnificent views were enjoyed by Mr. Dobell with an enthusiasm that was not of the loudly demonstrative kind, but that stirred the fountains of thought and feeling, and sometimes found vent in utterances that might be called poems in embryo. The 'Sketches from Nature,' which appear among the selections from his papers published after his death, show what a close observer he was of all the forms, tints and sounds of the external world. He had the eye and ear of a naturalist as well as of a poet.

A description is then given of a strawberry-and-cream feast (a favourite Edinburgh summer entertainment) at Mr. Dobell's rooms in Aber-

crombie Place, when among the guests were
Thomas Spencer Baynes, Eneas Dallas, Alexander
Smith, Alexander Nicolson, and George Cupples.

After the feast the whole party were driven
in open carriages to Craigcrook, at the foot of
Corstophine, once the classical retreat of Lord
Jeffrey, at that time the residence of Mr. Hunter.
'It was a delightful evening,' the writer says,
'everybody was in the best of spirits and the
drive was an eminently agreeable one.' Professor
Blackie was at Craigcrook when the party arrived.
'The learned, able, and versatile Professor had
evidently a high admiration of Mr. Dobell's noble
character and poetical powers. The latter, though
humour could hardly be considered his forte,
excited considerable merriment by making a slight
alteration in one of the lines of Mr. Smith's 'Life
Drama,' as an example how little was needed to
cause a descent from the tragic to the comic. The
line which ran—

> Like a pale martyr with his shirt *of* fire,

he changed into—

> Like a pale martyr with his shirt *on* fire.

It was also on this occasion, I think, that he
made a pat quotation from Milton's Sonnet ' on his

blindness.' In the act of assisting one of the party
to fruit, he made a long pause, holding the spoon
in his hand, until he had concluded a remark on
which his mind was engaged at the time. Recalled
from his fit of absent-mindedness by the touch of
a gentle hand, he quietly remarked, smiling blandly
the while,—

> ' They also *serve* who only stand and wait.'

The writer, also, recalls having been sometimes
present, later in the same year, when Alexander
Smith and Sydney Dobell met, in the quiet Lasswade Cottage Mr. and Mrs. Dobell were then
occupying, to read over what each had written (of
the ' Sonnets on the War '), to exchange criticism
and select new topics, and says :

> I can testify that their criticisms of each other's work
> were of a thoroughly honest and plain-spoken character,
> but I never witnessed a quarrel between them, and they
> almost invariably accepted each other's suggestions. So
> sweet was Mr. Dobell's disposition that a frown on his
> brow was as rare as the shadow of a cloud on halcyon
> seas. After the sonnet business was settled, and set aside
> for the day, the stream of conversation, which never be-
> came a brawling argumentative brook, flowed on pleasantly
> until the time came to part.

Many disappointments—in regard to obtaining

letters—have been experienced in preparing these
Memorials. Mr. Dobell's own rule was carefully
to preserve all letters—regarding the destruction
of records of the Past and Present as wrong done
to the Future. It cannot be unfair to remark that,
in a few instances, his correspondents may have
felt natural and justifiable reluctance to give up
letters which might, if used carelessly, have shown
them as they would not have wished to appear.
To these the Editors venture to say, that had more
confidence been shown, it would not have been
abused; so strong has been the desire to do
nothing, in the preparation of these pages, inconsistent with the tolerant charity which filled the
heart, and regulated the life, of him who is the
subject of them.

If, by his easy accessibility and wide sympathy,
he laid himself open to a large experience of
the selfishness, the indolence, the forgetfulness, the
ingratitude of human nature, he had, also, many
other and happier experiences, and it was on these
that he loved to dwell. The other things were not
only forgiven, but in many cases, both his own
good deed and the evil return for it, literally forgotten.

Accident, by fire or water, has destroyed his

part of more than one intimate and interesting correspondence. Of one of these—with a friend for whom he had the warm affection of an elder for a younger brother—it is peculiarly disappointing to get no trace; because these letters contained fuller, clearer, and more detailed statements of their writer's religious opinions, hopes, aims, and aspirations, at this time of his life, when he was described by a talented and speculative acquaintance as at once the most orthodox and the most transcendental man he knew—than can be given in any other manner.

There can be no impropriety in quoting, from the other side of the correspondence, a sentence or two to show the way in which this brotherly affection was returned; as affording one instance of the feeling he inspired in many a fine and ardent nature.

I should like to fill in a short pause in my daily work with a few words to you—somewhat as sailors love to fill the gaps in their toil with singing . . .

Remembering that your words written or spoken never yet reached me without my heart having thanked you for some new strength and some new good—so, I never think of you without a wondering thankfulness to God for our friendship, which has been more to me and for me than I can well tell in words. This is harping

upon an old string, which I should not think of sounding
to you were it so empty a thing as praise.   But I know,
to one who thinks as you do, it is no small matter to have
been one means of turning to simpler and nobler paths
feet which might, I sometimes think, have wandered far
and wide without finding what was sought.

CHAPTER IV.

PUBLICATION OF 'SONNETS ON THE WAR,' 1855.

AT the beginning of this year the little volume of
'Sonnets on the War, in which Sydney Dobell
and Alexander Smith appeared in literary partner-
ship, was published.   These poems were well
received ; and, in literary circles, gave rise to a
good deal of interested speculation as to the
respective authorship of each Sonnet.

One friend, himself both poet and critic, wrote,
in acknowledging the book :

I am more ready to say of a sonnet which I can at all
decide upon—that it is Smith's than that it is yours.
I suppose it is because you have many manners and do
not repeat yourself.

The same friend said :

How deeply I felt that second sonnet of dedication,
and I like Smith for writing it.   I knew he would feel it,
but I did not know whether he could thus express it.
And sure I am that there is not a soul who has seen the
ly Una' to whom the dedication refers who

would not breathe the same heart prayer that she might
be restored.

To a young Sister.

Lasswade: January 5, 1855.

I write my Sunday's letter to you to-day, in return for
the many welcome letters my kind mindful sister has
written me. And since a letter is but a poor acknowledgment of them all, I hope to send to-morrow a copy of
the Sonnets, with your name written in it. But you know
that book and letter are but the requital of your pen,
ink, paper and entertainment : your brother's love for you
and hopes in you are the only return for the feelings and
the remembrance which set pen, ink and paper in motion.

We have heard with great interest, I assure you, of the
new edition of ' Pups ' which have succeeded to your en-
thusiasms, and have not a doubt that they are all your
glowing affection describes them. If they are white and
of really pure breed, I wish you would bring up one for
me. I am sure all these new canine families will not
make you neglect little Jeannie. Give her many messages
from us, and pull her ears for me.   .

It was curious to read your account of the mild spring-
like English weather in the midst of the wintry snow-scene
around us. I shall want you to send me close accounts
of the progress of Spring in the dear remembered fields :
and you will, I know, send me word when the very first
snowdrop comes up in the garden. I don't care to have
any *garden* primroses, for tame primroses are faithless to

> the holy rites and customs due
> Of free unconquered seasons ;

and a little soft breath and fair seeming will win them over to Czar Winter as easily as the Lieutenant of ' The Tiger.' But I can't tell you how I should value one of the first you can find really wild. The banks of the stream (where they are tall and shaggy with dead grass), a little below Doweles' farm are where I have found them earliest. . . .

. . . How glad and thankful I was to receive at last that letter from ——. . . . I have so long felt that the question of whether he would realise all my hopes for his future, would be answered mainly by the fact of whether or not he could arrive at this religious estate into which he has now come, that it would be difficult to over-estimate my joy in his confession ; and in his confession not only of the estate itself, but of all the happy solutions, and clearing off of difficulties and mental fogs, which I knew would follow the one great achievement. God, Who has guided him so far and so early, direct him even to the end ! And how near the end may be ! the end that is of the present arrangement of society ; for the more I think on the matter, the more I feel convinced that the golden age of the coming Theocracy, under Christ, is not to be a thousand years only, but more than three hundred thousand.

Ask Papa if he has heard that Sebastopol is Greek for Armageddon. Sebasto, the august, polis, city— Greek. Arma, the august, geddon, city—Hebrew. It may be a coincidence only, but it is interesting to know that Armageddon relates to some one of the mighty cities of the world. But I must not enter on this subject to-day.

To his youngest Sister.

Lasswade : January 12.

After the stern rebuke I received from your high mightiness a few days ago—a repetition, too, of one which your majesty had previously administered—I suppose I must address my ' Sunday letter ' to your august and—dare I hope ?—propitiated acceptance. The offering would have been more in quantity—if less in quality—but that, instead of beginning to write at the proper time, I followed a voice that was singing to me in the air and learned from it another lyric for that collection of ' Lyrics on the War.' I will copy it for you at the end of this letter. You must fancy it the song of a solitary hopeless sadness—of some one of the many who are left lonely at home with hardly a chance of seeing the ' soldier-laddie ' again. . . .

. . . How the name of Rossley sends my imagination up the fields, and down the road above which, from the Coxhorne gate, its grey gable and nine elm trees, and glittering morning fields, made one of the views I loved best in the world. Spring hardly seems like Spring out of sight of those hills. You must kiss dear N. many times for me for her little box of primroses. I dared not hope to have any so soon. . . . The weather here is damp and mild, and I heard two thrushes singing to-day ! . . .

No artist has really learned the mysteries of clouds and skies till he has studied in Scotland. Our bedroom window looks towards the east, and many a sunrise as I have seen at home, I have never known anything so imperial—nay, so divine—as the god-like majesty of what we see here day by day. Was anything noticeable in the English sky on New Year's Eve ? Here there was the most marvellous—not the most beautiful—appearance I ever beheld. When the sun began to rise, the sky, at an enormous height, was delicately powdered over with those very small clouds which are called ' cirrhi.' Instead, however, of being separate clouds, they were woven like the thinnest of lace veils over the heavens. When the uprising sun sent his slanting beams into them, a quarter of the sky became of the colours of the rainbow, there was no arch—and the clouds when transfigured thus were not perceptible as clouds—but it seemed as though that part of Heaven were roofed with iridescent mother-of-pearl. Every colour of the prism was there in perfection, and you would have delighted to see in particular, the celestial violet-beds that stretched away, as it seemed, to immeasurable distances—kingdoms and continents of violets. This continued in full force from nine o'clock till nearly ten. The sun was white all day, and the moon rose green. . . .

When I do not write, you must be sure it is not because his dear little sister is absent from the remembrance of her loving brother,

SYDNEY.

' I remember ' he writes to a friend who had just passed through a crisis of anxiety,

how about this time last year I was looking forward to a physician's verdict—a verdict of ' cureable ' or ' cureless.' I remember how that day—the day of decision—hung like a black veil between me and the more distant future ; how I lifted my eyes towards the coming Spring, but could not see the primroses. . . . I think I shall one day write something on ' The First Eclipse ; ' for what the race felt then each individual of us has known more or less.

Early in the spring Mr. and Mrs. Dobell left Lasswade, and for a time remained in Edinburgh.

To his Father and Mother.

North Hanover Street.

I have learnt since leaving that romantic little valley, that you may add a new interest to the list of its illustrations which I sent you some time ago : Christopher North lived there till within a short time of his death. But one of the curiosities of this Scotland, is, that itself and its inhabitants, go where you will, are just a story or a flesh-and-blood history.

The other day somebody happened to mention that a son of Lord Something Douglas, who was next me at table, was the direct descendant of the man who brought home Robert Bruce's heart from Palestine. On my expressing some very natural interest at such a breathing chronicle,

a lady at my elbow said, ' What will you say to me then,
for I'm the lineal descendant of the Bruce himself!'
Not long ago I was pressed to come to a party because a
Mr. Something would be there, ' a great critic in art, and
the heir of the man who bore the banner at Chevy Chase.'
And these curious resurrections of the past are not rare
ghosts that walk in out-of-the-way places, but things that
spring up before you in the streets, or glare like old
gargoyles from all manner of unexpected walls.   You
walk along the ' old Town' with any antiquary, and,
passing a dark turning, say, ' Queer alley that.' ' Yes,'
says your companion, ' that is where Queen Mary waited
while Bothwell was lurking up yonder close the night he
killed Darnley.'

You see by my beginning to gossip again, that I am
putting off the invalid : though, to say sooth, I am hardly
in writing order. . . . You will be glad to know that the
Sonnets seem generally successful.   Did I tell you I had
a sweet-natured note from Tennyson about them ? . . .
The Dedicatory Sonnets seem especially popular : and
——'s sentiment, ' I could love Smith for having written
them,' appears to be very generally entertained.

Mr. Dobell was at this time warmly interesting
himself about a young poet, then personally unknown to him.

In one of his home letters he says :

—— has already some notion of coming to live in
Edinburgh ; and I am inclined to wish he may carry it out,

because I should, if he came soon, have an opportunity of getting a more definite personal estimate of him than by letter, and should probably be able to set him on a better method of life and arrangements : for he is evidently the creature of impulse, but has—quite as evidently I think—materials for wisdom, which a little wise training might turn to active prudence. Moreover, he would here enter on a new field and in a new atmosphere. In London he is lost in the multitude and immersed in his antecedents.

Here he would begin afresh in his present character, surrounded by much better influences, and with the certainty of a great deal of respectful appreciation, and enough sympathy to be valuable in his worst needs.

. . . I was interrupted, and could not finish before going out. Dr. Guthrie promises to interest the Duke of Argyle in -——, and I am to call on the Duke's sister, whom I have met. I have only time to finish this, for I found unexpectedly the room crowded and with interesting people—among whom three of unusual interest kept me in three hours of profound talk.

To the Rev. R. Glover.

. . . I enclose you Gerald Massey's 'War Waits,' and know how heartily you will respond to their fine flushing enthusiasm. . . . If you don't know his other works yet, by all means lose no time in seeing them, and in reading his Preface, which contains sentences of prose which

Milton might have written. One especially: ' I have known people in the poorest circumstances to whom heroism is a heritage, and to be noble a natural way of living.' . . .

With regard to what you said on Smith's Sonnet upon ' Napoleon III.' I would quite agree, but that I think you have not taken his meaning rightly. The Sonnet is not intended as a condemnation of the Emperor, for Smith is rather an admirer than an enemy of his. It is merely intended to set forth *alternatives*—the road of glory and the *Via mala.*

He sees in vision the possibilities of this dark, unknown, impenetrable man. Will he be the saviour or the tyrant? The oracle repeats—without answering—the question of mankind.

To his Father and Mother.—(After a hurried description of crowding engagements).

No. 36 North Hanover street, Edinburgh.

We hope to go out of Edinburgh for a week or two very shortly, for this sort of bustle is neither good for body nor soul. But you can direct here till Thursday— that is to say, we don't think of leaving these lodgings till then.

Thanks to my Father for his advice about ——. He need not fear I shall compromise myself at all. But I feel I ought not to stand by while he is suffering so acutely, and struggling with difficulties—material and mental—which must do desperate work on a nature like his before long.

By having him here, I can exercise a more direct influence over him and bring it to bear on the needful points. And for want of some such friend, he may go to wreck. . . .

A report came to Edinburgh last night that the Emperor of Russia is dead : but I fear it is mis-telegraphed for the Empress, who has been dying for some time. Till this solution struck me, my blood ran back cold with the divineness of the catastrophe.

It may still be true, and if true who shall foresee the next step of the Angel ? If true it casts a curious glare upon Louis Napoleon's indomitable determination to go to the Crimea. I should be inclined to think that Nicholas died of the ' disease of Russian Sovereigns,' and that the dark fateful French Emperor had warning of the conspiracy. . . .'

To a young Sister.

. . . Have you read ' Waverley?' I read it, I remember, before I was as venerable as you. Do you remember the ball at Pinkie House given by ' Bonnie Prince Charlie' to his chiefs ? The S——'s were going down there the other day, and on returning from a walk—lo! I found my nest empty and my little bird flown. They had carried her off ; and, after a drive by the sea, she dined at the strange old historic place, went into the Chevalier's bedroom, looked at the gallery which was used as a hospital after the battle, and saw so many funny things that she lay awake till two o'clock in the morning describing them to me.

To his eldest Sister.

What a daily problem the dear little fellow must be to you. I should enjoy to study that intermediate state between the receptive and the active power of speech. The mind seems now to lie before you like an unfinished seal, taking whatever image you grave upon it, and retaining that image as a recognised shape, but not yet exerting itself to stamp the same on the wax of the world. Or it is like a crystal cup which you are slowly filling, and through which you see the wine of life rising—rising. One day it will overflow.

To M——.

Edinburgh.

What do you think I have been doing this morning? Reading a novel by an unnamed authoress, who, if she could be struck with leprosy, or sent 'to eat grass like an ox,' or blessed with some trifling discipline of that sort, might be a great writer, perhaps a poet.

As it is, she is in unison with nothing in heaven above or the earth beneath ; but treads the carpet and breathes the air of a great, hot, scented drawing-room universe, full of consumptive patients in the most tingling state of mesmeric 'criddle.' The book is called 'Counterparts,' and is the history of a great poet who—I could stake my life—never did, nor by any possibility *could*, write a poem, and of a wonderful doctor who bears about the same relation to a great man that a fop bears to a gentleman. The whole tone and character of the work is, to the key of real

nature, as the perfumed atmosphere of a hot-house is to
the perfumed wind of spring. But, in the midst of all,
there are evidences of qualities in the authoress that, if
she is young, would make one look for very great things.
Only, I suspect, she has mistaken her art, and is a poetess.
In the present book you come upon line after line of
perfect metre, a most detestable interpolation in professed
prose; and she shows in some of these an *exquisiteness* of
expression that proves rhythm in her nature, and that
makes me think her mind works in the poetic mechanism.
There is also a nice acquaintance, sometimes, with spiritual
and mental facts and modes, which shows the poetic calibre,
and is, in the higher regions of experience, rare enough.
Altogether, I am half inclined to write to her—whomsoever she may be—and recommend her to go out as a
governess or a needlewoman for a year or two, and then
write a *Poem.* The book is worth reading; but if you
read it, don't forget to take a cold bath, or two chapters of
the Bible, after it, to restore you to the universe. The
best evidence of the 'I know not what' of ill health in
it was this—I was reading it to myself when E. said to me,
'I feel better—may I read to you a little?' I looked up,
saw that she had the Bible in her hand, and felt for a
moment *incongruous.* There is no better test for healthi-
ness and broad humanity than this.

To the same.

No date, but it must have been about 1855.

. . . I have hardly left room for the promised explanation with regard to that offending word which you were reluctant to omit. The rationale of the matter is, I think, somewhat this. There is a great social principle already acknowledged by some of the best and noblest; and requiring to be established through the whole mass of society; viz.—that a man's rank is determined, not by what he *does*, but by what he *is*. Every name, therefore, which implies a distinction founded upon *doing* is inconsistent with true nomenclature, which should classify solely with regard to inherent qualities. ' Gentleman' fulfils this requirement, and therefore must remain; ' Tradesman' does not, and therefore must be abolished. Words have certain natural relations to the mind which it is in vain to try to contravene, and if a word—as in the present case—is precisely adapted to express a false principle, it can never be converted to the use of a true, and its employment is a perpetual testimony to and propagation of the false. The ideas of most men and women depend altogether on the words they think with; and by changing their words, you may readily change their ideas. It is part of true general-ship always to storm the weakest point of the enemy, and in the case before us the word has, from trivial reasons, so many foes, that a very little additional impetus will push it out of society.

Before going to Granton, a few days were spent at Craigcrook—days which left bright, grateful, restful impressions on the guests: and which the kindly and courtly host commemorated by the following lines :

Two gracious visitants once lighted here,—
 A high-souled poet with his twin-souled wife—
 And rested on their winged way through life
For a brief season in our narrow sphere.
The place became a Bethel.   Too severe
 For our weak eyes had been his radiance bright,
 If not attempered to serener light
By the soft veiling of her atmosphere.
 Through their sweet blended influence, our home,
Within, without—its chambers, halls, and towers,
Its hills, vales, waters, rocks, lawns, trees and flowers—
 Bloomed into Eden under heaven's blue dome.
Return, fair spirits, ere the blessed light
Ye left around us wither from our sight !

To M——.

Granton : March, 1855.

. . . I am actually writing to you in full view of your beloved sea.   You will love it better than ever, I think, for E—— is soothed and strengthened by it ; and for me, I have not felt so well for months past as I felt yesterday in a walk by the shore . . .

. . . Within these few days it has run over every note of varying influences, and gone through its every attitude of grandeur and beauty.   Three days ago there was a

great storm of wind, hail, and breakers. The sea tore up
its depths, not metaphorically but in fact, and became
yellow with sand, and white with fury. The great waves
charged the parapet above the beach in long, separate lines,
and came over like a regiment of white lions, all mane
and tail. When they failed in the leap, the effect was
even finer, for they sprang in sheer strength upwards as
high as a house. The blows upon the shore were like a
cannonade. But all my theories about the sublimity of
the sea were confirmed by this new experience. The
highest waves, the greatest noise, the strongest force, was
poor compared to what one might rightfully demand from
these many, many miles of water. If all that had been
done by a river, it would have been sublime; but seen and
heard as the outcome of that vast visible ocean before me,
it was as though a giant laid himself out full length and
twiddled his ten toes. Finding that it had failed in the
sublime, it tried yesterday afternoon to bewitch me with
its beauty, and I may well say *bewitch*, for the effect of
what I saw was such as one might feel in an enchanted
heaven of magic. A heaven of magic, for it had all the
unreality of a vision and the marvellousness of the supernatural.

The sky cleared, soft winds blew gently, the sun shone
everywhere, and the sea, changed to a sea of pearl, lay
like something that had no deeps, no substance, but *surface*
—a plain of rainbows and of tints more delicate than
rainbows, and of whiteness, like pearly air, more fragile,
etherial, and exquisite than white. It was calm, calm with
hardly even a fresh-water ripple, and the gliding white-

sailed ships went over it slowly—not as if sailing in any
wind, but rather as if the mere necessity of beauty obliged
them into the grace of motion. You would have been
triumphant to see how I stood before it. This was its
first great revelation of the beautiful since we have been
here ; but the sea and I have got on very well together
every day   It makes a great deal of noise and rude play
as I walk along the shore, and I feel towards it very much
as if it were a big dog. The storm put this Ballad into
my head :

> My love he was the prince of men,
>   Sing heigho merrie and well-away—
> Merrily sings the little brown wren,
>   Sing heigho merrie and well-away.
>
> My love he was bonnie, my love he was bright,
>   Sing heigho merrie and well-away—
> The night it is black and the day it is white,
>   Sing heigho merrie and well away.
>
> His eyes they were blue, his locks they were brown,
>   Sing heigho merrie and well-away—
> The moon goes up and the moon goes down,
>   Sing heigho merrie and well-away.
>
> The breaker breaks—the sea-mew creaks,
>   Sing heigho merrie and well-way—
> The mew is in the air—the merry men are—where ?
>   Sing heigho merrie and well-away.

To a Brother-in-law.

Granton.

. . . We have heard of dear N——'s danger and
safety . . . How much older we grow in one day, or even
hour, of intense *mental* pain.   How the spiritual skeleton
seems to set and consolidate, and how, as though in a
bloody sweat, all that is unreal and unworthy seems to
roll off from the soul.   In such a state one is best fitted
to receive so great a happiness as you must have known
when, in the midst of such agonising anxiety, you had the
assurance that your wife was safe.   What strange extremes in how short a time.   May God indeed bless them
both to both of you—and every other trial He may see
fit to make the messenger of good.

To Dr. Samuel Brown.

Granton, near Edinburgh.

Every week, for I know not how long past, E. has said
to me: 'this week must not pass without a letter to
Samuel Brown;' and week after week I have given practically the same answer: 'Brown knows—and loves—me
well enough to trust me.'

After detailed explanation of the hindrances
—from changes of residence, and illness, his wife's
and his own—which had kept him silent,—of his
wife, he says:

She can now ride a little, walk a little, read a little, and write a little. You will readily understand that I almost fear to speak of these things. When I do not fully recognise them, I feel almost afraid to oblige them to give themselves names lest they prove their phantom nature by taking offence and disappearing; and when—as now and then—I am conscious of them all at once and know them for realities, the case is, if possible, more perplexing. Don't you know states of mind which seem as if they could have no expression but in music?

Though I have neither heard from you nor written to you lately, you will not suppose I could be content without hearing of you . . . I wish you were nearer, though I shall probably be away from Edinburgh a great deal this summer, for I should have so much liked to feel that you could be the central point of that small circle which I shall very much regret to leave and for whom my whole heart is interested. For Alexander Smith and Gerald Massey, in particular, you are precisely the friend whose atmosphere and unconscious influence I could, at this phasis of their development, most earnestly desire. . . .

Have you heard from Lady A—— lately? E. has had several letters; and in one received this week the dear old lady asks most anxiously about you. . . .

Is there any way of getting from Granton to Haddington by water? If so, we might hope to make a descent upon you. It is hardly possible, while we are three miles from friends, and in unaccustomed lodgings, to leave E. as long as would be necessary for the journey

by train, and she is not yet strong enough for so many
miles of railway shaking. . . .

To a young Sister.

Granton: April 13, 1855.

It seems hardly a month ago since I last wrote to you
on your birthday. I remember even the tenour of the
letter—chiefly about the beautiful and of my hope that
you would study and practise every branch of all the arts
that culture the sense of beauty. For the theory of beauty
cannot be taught: no man can give you rules by which
you shall decide that a thing is beautiful. But by loving,
pursuing and enjoying those that we are all agreed to call
' beautiful things ' that part of your nature which appre-
ciates and delights in beauty is developed and made
sensitive, and its increased ability to enjoy one manifes-
tation of beauty will make it additionally sentient to
others . . . By occupying yourself with beautiful forms
and beautiful sounds you have been increasing your taste
for beauty and your affinity with beauty ; and these two
qualities will not only enable you to find more and more
happiness in the perception of everything beautiful, and
to recognise more and more the Divineness of this wonderful universe in which we live, they will also dispose you
to behave beautifully—to be graceful in manner and
gracious in mind—and will incline you to the highest
beauty—even to goodness itself. Because goodness is the
highest kind of beauty the best preparation to be good is
to be beautiful—for in replenishing yourself with beauty
you are furnishing for goodness a home that is likest to

itself. So in Nature you will find that all the finer es-
sences are contained in those that most resemble them—
the insubstantial fragrance in the fragile flower, the in-
tangible light in the etherial air, the expressing human
soul in the expressive human body. And so in the Bible
you will find the sublimest messages of the Prophets have
always come to us in a vehicle of poetry, because poetry, as
the divinest kind of human thought, was the most congenial to a diviner inspiration still.

What I have said of the finest passages in the
Bible you will find to be true, in another way, of the whole
Book. The more exquisite your sense of beauty becomes
the dearer will the Bible become to you, the more natural
and indispensable will the wisest and grandest of its sayings become to your heart and mind. They will seem
proper to each other, as wings to the air, and feet to the
ground, and light to the eyes. You will feel certain
that the mind was created for the saying, and the saying
for the mind ; and you will be no more able to doubt the
truth of the one than of the other. And as the love and culture of beauty prepare the heart to appreciate Revelation,
so the Bible will be your best help to the love and culture
of beauty. As the sun brings flowers out of the dead
ground, and as God breathed into Adam the breath of life,
its words will warm and animate you till you are beautified
unaware, and till you rise up indeed 'a living soul' of
new perceptions. I know how dearly you already love it,
and that you will let the daily love and study of it through
the coming year go hand-in-hand with the continued

culture of all else that is beautiful. God send that it may indeed be so with all of us !

To M——.

Granton : April 1855.

Do you remember that I have often described to you how I was paralysed among the Alps, and how it was only after a year of absence that I began to *feel* concerning them ? I can, therefore, thoroughly understand your present sorrows, and know alas! that they are inevitable. . . . These are sufferings which are neither to be condemned nor indulged—the natural efflorescence which needs no culture or pruning, 'flowers in their seasons,' having their appointed work and beauty there, and passing away with them.

I don't think, therefore, you need care to say 'perhaps they are not quite right;' for I am sure your other qualities will not allow them to make an injurious desolation. There are afflictions from which no one ought to recover : but that which you have lately passed through, or rather that into which you have lately passed, is not one which Nature can recognise among them : and God is Nature, though Nature is not God. Therefore, since your character is unusually natural, there is no danger for the future . . . the true wisdom is rather to encourage on growth than to weed out the other.

Somewhat on this last principle I shall not answer much of my little sister's letter till she is less sad and 'aweary,' and will only speak to-day of those things that may amuse without seriously paining her.

And first of the —— s, who arrived in Edinburgh eight days ago, and on Monday entered upon the lodgings we had found for them at Trinity—where they now seem comfortably settled. I have seen them every day, and am pleased to the heart to find in him more even than I allowed myself to expect of beautiful and good. . . . The upper part of his face reminds me of Raphael's angels, and I catch myself dwelling upon him with a kind of optical fondness, as one looks upon a beautiful picture or a rare colour. And this, in spite of blue satin waistcoat! and a gold-coloured tie!

The second morning I came upon him early, *sans* neckerchief or collar, nursing his sickly baby, the grey wrapper in which he sat, being like the mist to the morning as regards his wonderful complexion, and it would be difficult to imagine more marvellous (masculine) beauty.

CHAPTER V.

HIGHLAND TRAVEL, 1855.

MRS. DOBELL's recovery had now so far advanced
that her physician considered she would benefit by
complete change. They went, therefore, for a time
to the Bridge of Allan ; then, when the summer
came, to Arran, where they were joined by some
of the Dobell family.

'Maida,' the deerhound spoken of in the following letter, was the gift of a direct descendant
of Flora Macdonald's, and was, for the future, an
important member of Sydney Dobell's household.

'Shall I tell you '—he wrote to a young sister
of my new and beautiful companion—Maida ? She came
more than a week ago, and is the most beautiful creature
of her kind I ever saw. Already, at ten months old, she
is bigger than a common greyhound, so you will imagine
what she will be full-grown. Her colour is a fine dun,
with markings of black upon the head, as delicate as the
tracery on a shell, and with an intermixture of a stern
dark colour all over, except the head, which shades the

dun without marking it. Her hair is rough : her form
faultless in strength and grace, so that my eye is never
tired as she goes beside me of the wonderful combinations
of line. Her temper is so sweet and feminine, that I love
her almost like a human being, and she is already very
much attached to us. Whenever I go out she walks
gravely at my heels or prances a little way in advance,
and her obedience is exemplary. When she sees me
coming to her she lies down and makes the funniest and
most graceful obeisance, and then jumps up for a cordial
welcome. In the evening I take her into the field behind
the house, and we have a game which she enjoys vastly,
sometimes in the height of her exultation clapping her
forepaws on my shoulders—but she is usually too well-
behaved to venture on such familiarity. . . . She will
make a magnificent study for C. some day. She is so
good-natured that I had some difficulty at first in keeping
her from being worried by the little troop of savages we
have about here—(I had to go out to them just now to save
a poor toad). But the little devils stand in considerable
awe of me, and, between lectures and sweetmeats, they keep
at some distance from the kennel . . . they know me by
a title which I at first supposed to be Ahriman—the
principle of Evil, but have since discovered as ' hairy man,'
in compliment to the terrors of my moustache. . . .

. . . I was specially pleased with what you said of
your love of flowers in your letter, because it was evidently
spoken not from mere admiration, but *love*. It is the
nature of the mind to grow like what it loves, and to love
beauty is therefore one way to become beautiful. All

kinds of beauty are manifestations of the same thing in
different ways. The beauty of a sound, of a flower, of a
virtuous and sweet mind, are the same great unknown
principle made apparent to us in different substances and
through different senses. What principle that is upon
which God constructs these various forms, it is probable
that no human mind will ever discover; but, meanwhile,
we can feel enough of *their* relationship to be sure of *its*
identity. Therefore, when you are looking on a flower
and loving it, and absorbing it into yourself, you are
really, while you seem only to be pleasing your eye,
communicating, by sympathy, its grace and exquisiteness to your whole nature. But this is only done by
loving it : not by criticising it, and displaying a ' knowing ' admiration. I often sit for poetry's sake—I mean
for the sake of improving my power of making poetry
—and look at an exquisite flower for a long while without a single *thought* about it, and in a way that many
people would think, I daresay, very idle; but I know that
my mind is stringing itself all that while like an instrument to a tuning-fork. . . .

To M——.

Bridge of Allan.

. . . Last week was certainly a shady time, but I dare
trust the sun is coming out again. E. had evidently
suffered from the journey here, more than the immediate
symptoms showed, and the fatigue remained with her in
a chronic way, like latent lightning that one feels but

does not see, and calls by mild electrical synonyms. And
there were no genial influences to soothe the vibrating
electrometer, or release imperceptibly the imprisoned
Afreet. A few hours showed us we were deceived in
place, house, and people. . . . The 'brae' faces west;
and when, at length, the sun is westering, a hill in front
throws us shadow instead of light, and makes the very
sunset 'ray darkness' on us.

Then, though 'the barbarous people showed us no little
kindness,' it was with a kind of rude assiduity that was
nearly as disastrous as ill-will. They made up in psalm
singing what they wanted in culinary skill, and between
the smell of garlic and the odour of sanctity my poor
invalid was very nearly starved.

To his Father and Mother.

Blaw Lowan, Bridge of Allan: May 11th.

. . . C. talks of the romance of this Scotch semi-
Highland lodging of ours, with its historic landlords and
neighbouring battle-fields; what will he say to the next
page in the chapter?

Some other lodgers have taken the remaining rooms
of the little farm-house, and they are—a young Indian
princess (a ward and god-child of Queen Victoria) and her
suite. It sounds quaint to hear shouted over the narrow
little stair: 'Jessie, come up, the princess wants you.' I
happen to have met the slender, pale, black-eyed elf (as
like an Assyrian sculpture as if some of the Museum
marbles had had a family) at mutual friends in Edinburgh,

and shall probably have some interesting walks with this
Queen of Sheba, if we stay here.   But I don't think we
shall remain long, for the Doctor recommends as much
change as possible, and it seems a pity, while in such a
district, we should miss the opportunity of seeing such
wonderful scenery as is now within reach.

After speaking of having taken a party of
ladies to see a picture, by an Edinburgh artist, just
then attracting a good deal of attention, he says:

Some of those poor peeresses, by the way, on whom dear
—— was so hard.   I was heartily amused at her contrast-
ing them with 'real men and women,' for so far as my little
experience goes, they—except bad specimens—are quite
as 'real' as, and in fact rather more 'real' than, other
people: as one, indeed, might infer from the fact of their
being put past question and therefore offering less temptations to self-assertion.

. . . Besides a good many letters, I have four MSS. to
see to and a proof or two to correct (for other people);
meanwhile, my Ballads are standing still.   I am tired this
evening. So—as the most objective and easy matter—I will
tell you of an expedition to the Abbey Craig—about two
miles from us, (E. riding a pony of the size and somewhat of
the character of a donkey, which is kept in the village for
such purposes).   It is a basaltic rock, famed for its noble
view.   To suggest something of that view, I will just stand
for a moment on the tip-top of the hill, and, turning round
on my own axis, call out the names of what I see.   I will

begin about South-east, looking over the links of Forth, and turn till I come to the same spot. Bannock-burn—where Bruce had his flag-staff—Stirling town—Stirling Castle—the ' hill o' the Gillies,' where the Bruce's camp-followers appearing through the trees caused the already wavering English to flee—the long high hill of Inche, not five miles away—Ben Lomond, white as an alp with un-melted snow—Ben Venue, also white, Ben Cruachan, Ben Auchray, Ben Ledi, Ben Humar, Ben Voirlich. I can't tell you the effect of this marvellous many-pointed barrier, which gives you the suggestion of infinite mystery regard-ing the strange other world beyond it. Ben Voirlich, forty miles off, is met in the landscape by the hills above the Allan, two miles hence, green sweet hills—the first of the Ochil range, three miles from where we stand, rather higher than the Malverns—then his long line of brethren, grey with rock, brown with whin and heather, black with fir, green with larch,—and at their feet such a little kingdom of milk and honey, corn and pasture, watered by the ever-winding Forth. Far away east are the Pentlands above Edinburgh. . . .

. . . Speaking of A—'s book. From the letters he sends me, I think there can be no doubt of its thorough success. I know he is too wise not to be amply satisfied if the ' thorough success' should even go no further than success as an *experiment on his own growth*, and on the present *status quo* of those powers which will one day secure the other ' success' of popularity. . . .

I am going to Stirling presently, to see the proprietor

of the principal paper there, who is in want of an Editor. I have seen him once already, and am in hopes to get the place for . . .

To M——.

Blaw Lowan : May.

. . . Till you are once more bran and bright, I must write only what will amuse you. . . .

I shall not easily forget the first sunset we were here, when, not knowing in what presence I was, I looked out of the open window towards the west, and was conscious suddenly, not of this mountain or that, but of a great awe as of a Divine *neighbourhood*. My eye was sufficiently accustomed to mountains to recognise, even at that distance, instantly, and without voluntary calculation, that I saw something greater than I had seen since the Alps. And at sunset, when they look like sheer precipices of their whole height, the effect is hardly less than Alpine. I can't describe to you the first unexpected impression—turning the eye carelessly on them as on common hills, and receiving the knowledge of their rank. It was like suddenly recognising an archangel, and . . . I could have stept back in Eastern fashion, and fallen on my face. . . . Our landlady is a grand old specimen of the Scottish dame. Her 'forbears' have been here for several generations; her mother remembered the Highlanders taking everything from the larder in 'the 45,' and she had an uncle 'wha mindit weel ganging wi' his father's pleughmen to see the battles and things.'

My proficiency in Scotch pronunciation (which would

astound the saucy little girl who so often laughed at my
vain efforts last year) is likely to receive great additions
in such company. For some months past—-having ' given
my whole mind to it' for more than a year—my skill has
been the astonishment of I know not how many who ' never
thought to hear those sounds from an English throat.'   I
can say Auchtermuchty, think nothing of Sloanachlachan,
and as for Loch, nicht, and trifles of that sort, might
give lessons with *éclat* to ' Edinburgh gutter-bluid' itself.

To the same.

Bridge of Allan : May 1855.

Tho' my little M—— is once more—what a blessing
to be able to write it—reviving in body and in mind, I
must not cease my ' amusing letters,'—are you laughing at
the title, you incorrigibly saucy girl ?—till she is again all
herself. Then, you know, I shall of course relapse into
all *myself*, and be as dull, subjective, spasmodic, and uninteresting as usual. Till then, let me make an effort,
and tell her something she cares to hear. What if I give
her the history of last Monday ? Hiring a fleet but safe
horse (for now that movement has become possible to the
poor prisoner to whom for so long it was forbidden, the
appetite for it, grown almost morbid by long abstinence,
has become nearly a passion, and I believe if she were
allowed to go without *me*, she would order an unbroken
colt), we drove along the foot of the Ochils to the banks
of the Devon, and pursued it as far as ' The De'il's Mill,'
the ' Rumbling Bridge,' and the ' Caldron Linn,' 17 miles
from Blaw Lowan. Oh, those wonderful Ochils—but I will

speak of them when I tell you of our ascent of Abbey
Craig. Just before we turned from them to the Devon,
we saw, seated on a woody subaltern hill that slopes up,
with slow, ample majesty, for two miles from the road,
and backed by the almost alpine masses of the Ochils,
(bare, brown and stern, with neither shrub, land-mark, nor
tree), that most romantic of ruins, the ' Castle of Gloom.'
Four hundred years ago it bore that title, tho' no legend
tells what pre-historic terrors sent down this name into
those days. To this moment the place about it is called
the ' Vale of Dolor,' and the burnies on each side ' the
Burn o' Sorrow,' and the ' Water o' Care.' Except those
evidences of an almost antediluvian grief which exist in
the *languages* of some nations and tribes, I know nothing
more pathetically suggestive than a spot of ground like
this—dyed, as it were, with the blood of a vast unknown
Calamity. The antiquaries try to analyse the coloured
soil, and to show that the purple stain means nothing after
all ; but their complex solution seems to me more difficult
than the difficulty. Stopping at the Inn at Rumbling
Bridge, we walked about half a mile down the Devon, and
saw the rushing rapid which from its sound is called ' The
De'il's Mill.' The Devon here makes its way through a
chasm as deep as a three-story house, and so narrow that
you might almost leap it. Afterwards, I walked—E——
being unable to attempt more on foot, and the path being
impassable for carriages—to the noble falls of the Caldron
Linn. The Devon, after winding as sweetly and calmly as
if it were a stream of the sky, which, as I walked, made it
blue, leaps suddenly into a gulf, falls thence into a Medi-

terranean dungeon, where it chafes, runs round, and throws
up white arms in agony, and finally springs, thro' the small
opening like a prison window, down a height of forty feet.
Seen from below, standing among rocks and wild trees and
a foaming stream that reminded me somewhat of Chamouni, the whole is really very unusual, and should be
visited by those who go many a thousand miles in search
of grandeurs not so great.

I must leave till another time—for I have more letters
than usual to write—our visit to Stirling Castle, when
E—— rode six miles on a pony, and then walked nearly a
mile, and to Abbey Craig when she rode three miles and
climbed one!

To the same.

Dunoon : May.

. . . We did not leave Blaw Lowan for a day after
the time arranged, as we could not deny ourselves the
blessing of another morning and evening in sight of the
nearest Scottish likeness to that divine wonder we call
Spring in England.

Here, in Dunoon, all is essentially Scotland, and bears
about the relation to the seasons of Blaw Lowan as those
little snowdrops we once had in miniature hyacinth
glasses, bore, in their poor and watery size and shape, to
the snowdrops of English woods and Coxhorne borders.

We started from Bridge of Allan on Tuesday about
eleven, and reached here safely, passing through Glasgow,
and sailing down the Clyde, by about four o'clock. The
Clyde, after you pass Greenock, deserves—for a few miles—
more than has ever been said of it.

There is nothing on the Rhine to compare with its grandeur as you draw near the mountains above Loch Long and the Haily Loch.

But Dunoon disappointed us very much. Imagine five or six hundred very small ' *neat willas*,' the multiplied paradises and ideals of the Glasgow man of business, clustered under a high range of moorland, and you have Dunoon.

. . . I don't think we shall stay long ; but use this as a central point for reconnoitring and discovering something better.

Yesterday we rowed up the Clyde to Strone, a much better place then Dunoon—but horribly willanous—situated on a promontory at the entrance of the Haily Loch. However, no eligible lodgings were to be had there.

To the same.

Dunoon : May.

You heard, I think, of our projected expedition to Loch Eck? We drove there on Sunday afternoon, and of all the poems in rock and water I ever saw I think it is one of the most complete. Loch Long, down which we sailed on Monday, is finer and larger in scale, but, except the lake of Thun in Switzerland, I have seen nothing so grandly sweet, so suggestively comprehensible as this Loch Eck. The Loch is hardly wider than a river, and you could walk without fatigue from end to end. The mountains are sublime in height, beautiful in shape, symmetrical in

position, and strewed as thickly with broken rocks as if
they had been bombarded from the skies.

But perhaps all the material grandeur of that afternoon was hardly more moving than a piece of human
emotion that happened to us as we drove home. Espying
a flag-staff on a hill-top, I asked the driver what it meant.
' It was put there by the Hermit, sir, when the Queen
went by.' 'The Hermit?' You may fancy who was
immediately in the highest state of excitement. So we
discovered the cell where the Hermit had dwelt for thirty
years—having retreated thither from the faithlessness of
woman—and set of to visit him on the wild mountain
side. I can't now give you a full, true and particular account
of the odd cabin he has built, with its tiny windows, dark
' *ben* ' and hard bed, and smaller ' *but*,' with its queer
one seat and streaming western light in which sat ' the
Hermit' like a figure in one of Rembrandt's corners.
Neither can I describe the absorbed and silent interest of
his visitor, whose whole soul seemed to have passed into
the senses of hearing and seeing. An idea of the size of
his palace you will get from the fact, that we sat in the
' ben' and he in the ' but,' and that even then there was
hardly room for us. What I want to tell you is this.
After a few words the Hermit began to ask us of the war ;
and when I commenced the latest news, this old worn man—
this voluntary exile who for thirty years had pastured his
cares and sympathies with his goats upon the hill-side, this
misanthrope who had broken the link with mankind so
bravely and thought himself dead and buried to the world—
drew his breath, bent forward in his seat, shut his eyes,

that he might hear the more, and was positively stiffened
and galvanised with the extent of his interest.   Was ever
a whole nation so at war ?

To the Rev. J. B. Paton.

Dunoon : May 27.

I have carried your last letter about with me ever since
I received it, and have not till this morning found a time
when the 'must be written' gave sufficient space to the
'may be written' to allow me the indulgence of a pen-and-
ink chat with you . . .

. . . To-day I am a little better from a fit of rheumatism, but not mentally clear and bright enough to *work*
(I have begun a book of Lyrics, which I trust to finish
this summer.) . . . I can't refer to your brotherly letter,
without telling you how heartily glad I was to know you
enjoyed the Sonnets so much.   From all I have heard and
seen, they have been very successful as regards public
opinion (which does not add, I confess, to my respect for
that opinion, remembering how it met 'Balder'). . .

. . . I know you will be anxious to hear more of the
'book of Lyrics' I mentioned just now ; so a few words
thereanent before passing to more interesting matters.
To attempt any description of the war in poetry while
the war itself is in full vigour I feel to be impossible.   The
great epical action is not yet developed, and anything in
the way of war-ballads would require appeals to more than
the noble instincts and passions of the soldier.   At all
events, I fear I could not write full-blooded and hot war-

lyrics without throwing the whole man into them and not
only the hero. The difficulty to the Christian warrior is
not so much to deduce a theoretical justification as to
ensure that the human nature under those terrible excitements shall not transgress the bounds of the theory.
Sitting here coldly I can blow a Russian army into the
air with the very kindest sympathies for the individuals
composing it; but what sort of figure would this warfare
make in a lyric? I fear that if all that is evil in warfare
were religiously abstracted from the war-song it would
have to be sung on other than Crimean battle-fields, and
to different legions than our rum-drinking, Russian-hating,
skewer-'em-to-the-wall John Bulls. Nevertheless, in these
days I could not bring out a book of ballads altogether
unconnected with the war; I intend, therefore, if God
please, so to catch the various *home-reflexions* of that
blazing affair in the East as to create quite a little ballad-
literature on the subject, and surround it with an atmosphere of domestic interests and emotions. I think about
fifty ballads, of very various calibre, expressing what is
most poetical in the sympathies of each class, age, and sex,
in regard to the great Eastern tragedy, will, if well done,
accomplish this plan. Nine or ten of these are already
done; and five of them, I think you will be amused to
hear, in your ain Scottish tongue. I mean to have a
little 'Highland brigade,' and your most jealous lovers
of the Doric are satisfied with my proficiency therein.

After speaking of the improvement in his

wife's health, of their past movements, and of
their preparation to sail for Arran, he continues :

I meant to have given you some account of Gerald
Massey, who was lodging near us on the Granton shore for
some weeks before we left. We were thoroughly pleased
with him in the highest sense: and felt convinced that as
a man his materials are as fine as he has proved his poetic
genius to be. But my time is too nearly spent to allow
me to say more than that his face—at least the upper
half—is more like Raffaelle's Angels than any man's I
ever saw, and that his conversation and *personnel* confirmed the best impressions his works and letters had made
on me.

You have probably heard this already; for I think I
mentioned it in a letter to our friend Vaughan. I take
for granted that he is gone on a tour after his illness, for I
have heard nothing from him for a long time past, and
E. has been in vain expecting a letter from that sweet-
natured wife of his, for whom we both—in our short meeting—formed such an affectionate interest. Tell us of
their welfare, my dear fellow, whenever your many duties
give you time for a letter: and above all, give us a history
of your own doings, sufferings, enjoyments and labours
during all this long silent space during which, be sure, the
remembrance of you was often in our minds and your
name not very seldom on our lips.

Any letters for me directed to Alexander Smith, would
be forwarded by him, as he always knows my whereabouts.

To M——.

Brodick ; Arran : June.

During an interval of lodging hunting, in a bedroom
twelve feet square (no sitting-room being vacant in the
inn) and on two up-piled boxes for a table, I will try to
give you some notion of our journey and environ-
ments. . . . It is raining at this moment, E—— (utterly
fagged and worn with a long, jolting ride in the rough
cars of the country, in search of what could hardly be
scarcer if the cottages hereabouts were built of the
Philosopher's stone) is lying on the bed to recover
strength, and your imagination will fill up what haste and
brevity compel me to leave out. The sea and wind were
tolerably quiet when we left Greenock ; but before we
reached Cambray both had risen to a height that foretold
bad weather, and we therefore arranged to stay at Millport, and wait for a favourable day to cross to Arran. But
as we neared Millport, an old gentleman on board, who
knew the place, announced that it was little frequented,
and that at the hotel the beds were not likely to be *well
aired* ! You don't need me to say more. You know to
whom sea-sickness and heavy seas were happy alternatives. As we passed Millport the wind rose to a storm,
the clouds lowered to the masts, the rain burst upon us,
and the sea met it with counter showers of spray. We
kept the deck, for, below, heat and sick ladies were worse
than 'the elements.' The ship leaped like a colossal
horse, and rolled like a giant's cradle . . . the storm grew
worse ; and with the engines roaring, the rain pelting, the

waters raging, the ship creaking and crying—now on her
side, so that our faces might have touched 'the brine,'
now staggering, as a cross-wave struck her flank, or came
dash upon her decks—we bored as through a cloud,
through the foam of the grey sea.   I was not at all sick:
but felt what, if I had not had the knowledge upon me of
the little sufferer at my side, might have been almost a
fierce exhilaration.   'Fierce' is not the word, either; but
I know no other.   It was nearly nine o'clock before we
were on shore, and the deep mists allowed us to see but
little of the land during the short walk, through heavy
rain, to the inn.   Fancy what it was to waken at five
o'clock to the heavenliest of June mornings, shining and
glittering and streaming and curling, on flowery orchards
and greenest grass, on seas, pools, and streams, and round
such misty mountains as I have not seen out of Switzerland.   Oh—this Poem-Island, the microcosm of all the
best things in the Cosmos!   But you will hear enough of
it, if we stay long here.

We arrived in darkness and storm to an unknown
somewhat, [says a letter to another correspondent].   We
wakened the next day, very early, to an Eden-Island of
sunshine, orchard-blossoms, streams, seas, pastures and
mountains. . . . The contrast of the two experiences was
like death and resurrection.

After a long fag of lodging hunting, he wrote:

You would be amused to see our palace—a cottage on
a hill overhanging the sea, in the midst of the weirdest

wilderness of heath and rock. We have two rooms, but the bedroom is far too small to sleep in, and we, therefore, sleep in the sitting-room. We stayed at the inn till yesterday, and this is our first day of cabin-life.

To M——.

C——, full of present content and anticipated pleasure, is busily mending and preparing, on a low wall outside the door, the lines and rods that are to do execution before sunset among the shoals upon the 'Haddy Rock.' How curiously, in this glorious region, the humblest interests are coloured by the highest; as in a temple upon which the sparrows are holy. The formula by which we find our fishing-place to-night almost does for the sport what the setting sun will do for the waters in which our lines are let down. 'Row till you see the corrie and corriegills, and then bring the top of the Goat-fell to the middle of the Mell Dhaun.' Have I told you that the hill on which we live is the Mell Dhaun? What a name for a legend! what a title for an apparition! 'I am,' said the Spectre, 'the Mell Dhaun!'

To the same.

I hope to send some heather blossom in this letter. If I could send you a sight of the mountains that bear it and the sea that reflects them! If you could have seen that sea last night as we rowed through the liquid sunset—for the water was as golden as the clouds and air—

in fact, seemed a mere extension of the western sky—and saw above us, round the summits of the Goatfell and Glen Rosa, such things as I had hardly thought to see with eyes of the flesh.

Sometimes one does meet with these rare perfections, which seem to leave the intellect diviner ever after; but I have seldom seen so ideal a combination of the most subtle and difficult of such, as appeared to us last evening the instant the sun sank.

His youngest brother had joined him at Arran, and was the companion of the fishing expeditions which Mrs. Dobell, also, was often able to join, having a couch made for her at the bottom of the boat.

The following letter was written in expectation of the arrival of his father and mother, and another, his favourite, brother:

To his Mother.

This is not a Birthday letter, for in the happy hope of so soon giving you with actual voice and lips what no pen and ink can worthily counterfeit, we have all three voted that your birthday is no birthday; and, summarily depriving it of its hereditary estates in wishes, and possessions in kisses, intend to hold them, as it were in Chancery, for the benefit of some more fortunate successor, whom we shall elevate by patent to its place and dignity.

But ' Hail to thee, twenty-sixth July!' [1] has become too much a habit of the heart for any amount of theory effectually to absolve it, and you will take this note, dearest mother, as a kind of echo of the thoughts and prayers without which the day will not go by us.

Nevertheless, as I said before, you must not think it is a birthday letter, for we have to keep your birthday here, personally, visibly, practically, the first fine day we spend all together in Arran.   We are looking out eagerly for some definite news of your intentions. . . .

To Dr. Samuel Brown.

Brodick, Isle of Arran : August 1.

That law of the body politic by virtue of which ' Agitate, agitate, agitate,' has become a received maxim, must certainly be in force also in the individual corpus. How often, by the way, one may solve social problems by just considering one's mind a federation of faculties, and observing how said problems are disposed of there . . . I have heard nothing of you for a very long time, but have had so many thoughts of you, at gradually decreasing intervals, that, though I have a weary deal to do (a weary deal, I mean, to brains easily wearied), I must of necessity take up a pen and begin a sheet of paper with ' My dear Galileo.' This crisis would have come much sooner but that our wandering life made it almost physically impossible.   To get through unavoidable correspondence and to

[1] The first line of one of his childish poems, ' To Mama, on her Birthday.'

secure occasional leisure for my Ballads (I find the conditions of a migratory existence too desultory for 'Balder:
Part II.') was as much as 'objective' business allowed.
Here in this Prospero's Island (we are lodging with 'the
d—d witch Sycorax,' who retains her moustaches, I confess,
but has otherwise ameliorated into the kindest of land-
ladies), we rest awhile from our labours: and sometimes as
I look upon the wondrous little world of sea and mountain,
rock and garden, forest and torrent—with its streams so
streaming, its skies so celestial, its gladed wood so very
sylvan, its very precipices so singularly precipitous, all its
grandeur so unmistakeably great and its softness so ideally
tender, everything about it having that quality of *bestness*
which makes it such a Poem-Island, I could almost fancy
we had entered into another 'rest,' and look out to see if
any 'works do follow' me.   Other things, at all events,
are following us . . . One of my brothers is already here,
and my favourite brother and my father and mother are,
I trust, to arrive to-morrow.   In prospect of all this happiness and the occupation it will bring, I can't let the last
quiet morning pass without a letter to you. . . .

I hope you like Massey's Poems.   I have not seen
Meredith's, but just before reading your praise of them
had been hearing a critic of extensive poetical reading
pronounce all the good things were borrowed . . . Patmore's 'Angel' I had not seen when you spoke of it; but
I have since read it, and, without going so far as Tennyson's verdict to De Vere, I must say that another element
(I know not what it is, but *that* it is) would have made it
worthy even of so high a sentence.   At present there is

something lacking which (I think) leaves it less than a
'great poem,' but there are chapters—such as the one
entitled 'Honoria'—that seem in their way almost perfect. As a whole, it seems to me immeasurably beyond
anything Patmore has before accomplished.

You will be glad to know that —— has got a good
appointment in Edinburgh. He is in great grief just
now, poor fellow, for the death of his youngest child.
Another death, which has shocked me more, is that of poor
Mrs. ——. Perhaps I see the darkness of her husband's be-
reavement the more blackly from its contrast with that
gracious light which continues to expand over my own
prospects. . . .

When I contrast what she can do and bear to-day
with what was possible to her on the first of last August,
I am astonished that her progress has seemed slow.

CHAPTER VI.

GRANTON, 1855.

THE anticipated happiness of the family meeting was marred, and the plans which had been formed were interfered with, by the serious illness of his youngest brother.

The invalid was, by and by, removed from the Island to the Bridge of Allan, where his mother remained with him, while his father and the artist-brother made, with Sydney Dobell and his wife, a brief tour in the Highlands.

From Inverness, when again alone with his wife, he wrote:

To-day we have been on a pilgrimage to Culloden, and stood by the yet green graves of the Clans—conducted by an old Highlander, who 'mindit weel,' speaking to the very men who buried them. We break the distance to Dunkeld by staying at Kingusie for a night. We should have stayed at Inverness, instead of Dunkeld, but the great Highland games are held here next week, and lodgings are to be a guinea a day while they last. Much as I

should have liked to see them, I don't feel I can afford to
pay so dearly for the experience.   E. is very much fagged,
and we are both in much need of rest, and shall be heartily
glad to repose awhile at Dunkeld.   The mere succession
of objects of wonder for so many days and miles is of itself
an exhaustion. . . .

To M——.

. . . I must tell you a vision I had the night of the
fall of Sebastopol—a vision told next morning to credible
witnesses, and enough to make the fortune of a would-be
clairvoyant.   I thought I was talking with an unbeliever
on the signs of 'the last days.'   It was evening: he
pointed to it, and scoffingly asked: 'When there shall
be no night there'?   As he spoke, the evening star, which
was hanging in the clear sky before us—large, full, fruity,
like a Scottish star—began to swell and swell, till, as it
reached the stature of the sun, and the whole earth lay
in glaring day beneath it—it set off swift as a meteor
in a perpetual circuit round the heavens.   Every corner of
the land was scorched as by a day of incessant lightnings.
The people flooded out, as at the opening of the sixth seal.
Oh—the upturned faces with that light on them—the
gestures, the voices!   I leapt out of bed and went to the
window to see *that it was not real.*   I came back, and
said—'I have had, not a dream, but a *vision.*'   This
happened on the night of Saturday, the eighth, while the
Russians were burning Sebastopol.

To his Father and Mother.

Aberfeldie, Perthshire: September 20.

Once more I sit down to a 'Sunday letter.' Is it possible that, since I last wrote one, you have been with us, we have seen you and heard you, and that meeting— so much longed for, so brightly commenced, so suddenly interrupted—is really over and gone? It seems already so strange and visionary, so near and yet so far, so actual and yet so incredible, that I could believe it one of those dreams which thirsty men have in fever when they fancy only they have drunk, and wake as parched and unsatisfied as before.

But I must not discourse upon the past, or this 'Sunday letter' would even exceed my former despatches in length; while I think that for some little time I ought to make them briefer than ordinary; for that great mental difficulty in letter-writing, which I spoke of to you, increases, though I can write poetry with even less labour than usual. . . . I will give you, therefore, the merest jottings of objective news, till a holiday from anything epistolary has restored that refractory brain of mine to proper obedience.

You know that we have left Dunkeld, and established ourselves comfortably here, close by the entrance to Burns's 'Birks o' Aberfeldie,' the most exquisite waterfall I have seen. Burns's song describes the spot minutely, but no song can convey the marvellous exuberance of the scene or the etherial grace of that abundance. It is a miniature of the great Pass of the Tête Noire in Switzerland; but, as in a miniature, all that is grand in the one has become in the other delicate and beautiful to an extent that seems impossible, and therefore unearthly. The waterfalls themselves are singularly exquisite, and seen from below, up the steep bed of the burn, wave like the waving of a hundred locks of hair. I think I told you, in my hurried itineraries, of our stay at the foot of Ben Nevis, and my ascent of the mountain. My father need not feel his laurels in danger, for though the ascent is far more difficult than that of Ben Lomond, the view from the top is not finer. More extensive, but not more beautiful—perhaps less so. . . . Glen Nevis, at the foot of the Ben, is far more worth seeing, and is indeed the most perfect thing I have seen in Scotland. Altogether, the district of Lochaber—along the base of Ben Nevis— is one of the most characteristic in the Highlands; and if I wished to recommend a journey which should give the most intensely *Highland* impressions, it would be to Bannavie, and through Lochaber, Strathspey and Badenoch. These last districts I think pleased me more than even the grander mountain scenery, or than the richly wooded rocks of the Dunkeld and Blair Athol tracts. These (Dunkeld and Blair Athol) you can understand by having seen the Trossachs; but there is nothing anywhere else exactly like the monotonous variety of the many-figured many-tinted wastes and corny straths of Badenoch. We came through Strathspey and Badenoch at more leisure than by coach, having fallen in with —— . . . who proposed that we should unite in posting from Inverness. . . .

Dear C. will be interested to know that Richardson, the eminent water-colour painter, was staying in the hotel with us at Bannavie.   He and his wife were very friendly. Here is a letter of gossip for you—but its justification is the fact with which I commenced. . . .

At the end of this Highland tour, after a brief stay in Edinburgh, Mr. and Mrs. Dobell settled themselves at Granton for the winter months.

During a period of illness here he wrote, to one of his sisters :

I have been trying to make the most of my invalid hours by reading novels, and have just finished ' Bleak House '—that is to say have just commenced it, having taken my ' initiative ' at the end, and receded with rapture to the opening of the first volume.   I am heartily glad that I have been drawn into reading it, for it has given me such an estimation of Dickens as none of his former writings would justify.   I felt as once, when a boy of fourteen, I felt on first reading Tennyson's ' Mariana '— a disposition to throw up ' authorship ' as a thing thenceforth superfluous.   I know that, on going through it again, this feeling would abate, because the faults of the work would grow more and more perceptible, and gradually open sores of taste, and show the strange fallibility of that so-wonderful instinct; but, whatever the subtractions from general perfection, there are passages and performances in the book which prove not only the most marvellous talent —for I knew Dickens had that—but the most transcendant

genius. And of such genius his former works show no
conclusive demonstration.

To a young Art Student in London.

Granton, near Edinburgh.

. . . The forces of character are something like the
forces of a siege. The garrison first shows in quiet
resistance the strength which will, by and by, over-
whelm the worn-out enemy in the field.

An insidious danger is more to be feared than an open
one, and a highwayman is much less formidable than an
epidemic. A brave man might escape uninjured from
Calypso's Island more easily than a young man could resist
becoming 'young-mannish' in the continual company of
ordinary young men.

The evil in the last case is so gradual, so unrepulsive,
so imperceptible, when once the contagion is taken, so
apparently unamenable to any one of the Ten Command-
ments, that the victim feels insulted at the idea that he
is a victim.

And yet, if after listening to Mr. Arthur Pendennis,
or Mr. Clive Newcome, one says to oneself 'the beauty of
holiness,' it feels as when the cool sweet face of a pure
woman comes in upon a seducing dream.

I was very much amused and interested with your
description of the young fellows at Leigh's, and at the
R. A., it was so completely what one would expect. Only
we must not call it 'art-talk,' for the best among them
can have about as much notion of Art, as yet, as signet

eaglets on their ledge of the eyrie-rock can know of the skiey heights and wide horizons, the sense of supporting air, the cold of super-Alpine winds, or the look of the sun in those rare regions where he neither has warmth nor rays.

But all these things and more, the eagle knows, and they shall know. Meantime, the talk which those young 'Painterkins' think artistic bears about the same relation, for the most part, to Art, as the gossip of the masons over their work bears to architecture. The best stones and mortar will not build St. Peter's.

To a young Sister.

Granton, near Edinburgh : November 27.

You have been such a dear good girl in writing to me so often, without expectation of a reply, that I can be silent no longer, and will indite this 'Sunday letter' to you—though other occupations must make it shorter than your three or four welcome letters deserve.

Believe me, every detail of those letters had our warmest interest, from the history of your lessons to the state of the 'one tree,' and from the last farm news to the account of your walks in the autumn twilight. I am heartily pleased to know that you are working so perseveringly and thoroughly at your various 'lessons' . . . The intellectual fault of our family has been its tendency to smatter; and you can hardly tell how great a blessing you are receiving in the power and opportunity to learn things through and through, and up and down, and in and

in. The advantage of learning elaborately and completely
is not merely in the superiority of the things learned and
the finer effect they have upon your general knowledge,
but still more in the habit of mind which is produced in
the process of such learning. Having, therefore, such
invaluable opportunities given you, I am sure you will
spare no pains or perseverance in using them rightly ;
that you will go to each department of study with a
resolve that no one who ever undertook it shall have
learned more thoroughly and *genuinely* than you. I
cannot tell you how deeply I was pleased and interested
with what you told me of your feelings in your walk by
night. God indeed grant you a long youth of such ! They
are to the soul what early love is to the heart, and none
can tell how precious, in after times of darkness and
tumult, may be the remembrance of such hours. ' Can
one who has once been in a state of grace be lost ? ' said
the dying Cromwell. And when the minister answered :
' No,' ' Then,' said he, ' I am safe, for I am sure that *once*
I was in a state of grace.'

As love in its later years becomes something brighter,
dearer, more wonderful, more estimable than in its early
' rosy dawn,' yet we still look back in exquisite poetry to
those rose-hues of its first hours ; so the soul, long accustomed to God's presence, loses in the course of years the
first ecstasies of its recognition, and turns, in its clear sight
and calm knowledge and more equal blessedness, to be
refreshed by the memory of those early times when it first
thrilled to the voice—and flushed to the unaccustomed
face—of its Creator. Enjoy that 'sense of awful happi-

ness' while yet it is the time of day with you—and long indeed may your 'sun stand upon Gideon.'

But I have been interrupted, and must talk no more on these things, whereon I hope we shall really 'talk' some day.

To M——.

Granton : December 4, 1855.

Thanks for your 'impulse' with regard to the ballad. It was just what I expected, for that 'farewell' is rather a sonata (a sonata may be bad or good, you know) than a song, and I thought it would appeal to the musician within you.

For that matter, though, anyone who would wholly understand any of my poetry—lyrical or otherwise—must read it with the mind of a musician. I don't mean that it is *musical*, in the common sense, but that it is written on the principles of music, *i.e.* as a series of combinations that shall produce certain *states* in the hearer, and not a succession of words which he is separately to 'intellectuate' by the dictionary. In that lecture, or rather those lectures, of which E. spoke I hope to develope a theory on this head.

. . . What I propose to myself is two lectures on poetry and poets wherein I shall try to think out, so far as that be possible, the whole truth concerning the nature of these, making it grow like a tree into all the ramifications that depend upon it. I have been slowly cultivating it for more than a year, and I see it gradually organise into cosmical and living order. This line of thought I can carry on without hindrance to the Ballads, and they do not interfere with it.

To a young Sister.

I wish I were as confident that 'our ally,' the king of Sardinia, is a 'good man' as my dear correspondent seems to be. Or rather I should be sorry to feel sure of his goodness, because a good King in Italy just now would put back the poor Italians a quarter of a century. The worse their kings are the better for them: 'high pressure' engines are most likely to blow up, you know, and it is the iron round the gunpowder that makes the shell explode. Did you see your Sardinian friend's speeches? It was amusing—rather grim amusement, for it stirred one's blood—to turn from the newspaper-and-corporation fuss about him to his own actual words and thoughts. He could not even *think* on English principles, he did not, evidently, live in the same world with us. It was ludicrous to see, when he had to answer a popular deputation, how his very attempts to be civil betrayed him. It was like a man determining to be polite to dogs, and saying 'good,' 'kind,' 'excellent,' certainly—but always 'dogs.' I hope you admired his moustaches? We talk about 'bearding' a person, but it would need three men to 'beard' your friend : one on each side and one in front. Winter and he have created a *furore* for moustache in Edinburgh. I shall soon be the only shaven man in the city. Old and young, grave and gay, grooms and grandees, are all 'hare-lipped!' I can't think where the crop has come from: it seems to have sprung up like grass in a June night.

Friday morning. As I finished the last words, yesterday evening, in came (and with a moustache!) D. B——, who, finding himself in Yorkshire on business, made a pilgrimage to us. Of course I asked him to stay a day or two, and you will therefore forgive a much briefer letter than I meant to have written. And before I forget, let me say how rightly you made sure that I should be truly glad to help in anything you are doing for the mental welfare of the dear old parish . . . I calculated the other day that we give away more than a tenth of our income and so fulfil unintentionally the old Mosaic law of tithes. I say this, dearest N., that you may not misunderstand me, when I only offer a guinea a year to your scheme. . . .

Another time I will tell you what my new friend B—— is like . . . I like what he says and his mode of thinking and feeling very much, so far as I have yet seen.

The following short letters or extracts from letters, the beginning of a long correspondence, tell their own story, if given together—and all belong to the year 1855.

An intimate friend of the young poet, to whom they were addressed, writing to Mr. Dobell after the death of his correspondent, said: 'I was not surprised to find how little you had known of the feeling with which he regarded you, for it was too reverent to be much on the surface, or to show itself very readily to you.'

To D. B——, Esq.

North Hanover Street, Edinburgh: February 5, 1855.

'Dear Sir,—Your lines have much more promise and performance than most of the many MS. sent to me. Indeed, taking what you tell me of your age into account, I think they are unusually hopeful; and I shall have pleasure in getting them into some Magazine. At the same time I ought to warn you that their *appearance* is all you can expect from an editor: *payment* for poetry, except in the case of long-established writers, being almost unknown in literature.

I will send your MS. back to you (for I have not time to write *in extenso* criticisms) with some pencil-notes- - which you can easily erase—on the back of it. Not that you can do much to the present piece in the way of emendations, for such faults as it has are chiefly intrinsic and to be cured only by rewriting; but I think from the tone both of your note and poetry that you are in earnest in your wish to write well and that you may be glad, therefore, of some hints kindly given. I don't send back your poem at this moment that you may be saved from the needless pang (which, as I well remember, every young author feels) of opening a returned MS. When you have considered my few notes, and made what alterations you

like (or none), you can re-send me the paper, and I will see
what can be done.

Sincerely yours,
SYDNEY DOBELL.

The letters which answered the foregoing gave
a pathetic picture of the writer's estate, and, of
course, deepened Mr. Dobell's feelings of interest.

Men in your position, [the young man wrote] have
great power of giving comfort, and I could wish for your
own sake that you could have witnessed the rapturous heart-
content you bestowed to-day. I need not say I am somewhat in advance of my years. Having lived the last three
years invalid, very much alone, or in the company of
women, with Death, from time to time, staring me in the
face, I have ripened a little prematurely. My disease is
pulmonary consumption, but I have so falsified all the predictions of my physicians that I begin to hope my life
may be prolonged.

When about fifteen I settled on my line of life, since
when neither discouragement, nor want of success, nor
opposition, have for one moment made me unfaithful to
my belief that I should, and determination that I would,
succeed in poetry. Don't laugh at me. Plenty of idle
fellows say the same; but I did and do so with feelings of
sad earnestness . . . I tell you all this because I hope that
when I need advice you ('by far my elder brother in the
Muse') will let me come to you for it. I will not bore
you, nor seek you unnecessarily, but though I know some

literally have scribbled this letter the instant I laid down
your MS. as the best reparation for so tardy a verdict upon
a ballad of such exceeding merit.

To the same.

Granton, Edinburgh : November 23.

I am sorry that I have not time for such a discursion
among your affairs as I should heartily like to take, and
wish sincerely we could chat them over in some of those
leisure intervals when my head is too tired even to write
letters.

In what I shall briefly say on this sheet of paper give
me credit for much more interest and much more thought
than is actually set down.   It seems to me, revolving your
age, talents, and power of work, that you ought, being
' unencumbered ' and willing for patient gradual progress
—to make a living—and, in time, something more, by
literature.   I think that the editorship or subeditorship of
a Scottish newspaper would be an excellent field of action.
You would, if you proved yourself a competent person,
get eighty or a hundred pounds a year by *half-a-week's*
work, and would have the remainder of your time for
study, and Magazine employment.   Acting on this idea, I
have written to a newspaper proprietor whom I know, and
enclose you his answer.   From that answer I think there
is reason to hope you would get the appointment when the
vacancy occurs. . . .   Meanwhile, if among your friends you
could obtain admittance in some capacity or other to the
office of a country paper, for the mere purpose of getting

an insight into the mechanical part of an editor's duties (a clever man of quick perceptions, and a determination to work, would readily make himself thoroughly *au fait* of the whole thing in a short time), you would be ready to step into the present editor's place. . .

. . . If you feel inclined to enter heartily into this line of action, I will make enquiries among my friends in other directions.

There is no sphere of exertion that seems to me so desirable for a young man of literary ambitions who requires to live by literature as that of the editor of a modern newspaper. Whether you look at it as a post of present influence and popular benefit, or as a stepping stone to other and higher advancement, it seems equally eligible. But let me entreat you, while keeping your eye on these things, not to neglect any good or moderate business offers that may be made to you. You are not perhaps aware how very scarce even clerkships of fifty pounds a year are in these days of abounding mediocrity and intelligence : and I am certain that even posting a ledger may be—as a counteraction—a great and valuable help to an author and a poet. But more of this at some other time. I scribble now because I know with what anxiety you must be looking for the return of such doves of enquiry as you have sent out from your ark. I wish from my heart that the olive leaf, in this case, were larger and greener.

Towards the close of this year, the young poet, to whom the foregoing letters were addressed, being in Yorkshire, came on to Scotland and Granton, to make Mr. Dobell's personal acquaintance. The visit proved a long one, owing to the dangerous illness of the guest. A cold caught on the snowy journey through a December night, brought on a severe attack of inflammation of the lungs; and what Mr. Dobell then learnt of the state of his correspondent's health altered his views with regard to what was advisable in his case. Any Scotch engagement was out of the question: the only prudent course seemed a return to the mild climate of his Devonshire home, as soon as his health was sufficiently re-established for him to travel.

END OF THE FIRST VOLUME.

LONDON : PRINTED BY
SPOTTISWOODE AND CO., NEW-STREET SQUARE
AND PARLIAMENT STREET